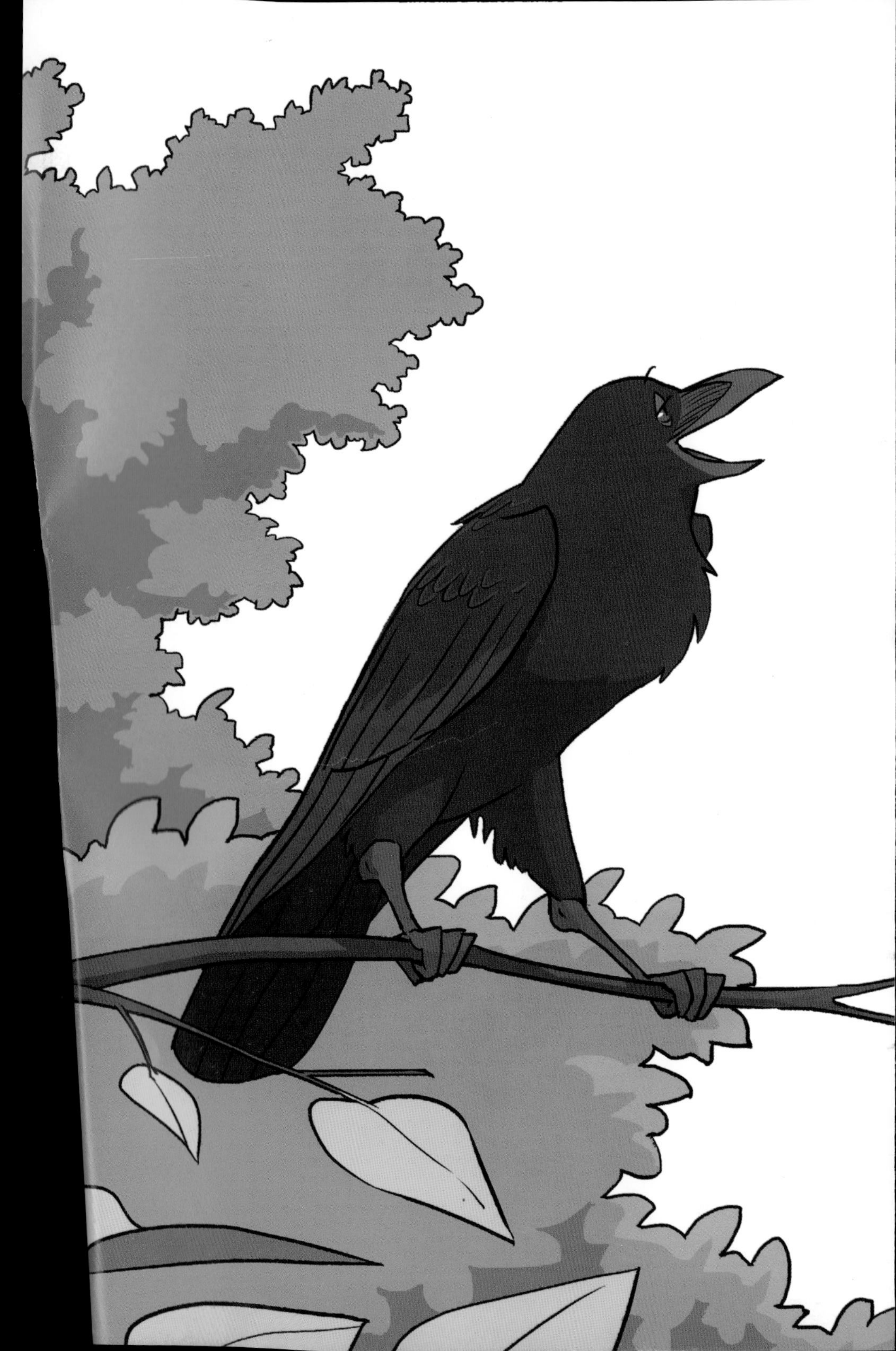

SCIENCE COMICS

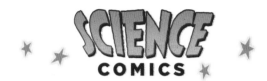

CROWS

Genius Birds

CROWS
Genius Birds

KYLA VANDERKLUGT

:01

First Second
New York

For Maxwell, who loved birds,
and for Merlin, who loved to eat them.

First Second

Copyright © 2020 by Kyla Vanderklugt

Published by First Second
First Second is an imprint of Roaring Brook Press,
a division of Holtzbrinck Publishing Holdings Limited Partnership
120 Broadway, New York, NY 10271

Don't miss your next favorite book from First Second! For the latest updates
go to firstsecondnewsletter.com and sign up for our enewsletter.

Library of Congress Control Number: 2019930674

Hardcover ISBN: 978-1-62672-803-5
Paperback ISBN: 978-1-62672-802-8

Our books may be purchased in bulk for promotional, educational, or business use. Please
contact your local bookseller or the Macmillan Corporate and Premium Sales Department
at (800) 221-7945 ext. 5442 or by email at MacmillanSpecialMarkets@macmillan.com.

First edition, 2020
Edited by Dave Roman
Cover design by Andrew Arnold and Molly Johanson
Interior book design by Laura Berry
Crows consultant: Kevin J. McGowan, Cornell Lab of Ornithology

Printed in China by Toppan Leefung Printing Ltd., Dongguan City, Guangdong Province

Penciled, inked, and colored in Adobe Photoshop.

10 9 8 7 6 5 4 3 2 1

Most days I'm sure I have the best job in the world. Not only do I get to work with terrific students, but I also get to learn from the truly amazing birds that are featured in the book you are now holding. Thanks to a great high school biology teacher who instilled in me a love of nature and science, I've been able to study crows and their close relatives (jays, nutcrackers, and ravens) for almost 40 years. During my career, I've watched these birds do many of the things you will read about. Yes, they really are as smart as chimps or even small kids! They do make tools, learn rules, speak, and even command dogs! My friend Kevin Smith actually almost lost his dog, Vampire, to a crow that famously made the rounds in Missoula, Montana. The crow was apparently raised by a person and, as they will do, learned to repeat what it must have often heard. In this case the crow approached dogs and called forth in plain English: "Here, boy, here, boy." Most dogs followed the crow's instructions, but fortunately Kevin got out to his kennel before the crow coaxed his big German shepherd away.

Crows are able to do such amazing things because they learn from personal encounters and by watching other crows. They use their sophisticated brains to remember what they've experienced and to think before they act. Sound familiar? Yes, as social beings, crows use their brains in much the same way we do. The mental ability of crows is important because it allows them to solve real problems, such as where to hide surplus food and how to coordinate the movements of their family when a predator lurks nearby. As we create cities and farms, many animals go extinct or retreat to more natural settings, but not the crow. Living close to people is not an easy task; for example, while some folks feed crows, others harass or even hunt them. Crows are able to meet this challenge because they can recognize us and remember how we've treated them in the past. I discovered this the hard way. After I captured crows and put identifying bracelets on their legs, I realized that they treated me differently. Once released, the crow would rarely approach its nest if I was watching, and sometimes the bird would aggressively dive at me and scold me with harsh calls. This made studying them tough! But it also suggested an experiment I'm glad to have done. My students and I wore caveman masks the next time we caught crows. After we released them, we tested their reactions to us when we wore the caveman masks, no masks, or different masks. The crows immediately recognized us when we wore the caveman masks, but ignored us otherwise. Now 11 years after catching those crows, they still recognize the caveman, and they've taught their kids, mates, and neighbors about the dangerous caveman, as well!

Lately, my research team has looked within the head of a crow to discover how its brain stores and recalls information about particular people. We've done this without harming the bird, by using a brain imaging technique called a PET scan. This research showed us that crows use the same parts of their brains as we do—the hippocampus and amygdala—to learn and respond to fearful events. We are continuing our brain scanning research in the hope of discovering how the crows' brains function during tool use and how they decode their rich language.

I admit that I'm pretty possessed by crows, but I'm far from alone. Crows and ravens have challenged and inspired humans for a millennia. There are raven images in Lascaux cave art! Our close and personal interactions with these birds have shaped our beliefs, arts, and language. You know what a "crowbar" is and what it means to be "ravenous," right? Given the intelligence of crows and their relatives, it's no wonder that many Native American tribes consider the crow or raven to be their creator, that the Norse god Odin was informed daily by two ravens, or that, according to the Bible, God saved his servant Elijah by commanding a raven to bring him food.

I hope you enjoy reading about these powerful birds as much as I've enjoyed studying them. As you wonder about crows, step outside and watch your local corvids. Unless you live in Antarctica, there will be a family of crows, jays, ravens, or magpies, which are guaranteed to delight you with their cleverness, varied voice, or social antics. I'll bet that spending time among your brainy bird neighbors will give you something to crow about. Just keep a careful eye on your dog.

John M. Marzluff
Professor of Wildlife Science
University of Washington

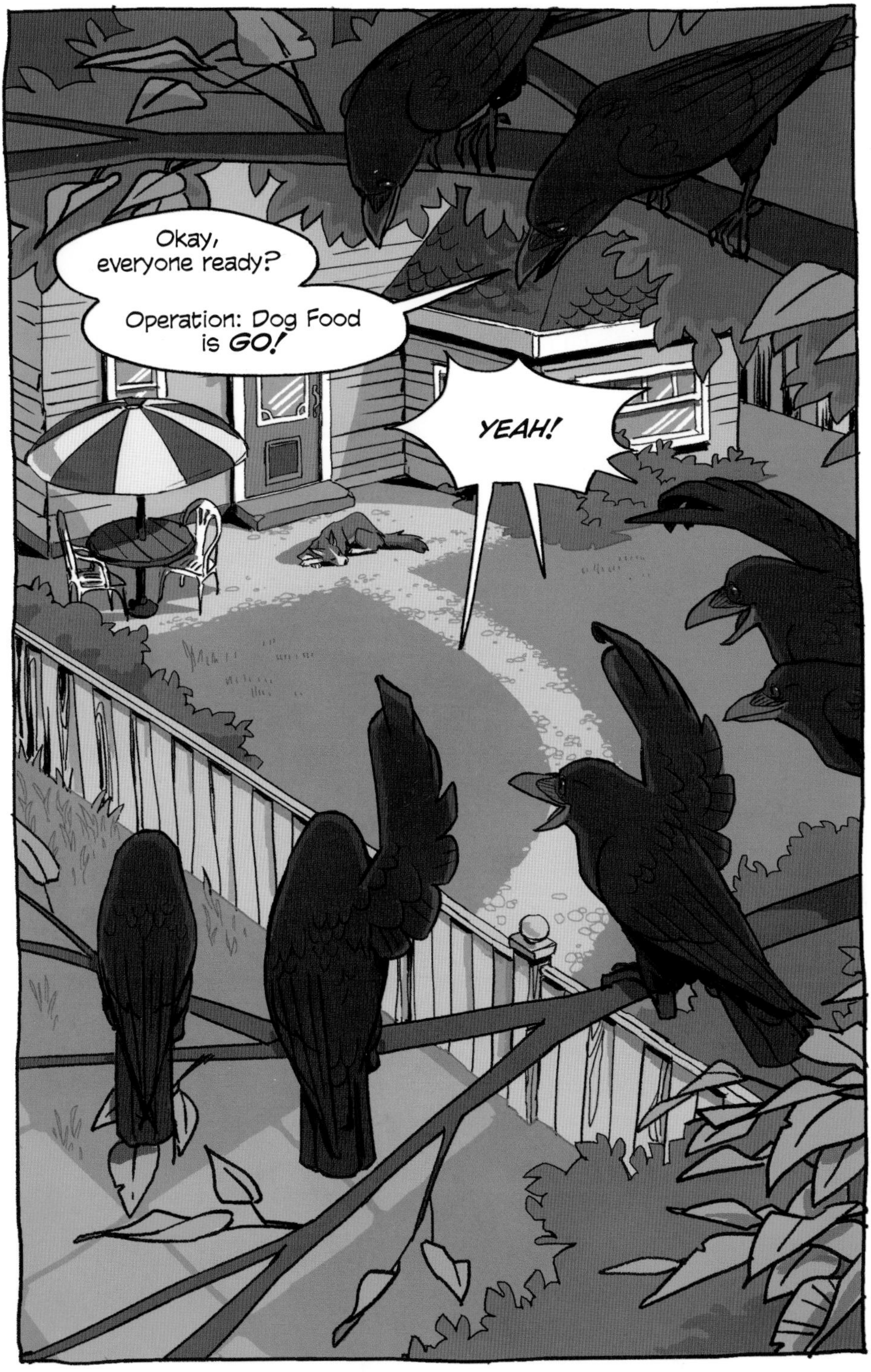
Okay, everyone ready?
Operation: Dog Food is GO!
YEAH!

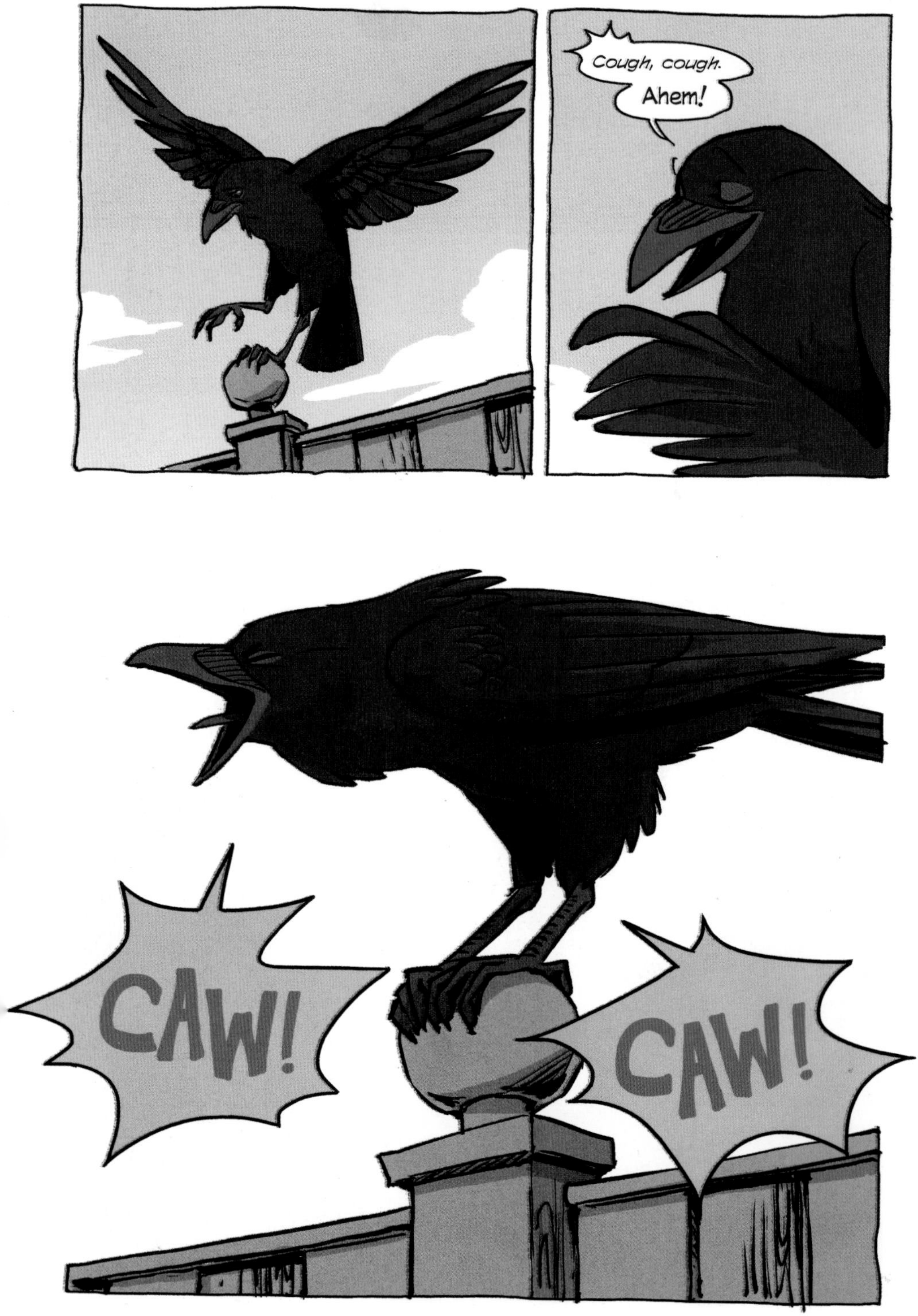
Cough, cough.
Ahem!
CAW!
CAW!

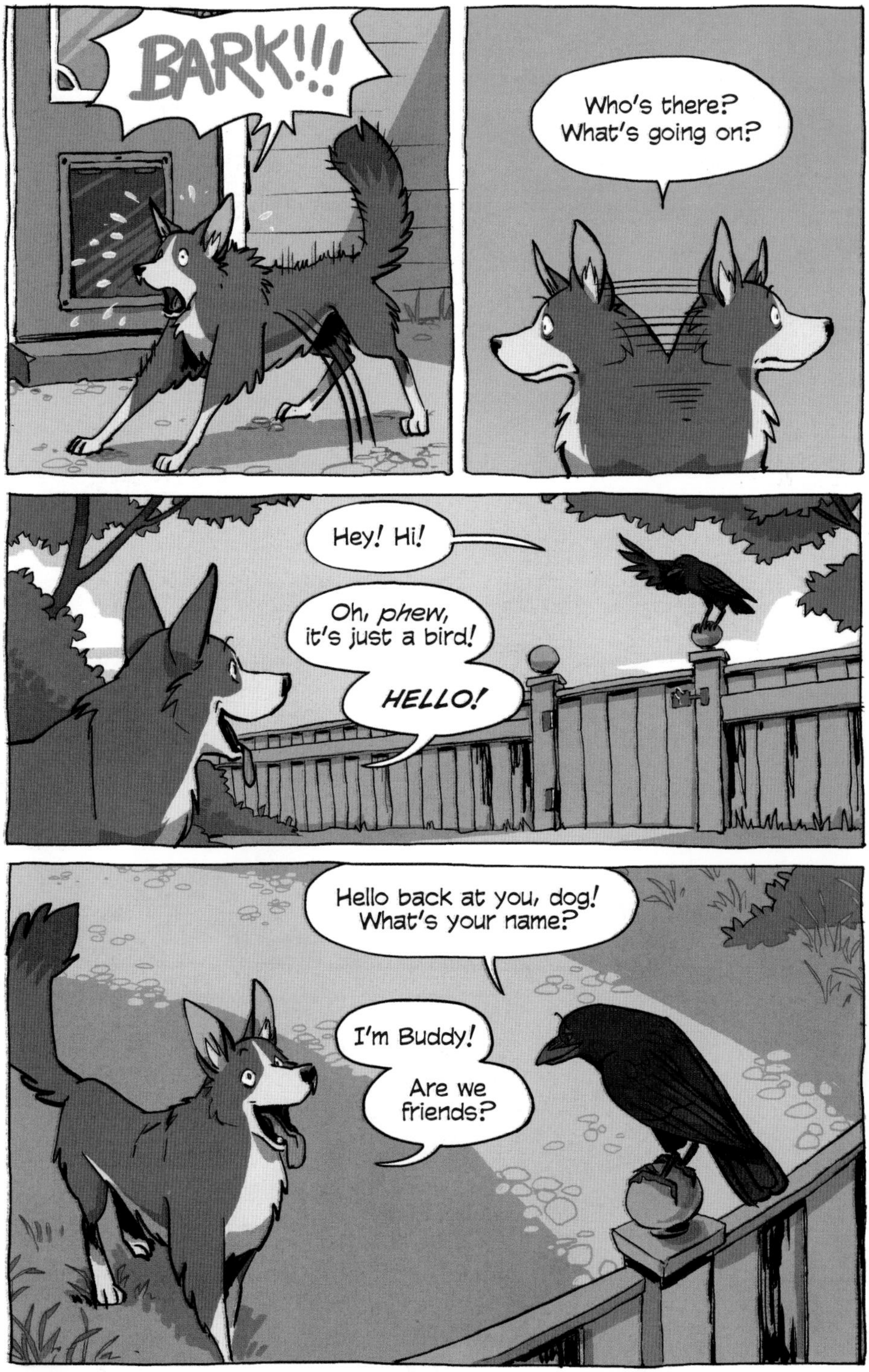
BARK!!!
Who's there? What's going on?
Hey! Hi!
Oh, *phew*, it's just a bird!
HELLO!
Hello back at you, dog! What's your name?
I'm Buddy!
Are we friends?

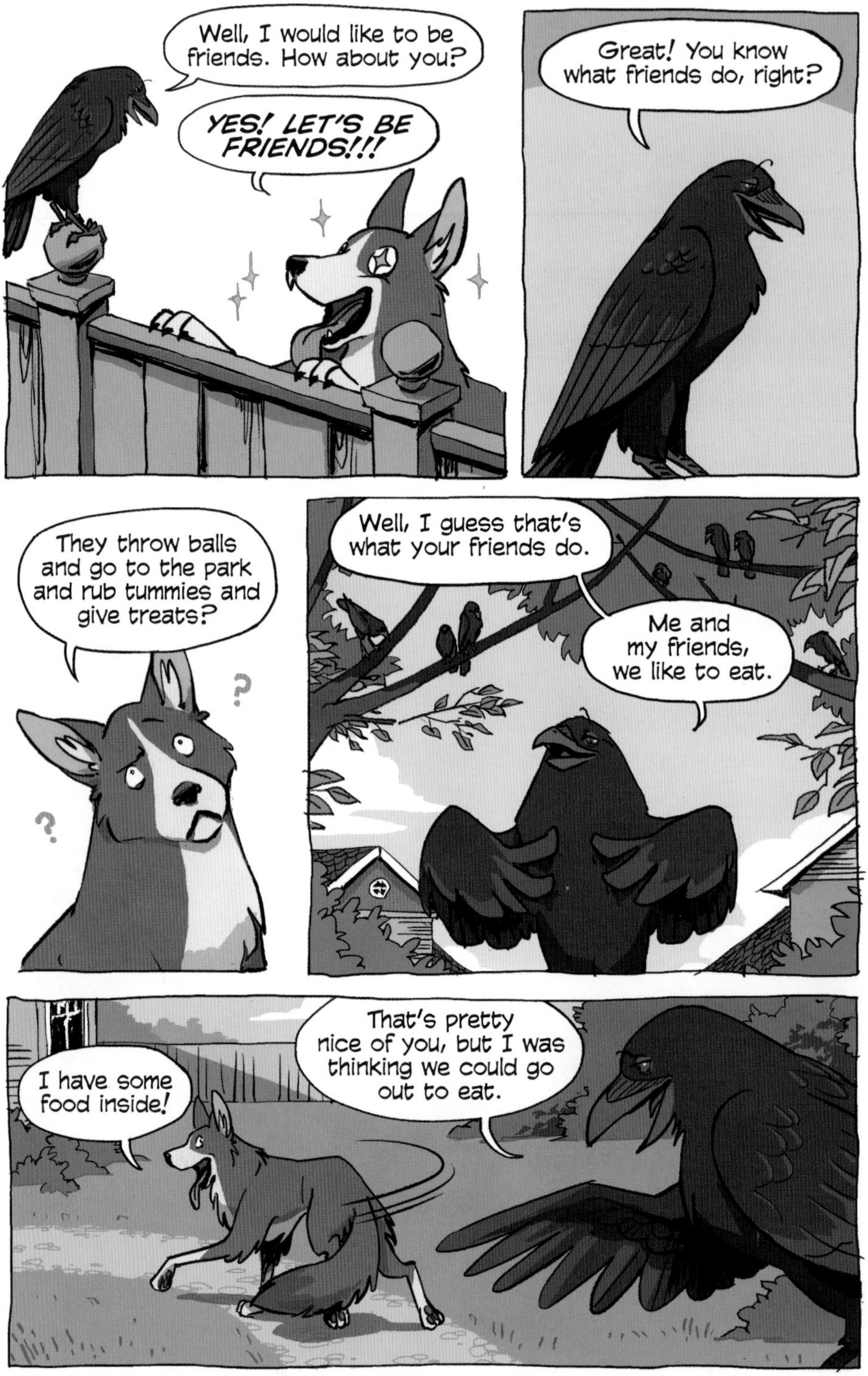
Well, I would like to be friends. How about you?
YES! LET'S BE FRIENDS!!!
Great! You know what friends do, right?
They throw balls and go to the park and rub tummies and give treats?
Well, I guess that's what your friends do.
Me and my friends, we like to eat.
I have some food inside!
That's pretty nice of you, but I was thinking we could go out to eat.

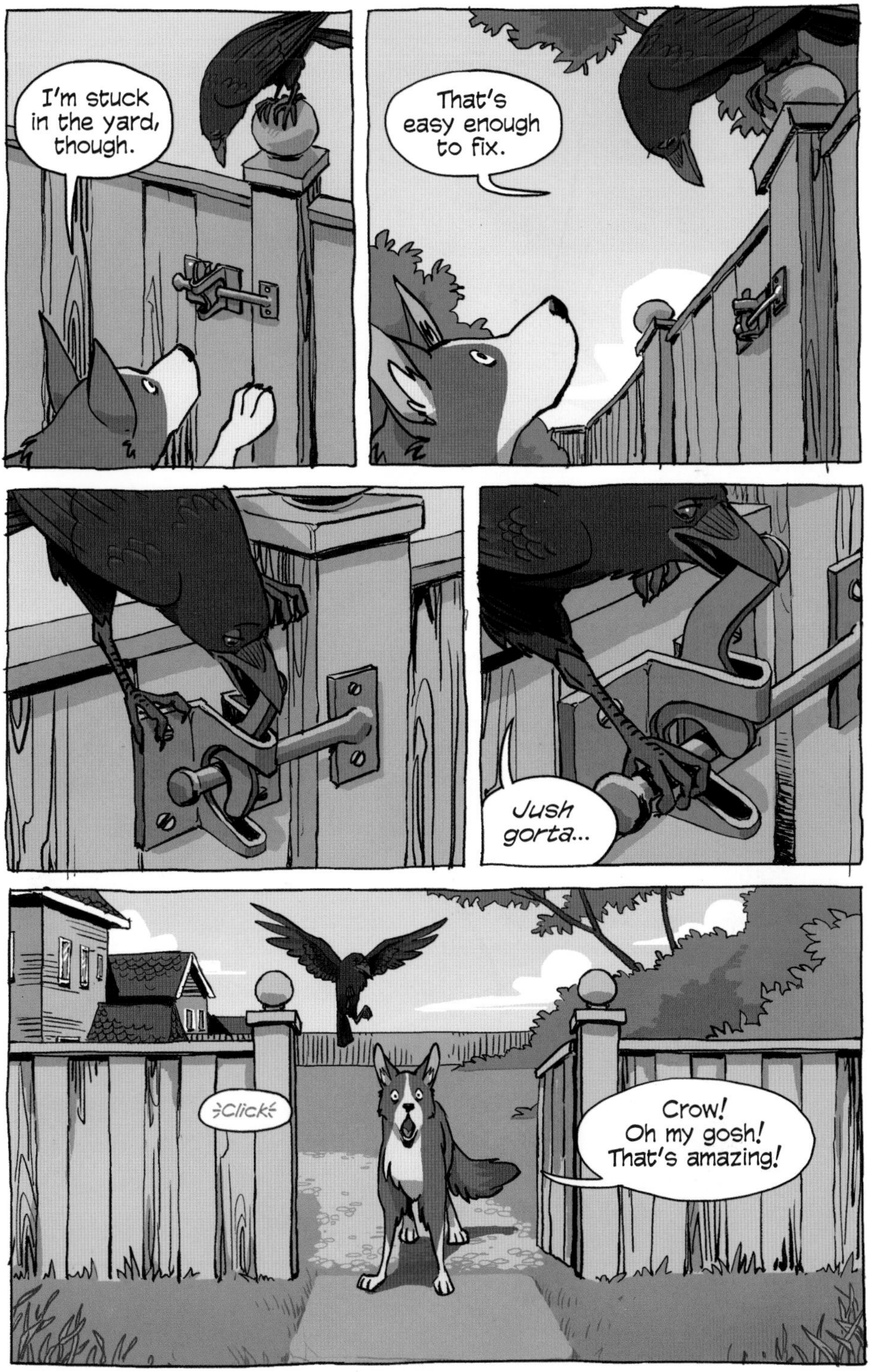
I'm stuck in the yard, though.
That's easy enough to fix.
Jush gorta...
Click
Crow! Oh my gosh! That's amazing!

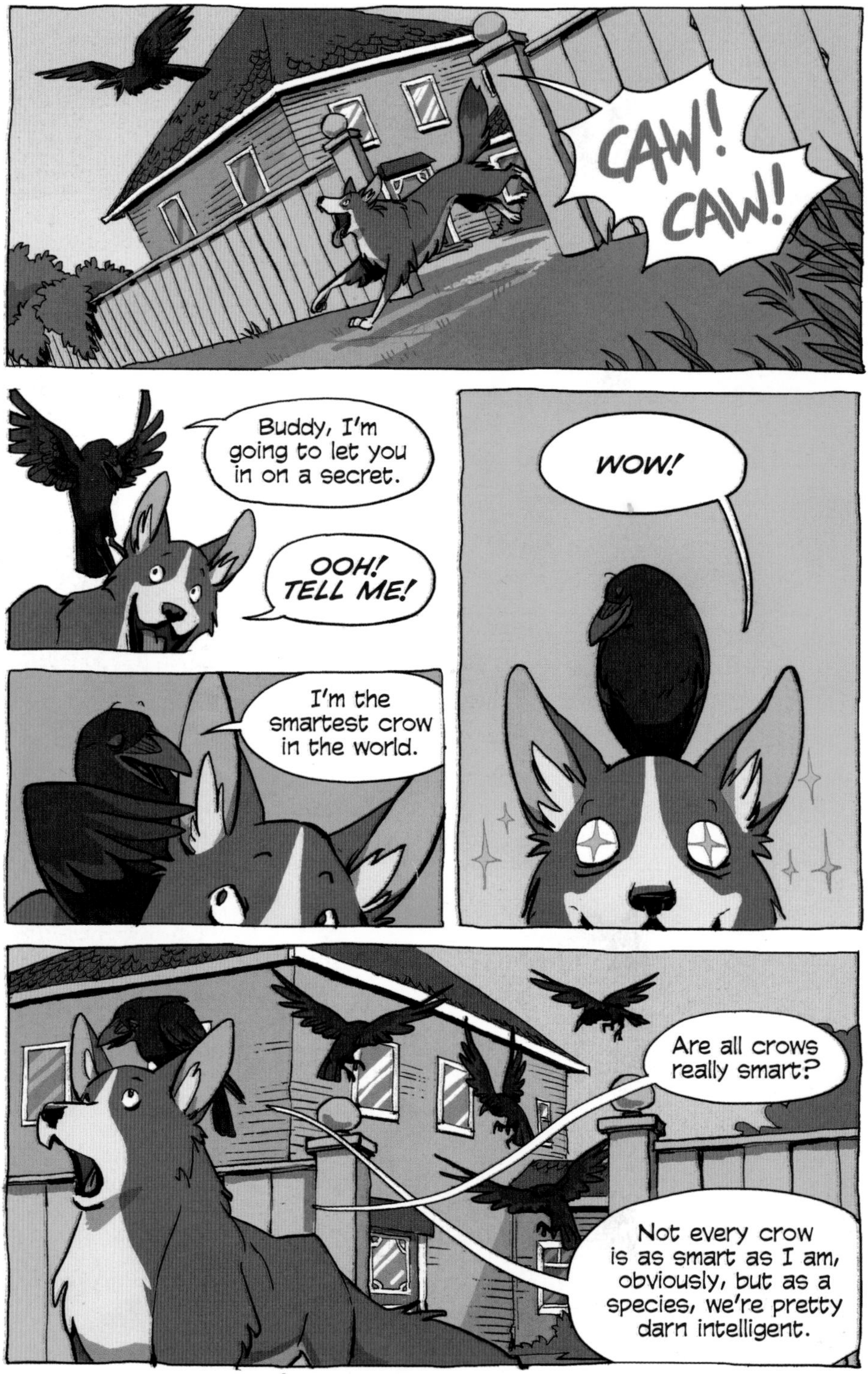
CAW! CAW!
Buddy, I'm going to let you in on a secret.
OOH! TELL ME!
I'm the smartest crow in the world.
WOW!
Are all crows really smart?
Not every crow is as smart as I am, obviously, but as a species, we're pretty darn intelligent.

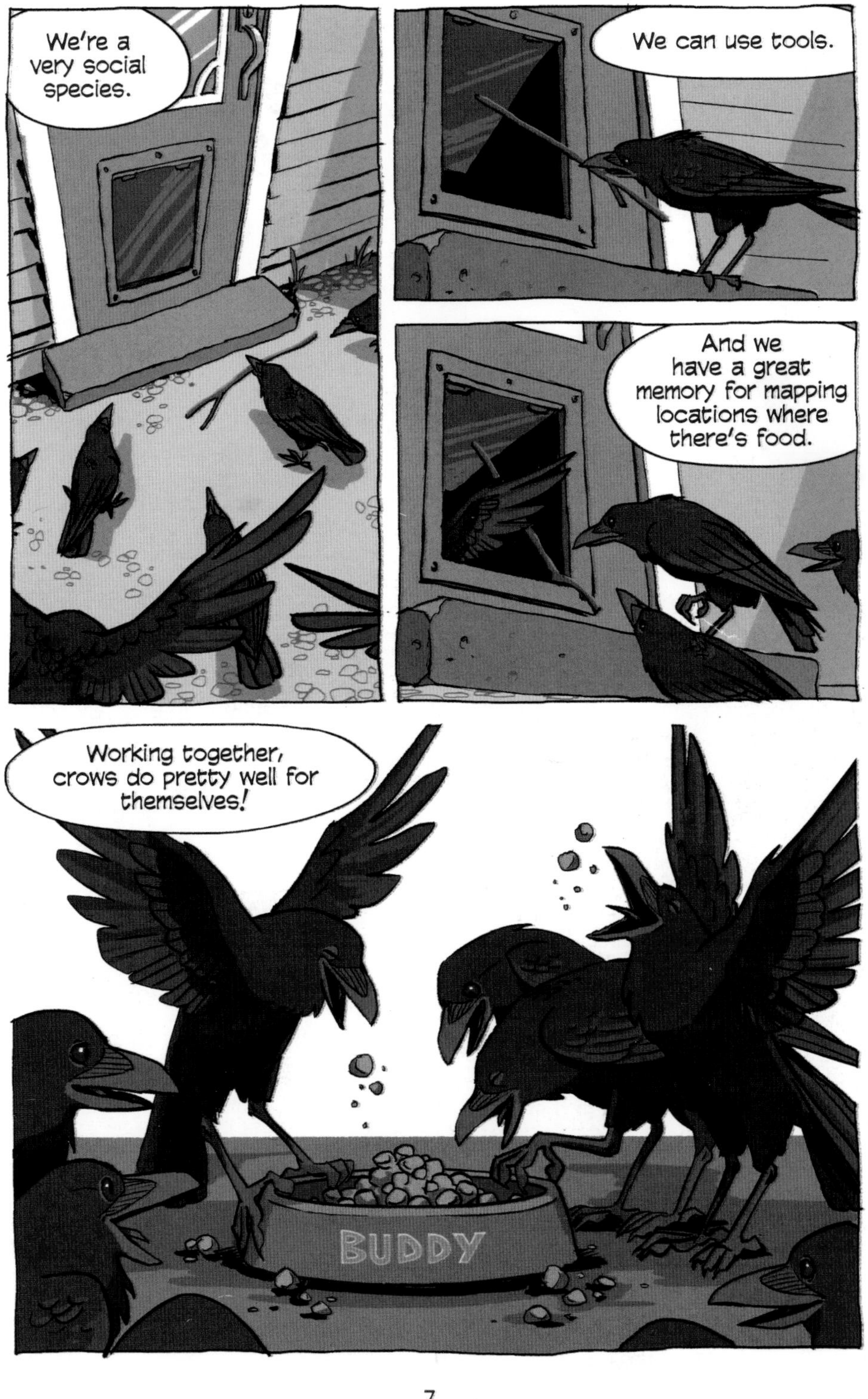
We're a very social species.
We can use tools.
And we have a great memory for mapping locations where there's food.
Working together, crows do pretty well for themselves!
BUDDY

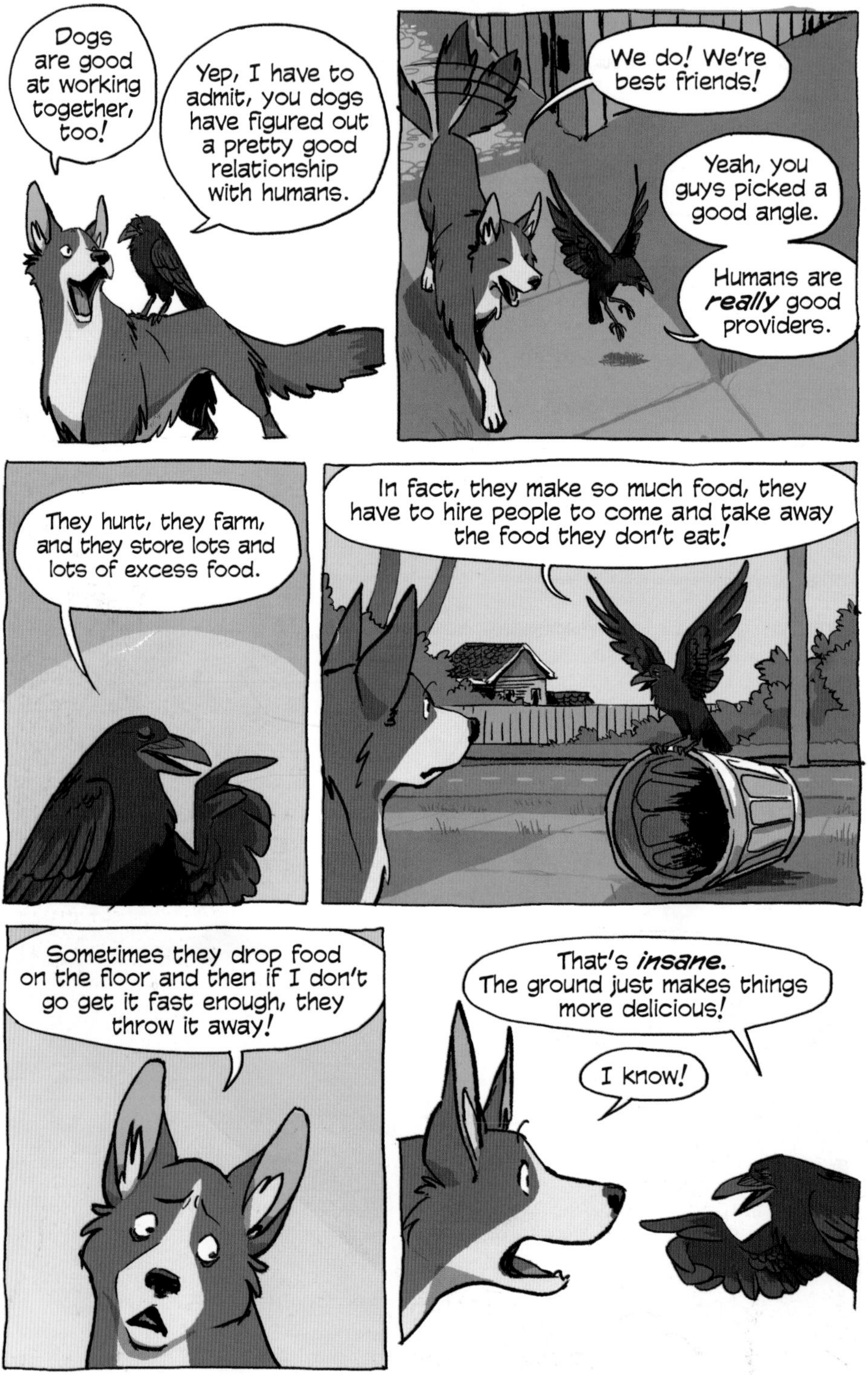

Dogs are good at working together, too!
Yep, I have to admit, you dogs have figured out a pretty good relationship with humans.
We do! We're best friends!
Yeah, you guys picked a good angle.
Humans are ***really*** good providers.
They hunt, they farm, and they store lots and lots of excess food.
In fact, they make so much food, they have to hire people to come and take away the food they don't eat!
Sometimes they drop food on the floor and then if I don't go get it fast enough, they throw it away!
That's ***insane.*** The ground just makes things more delicious!
I know!

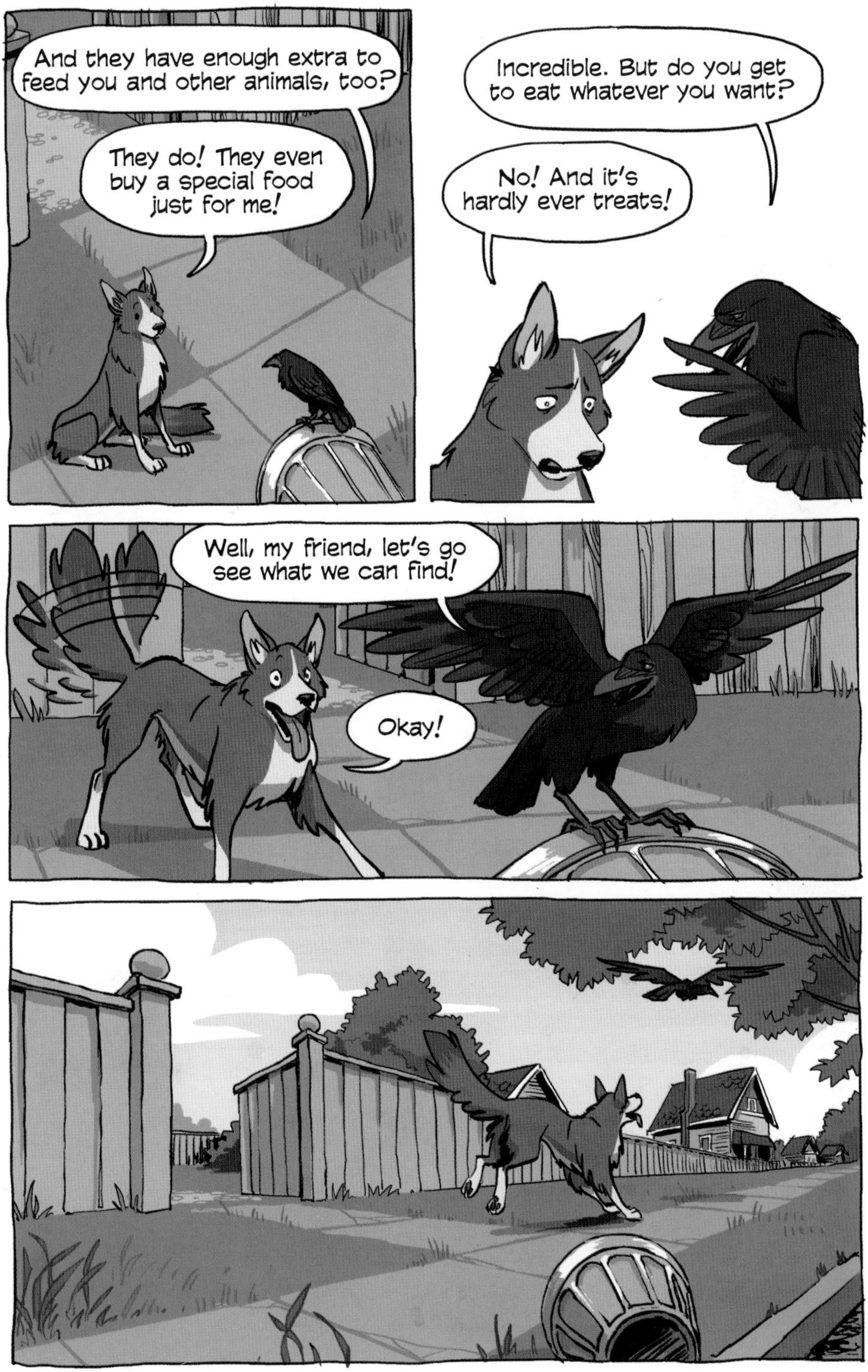

And they have enough extra to feed you and other animals, too?
They do! They even buy a special food just for me!
Incredible. But do you get to eat whatever you want?
No! And it's hardly ever treats!
Well, my friend, let's go see what we can find!
Okay!

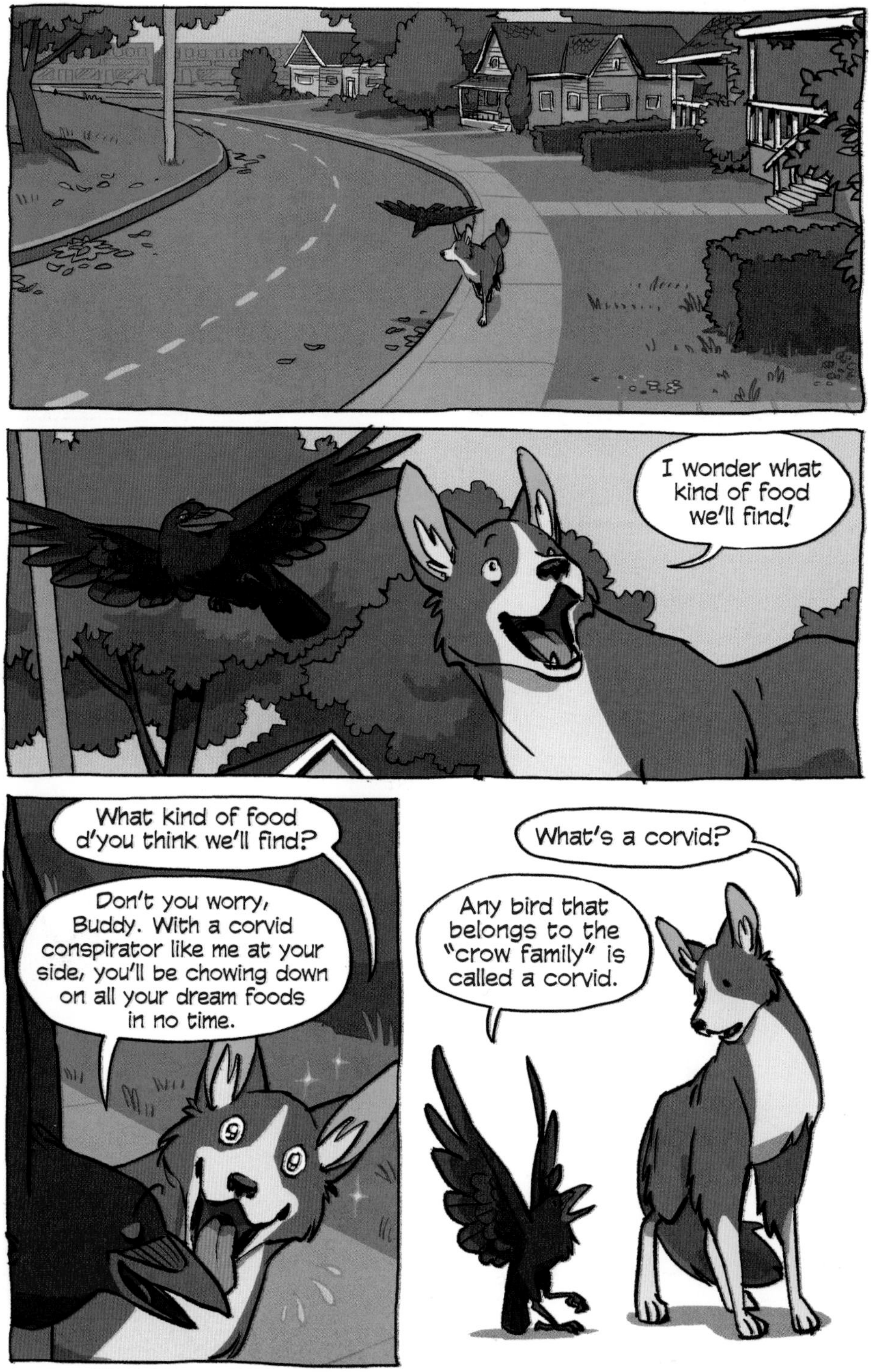
I wonder what kind of food we'll find!
What kind of food d'you think we'll find?
Don't you worry, Buddy. With a corvid conspirator like me at your side, you'll be chowing down on all your dream foods in no time.
What's a corvid?
Any bird that belongs to the "crow family" is called a corvid.

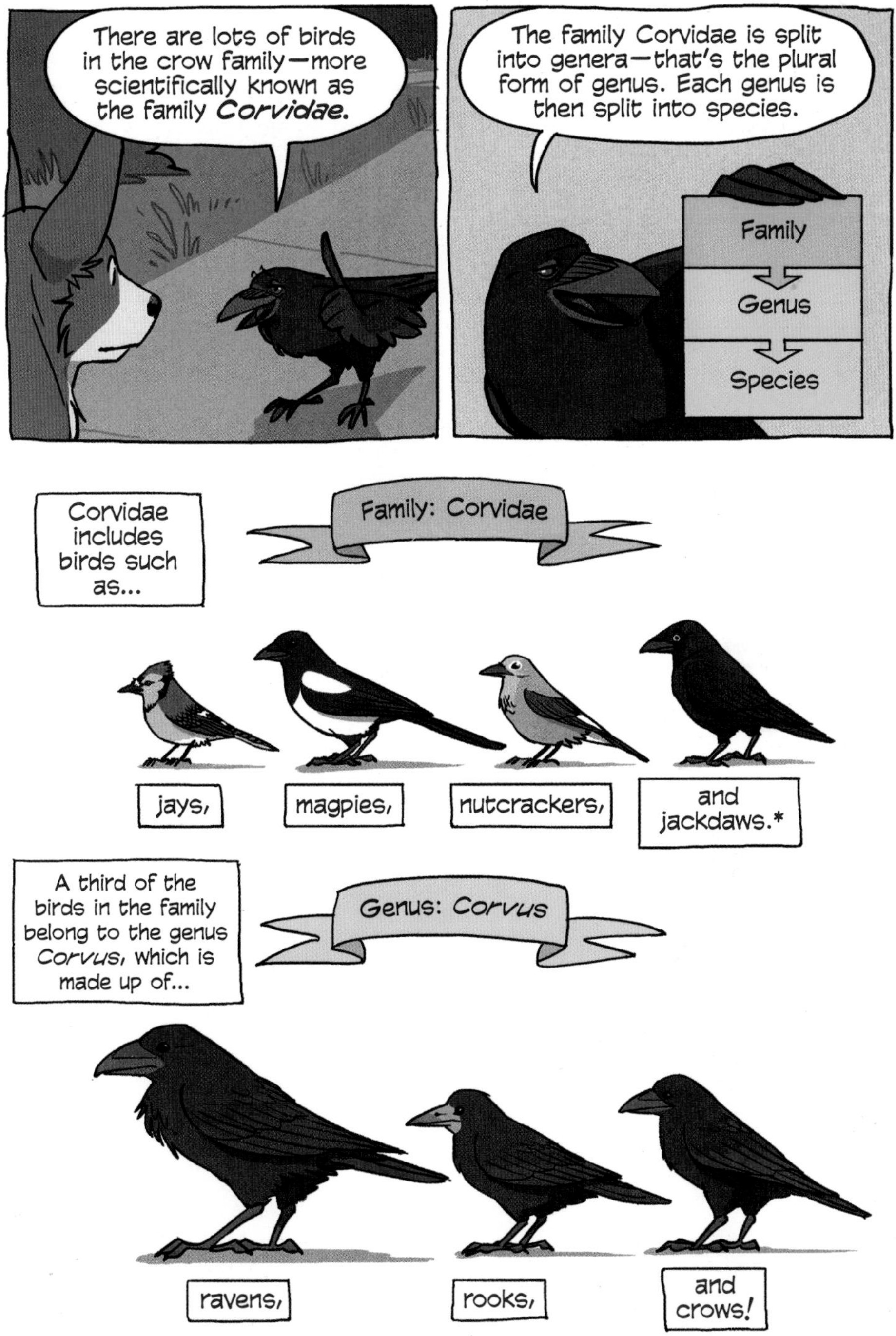
There are lots of birds in the crow family—more scientifically known as the family ***Corvidae.***
The family Corvidae is split into genera—that's the plural form of genus. Each genus is then split into species.
Family
Genus
Species
Corvidae includes birds such as...
Family: Corvidae
jays,
magpies,
nutcrackers,
and jackdaws.*
A third of the birds in the family belong to the genus *Corvus*, which is made up of...
Genus: *Corvus*
ravens,
rooks,
and crows!

*Although some experts still think jackdaws should belong in the *Corvus* genus, they were removed from it by the International Ornithological Congress in 2011.

I belong to **Species: *Corvus brachyrhynchos***

In plain English, that's the American crow!

Usually the smaller species in the *Corvus* genus are called crows, and the bigger species are called ravens.

Take the American crow and the common raven, for instance.

The ravens are a lot bigger.

Croak!

Caw!

Corvus brachyrhynchos / American Crow

Corvus corax / Common Raven

They also have thicker bills, longer nasal bristles, and shaggier throat feathers...

Raven

Crow

...and their tails are shaped like wedges, where a crow's is square.

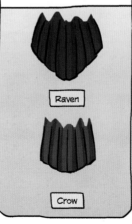

Raven

Crow

Rooks are easy to tell apart because of their bald faces.

You can see their nostrils!

And they're only found in Europe and Asia.

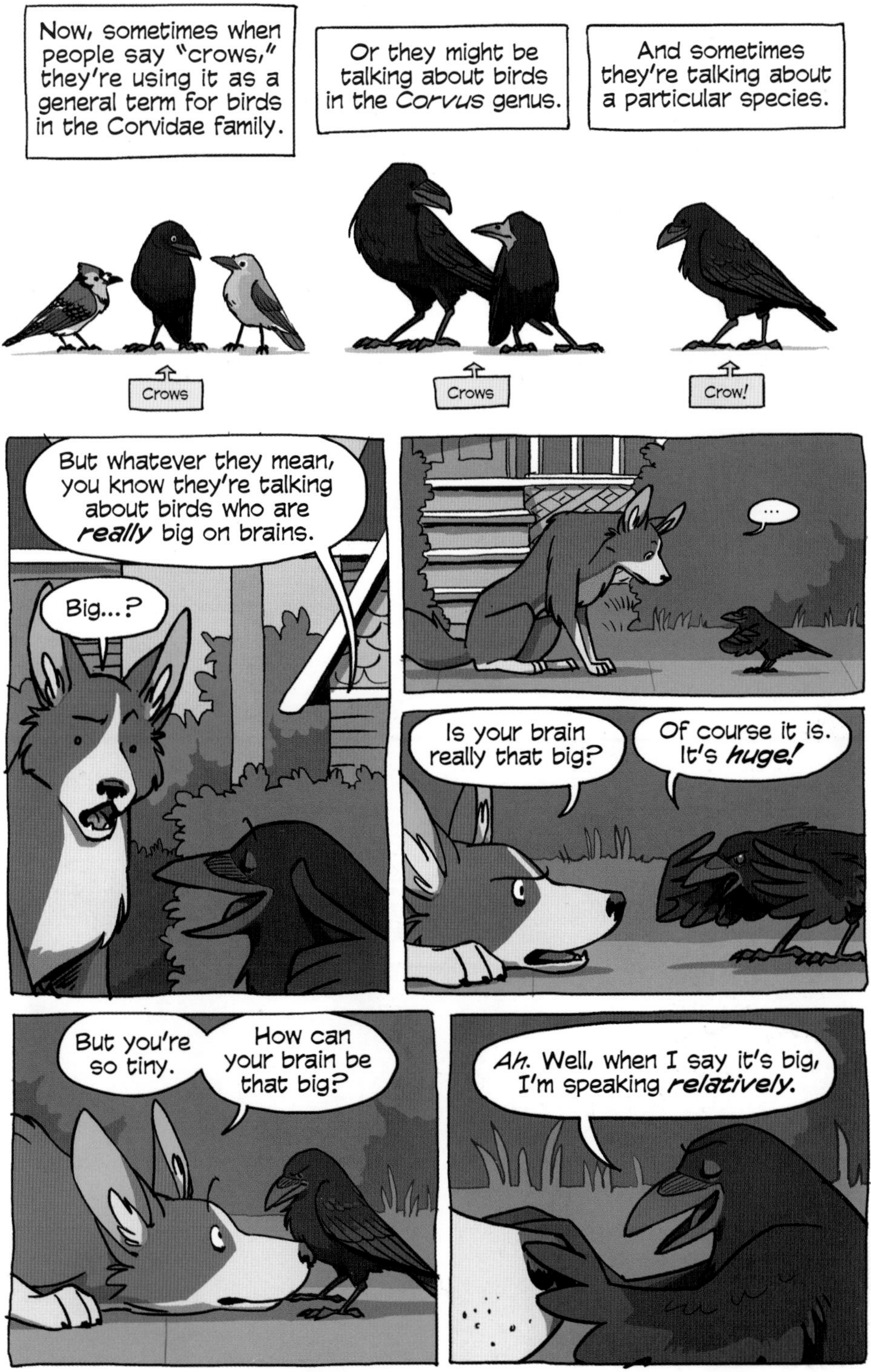
Now, sometimes when people say "crows," they're using it as a general term for birds in the Corvidae family.
Or they might be talking about birds in the *Corvus* genus.
And sometimes they're talking about a particular species.
Crows
Crows
Crow!
But whatever they mean, you know they're talking about birds who are *really* big on brains.
Big...?
...
Is your brain really that big?
Of course it is. It's *huge!*
But you're so tiny.
How can your brain be that big?
Ah. Well, when I say it's big, I'm speaking *relatively*.

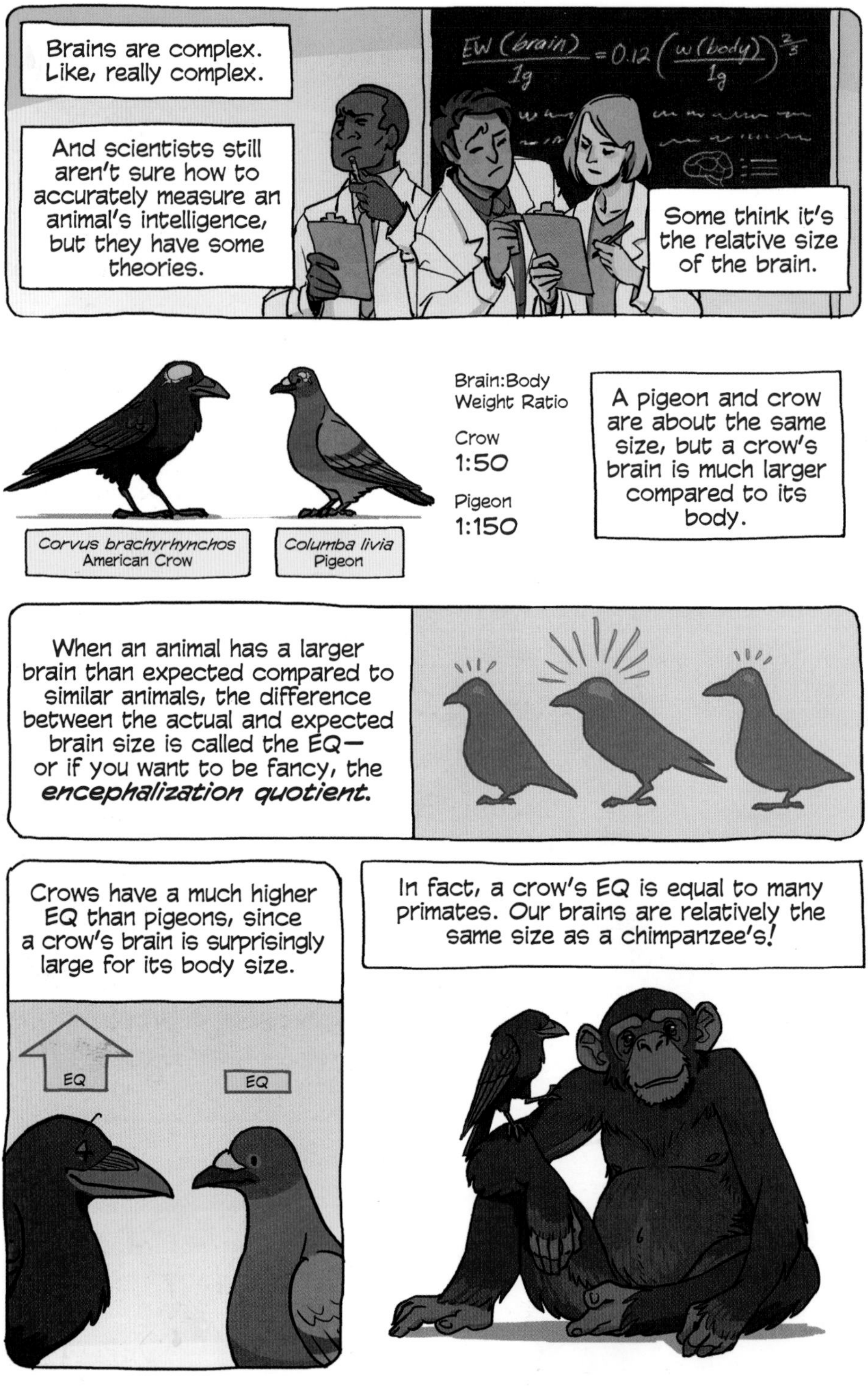
Brains are complex. Like, really complex.
EW (brain) / 1g = 0.12 (w (body) / 1g) 2/3
And scientists still aren't sure how to accurately measure an animal's intelligence, but they have some theories.
Some think it's the relative size of the brain.
Corvus brachyrhynchos
American Crow
Columba livia
Pigeon
Brain:Body Weight Ratio
Crow
1:50
Pigeon
1:150
A pigeon and crow are about the same size, but a crow's brain is much larger compared to its body.
When an animal has a larger brain than expected compared to similar animals, the difference between the actual and expected brain size is called the EQ— or if you want to be fancy, the encephalization quotient.
Crows have a much higher EQ than pigeons, since a crow's brain is surprisingly large for its body size.
EQ
EQ
In fact, a crow's EQ is equal to many primates. Our brains are relatively the same size as a chimpanzee's!

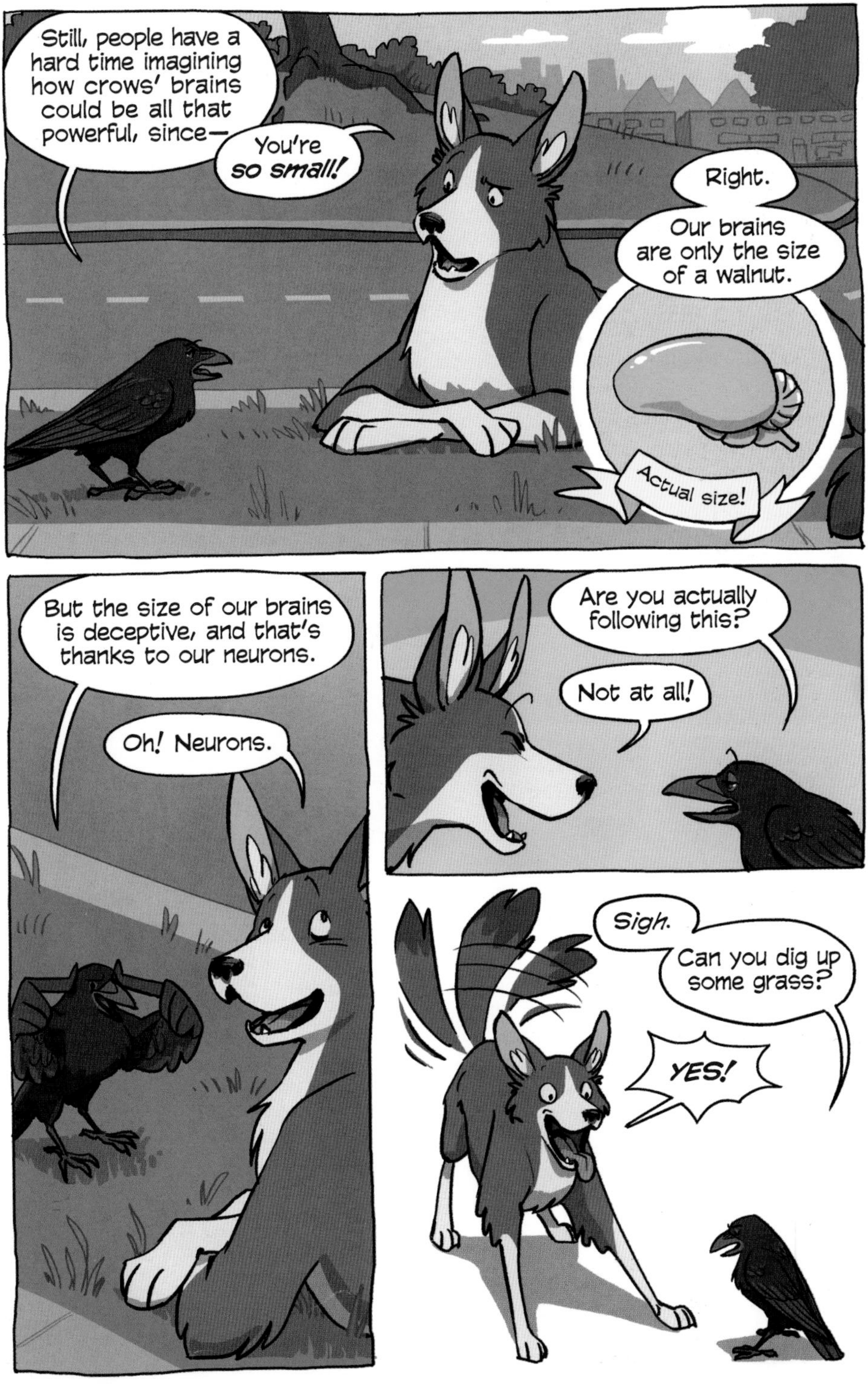
Still, people have a hard time imagining how crows' brains could be all that powerful, since—
You're *so small!*
Right.
Our brains are only the size of a walnut.
Actual size!
But the size of our brains is deceptive, and that's thanks to our neurons.
Oh! Neurons.
Are you actually following this?
Not at all!
Sigh.
Can you dig up some grass?
YES!

That's good.

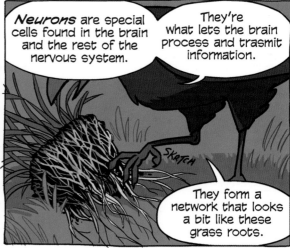

Neurons are special cells found in the brain and the rest of the nervous system.

They're what lets the brain process and transmit information.

They form a network that looks a bit like these grass roots.

Bird brains pack in neurons way more densely...

...compared to mammal brains.

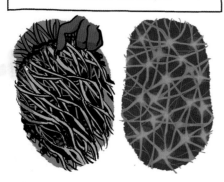

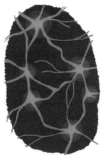

That means that, ounce for ounce, a bird brain could pack more cognitive firepower than a mammalian brain.

Not only that, but they're most dense in the forebrain.

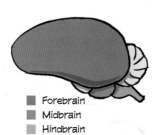

Forebrain
Midbrain
Hindbrain

And that's important.

It is?

The forebrain is where the *prefrontal cortex*, or PFC, is found in the brains of mammals, like humans and other primates.

SKRT

SKRTCH

This area is responsible for things like problem solving, flexible thinking, self-awareness, and memory.

SKRTCH

SKRTCH

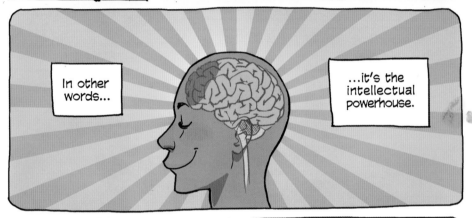

In other words...

...it's the intellectual powerhouse.

But birds don't have a PFC. Our brains are built totally differently from a mammal's brain.

SCRIBBLE

So scientists used to believe that birds must act totally on pre-wired instincts, like robots, since they didn't have anything in their brain that would let them really "think."

CREAK

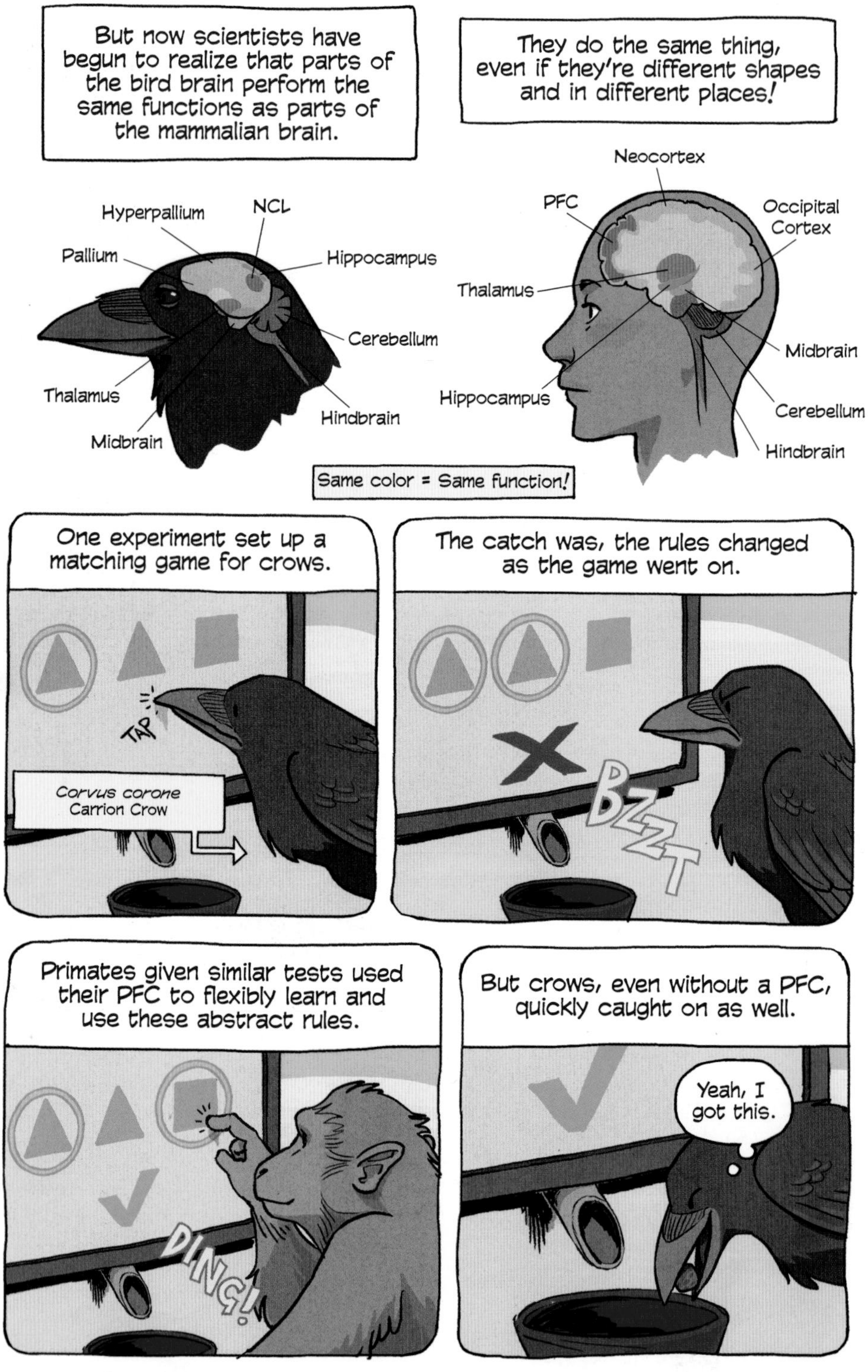
But now scientists have begun to realize that parts of the bird brain perform the same functions as parts of the mammalian brain.
They do the same thing, even if they're different shapes and in different places!
Hyperpallium
NCL
Pallium
Hippocampus
Cerebellum
Thalamus
Midbrain
Hindbrain
Neocortex
PFC
Occipital Cortex
Thalamus
Midbrain
Hippocampus
Cerebellum
Hindbrain
Same color = Same function!
One experiment set up a matching game for crows.
TAP
Corvus corone
Carrion Crow
The catch was, the rules changed as the game went on.
BZZT
Primates given similar tests used their PFC to flexibly learn and use these abstract rules.
DING!
But crows, even without a PFC, quickly caught on as well.
Yeah, I got this.

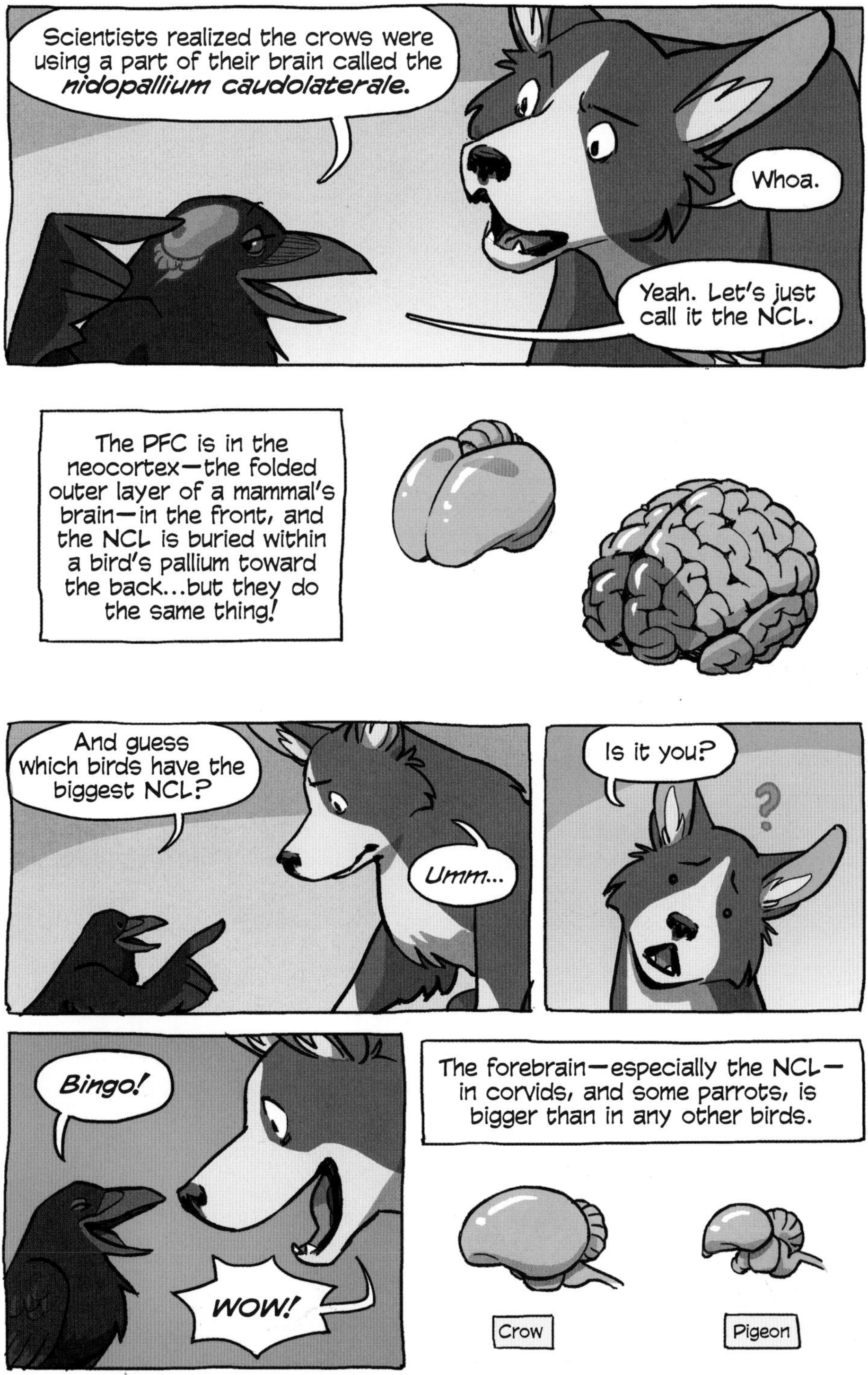
Scientists realized the crows were using a part of their brain called the *nidopallium caudolaterale.*
Whoa.
Yeah. Let's just call it the NCL.
The PFC is in the neocortex—the folded outer layer of a mammal's brain—in the front, and the NCL is buried within a bird's pallium toward the back...but they do the same thing!
And guess which birds have the biggest NCL?
Umm...
Is it you?
?
Bingo!
WOW!
The forebrain—especially the NCL—in corvids, and some parrots, is bigger than in any other birds.
Crow
Pigeon

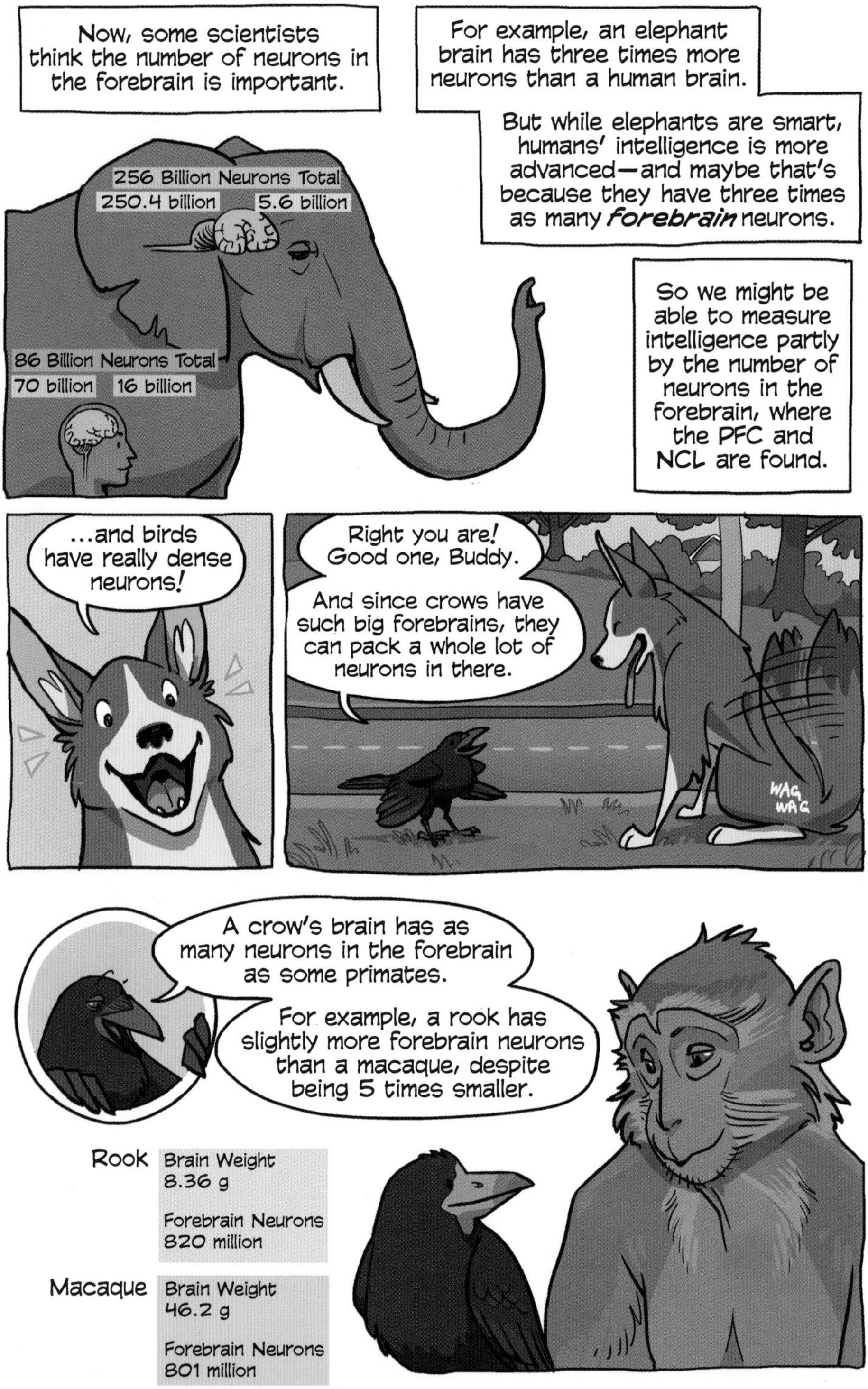
Now, some scientists think the number of neurons in the forebrain is important.
For example, an elephant brain has three times more neurons than a human brain.
But while elephants are smart, humans' intelligence is more advanced—and maybe that's because they have three times as many *forebrain* neurons.
256 Billion Neurons Total
250.4 billion
5.6 billion
86 Billion Neurons Total
70 billion
16 billion
So we might be able to measure intelligence partly by the number of neurons in the forebrain, where the PFC and NCL are found.
...and birds have really dense neurons!
Right you are! Good one, Buddy.
And since crows have such big forebrains, they can pack a whole lot of neurons in there.
WAG WAG
A crow's brain has as many neurons in the forebrain as some primates.
For example, a rook has slightly more forebrain neurons than a macaque, despite being 5 times smaller.
Rook
Brain Weight
8.36 g
Forebrain Neurons
820 million
Macaque
Brain Weight
46.2 g
Forebrain Neurons
801 million

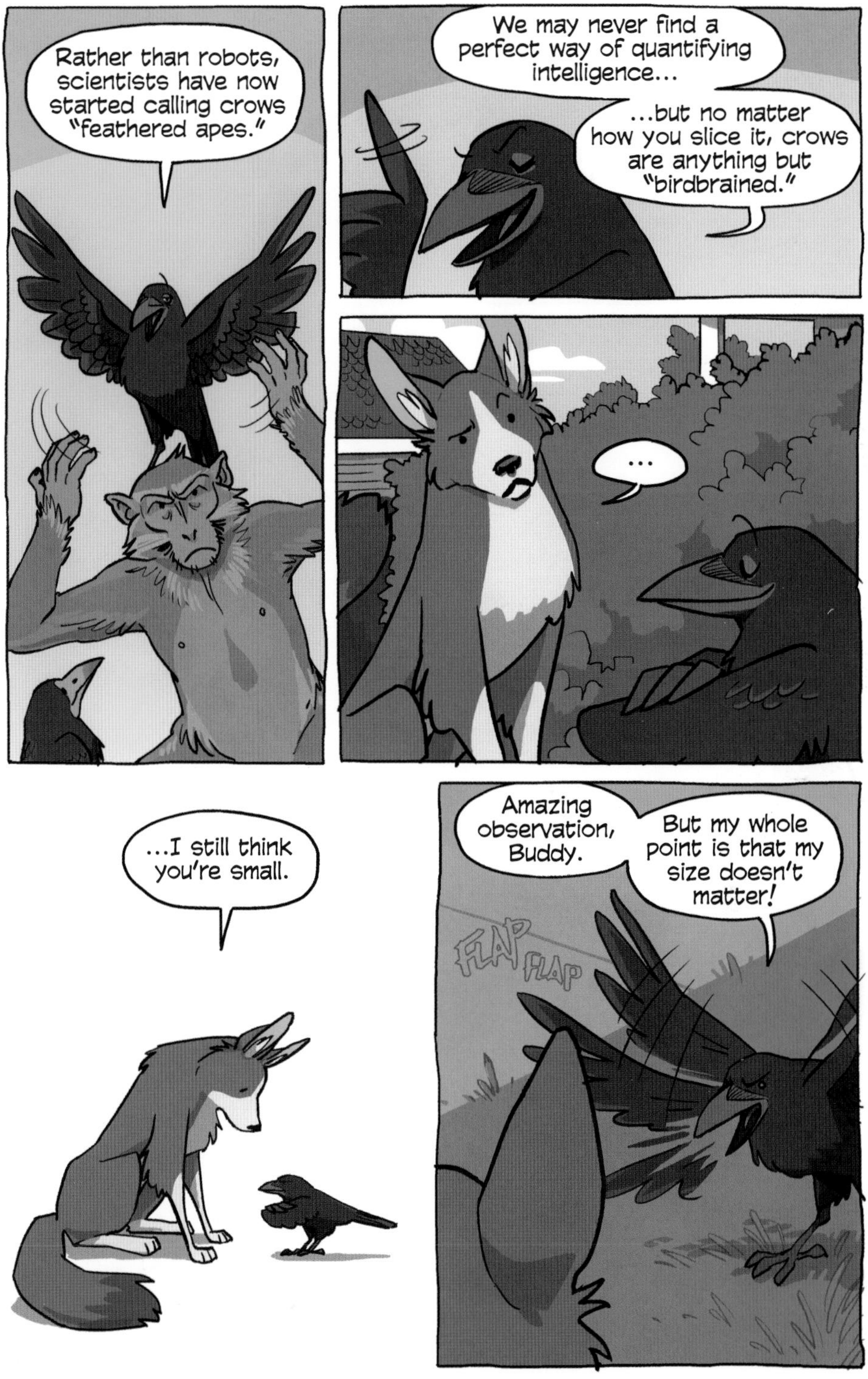
Rather than robots, scientists have now started calling crows "feathered apes."
We may never find a perfect way of quantifying intelligence...
...but no matter how you slice it, crows are anything but "birdbrained."
...
...I still think you're small.
Amazing observation, Buddy.
But my whole point is that my size doesn't matter!
FLAP FLAP

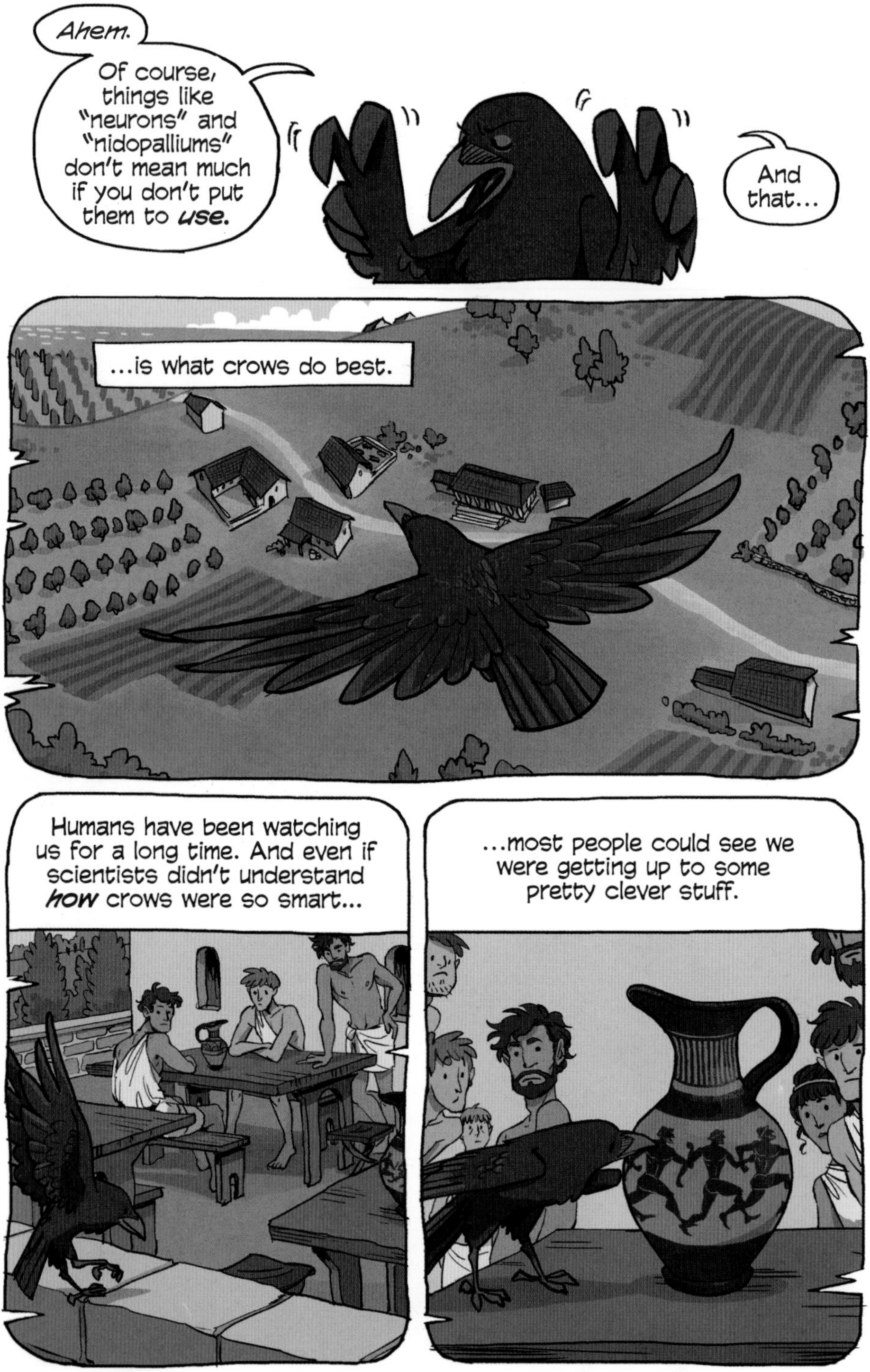
Ahem.
Of course, things like "neurons" and "nidopalliums" don't mean much if you don't put them to use.
And that...
...is what crows do best.
Humans have been watching us for a long time. And even if scientists didn't understand how crows were so smart...
...most people could see we were getting up to some pretty clever stuff.

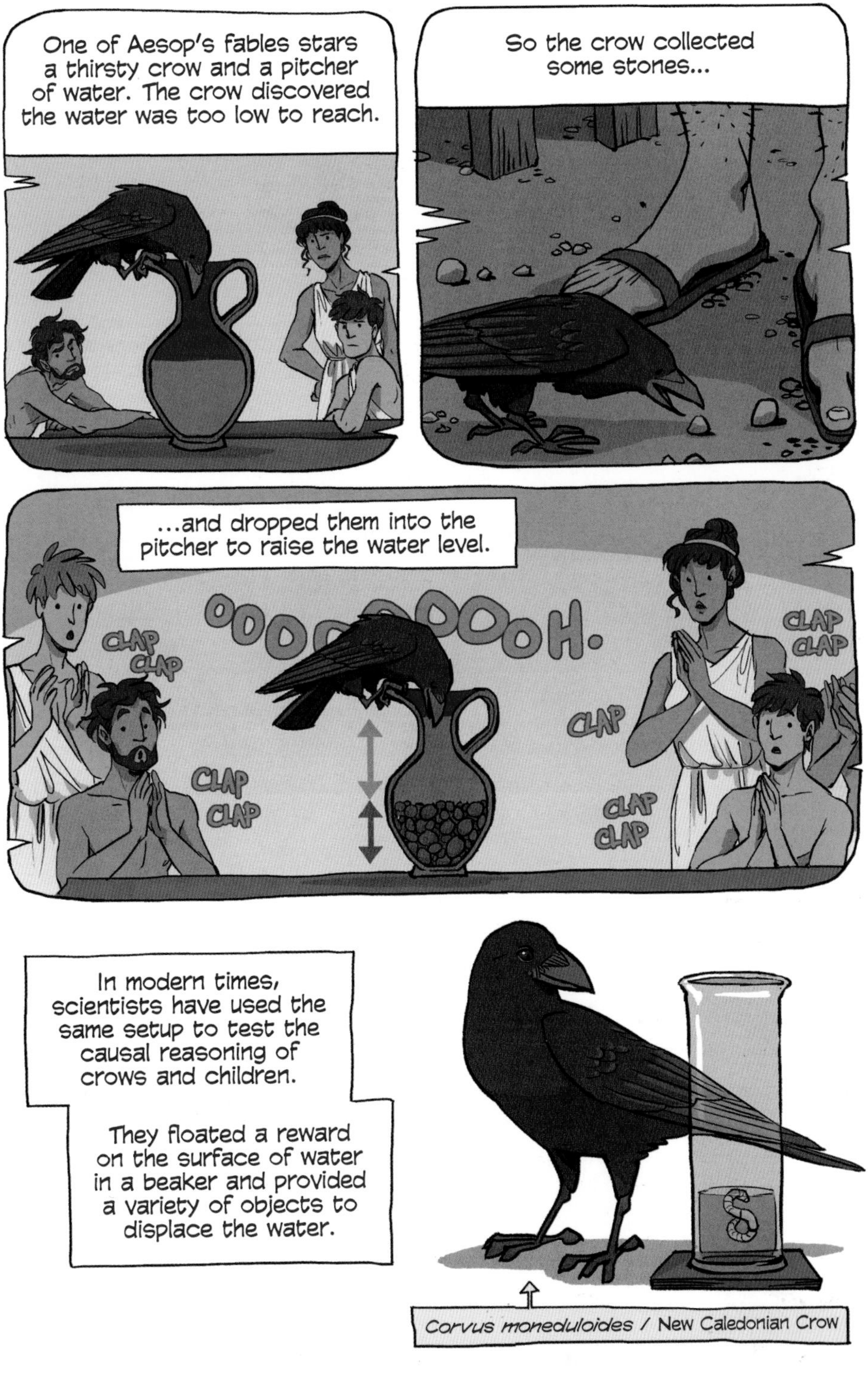
One of Aesop's fables stars a thirsty crow and a pitcher of water. The crow discovered the water was too low to reach.
So the crow collected some stones...
...and dropped them into the pitcher to raise the water level.
CLAP CLAP
OOOOOOOOH.
CLAP CLAP
CLAP
CLAP CLAP
CLAP CLAP
In modern times, scientists have used the same setup to test the causal reasoning of crows and children.
They floated a reward on the surface of water in a beaker and provided a variety of objects to displace the water.
Corvus moneduloides / New Caledonian Crow

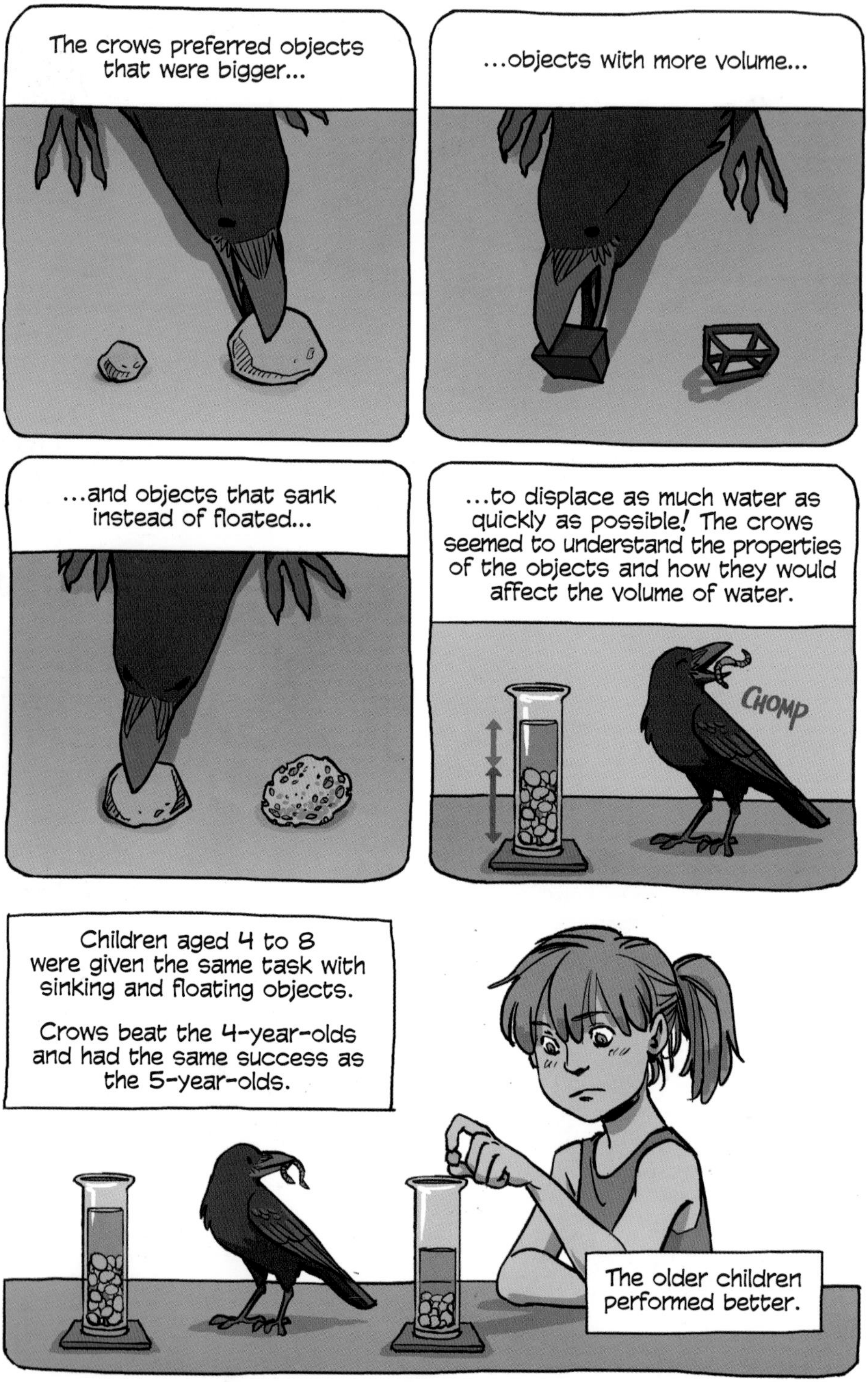
The crows preferred objects that were bigger...
...objects with more volume...
...and objects that sank instead of floated...
...to displace as much water as quickly as possible! The crows seemed to understand the properties of the objects and how they would affect the volume of water.
CHOMP
Children aged 4 to 8 were given the same task with sinking and floating objects.
Crows beat the 4-year-olds and had the same success as the 5-year-olds.
The older children performed better.

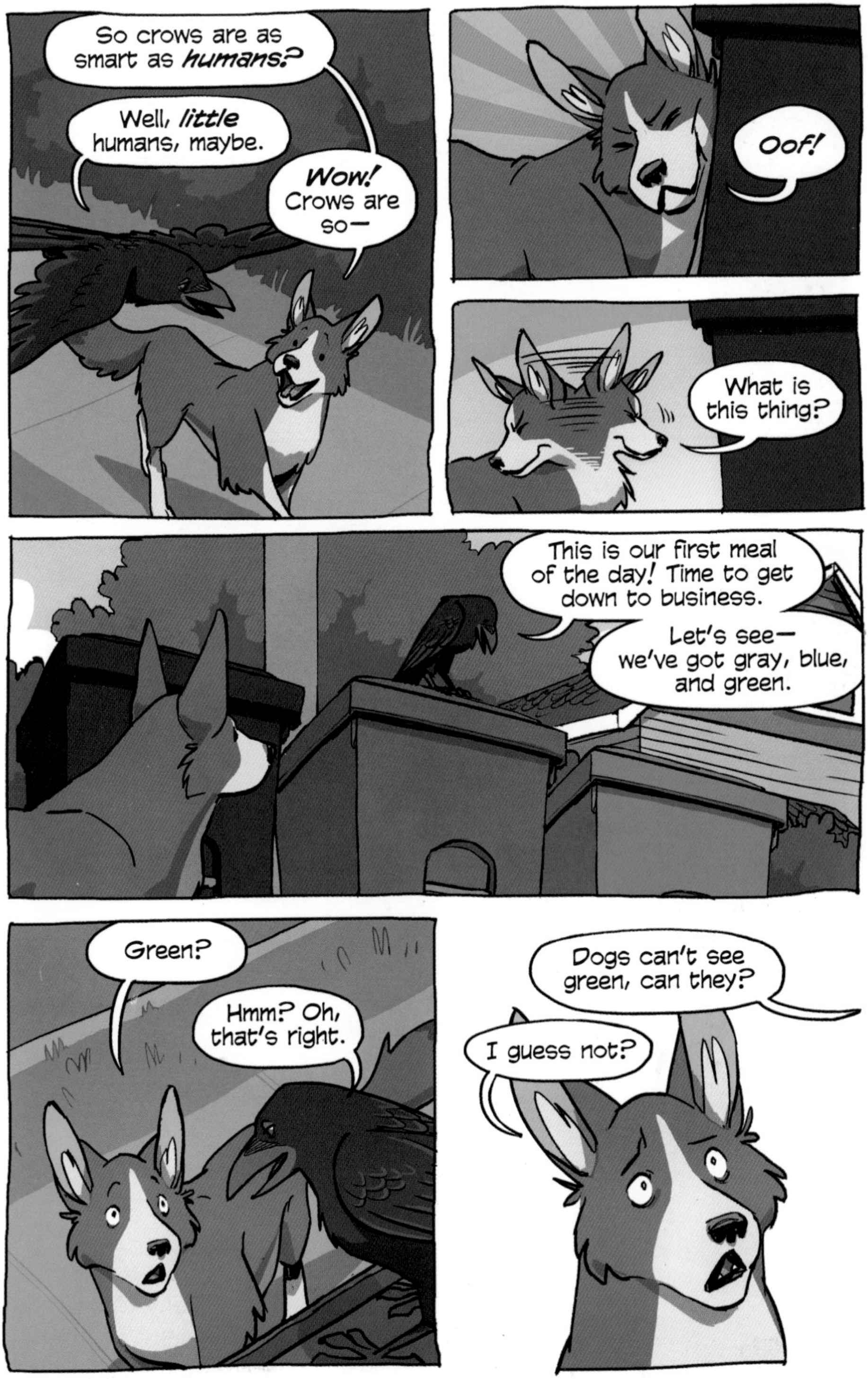
So crows are as smart as ***humans?***
Well, ***little*** humans, maybe.
Wow! Crows are so—
Oof!
What is this thing?
This is our first meal of the day! Time to get down to business.
Let's see— we've got gray, blue, and green.
Green?
Hmm? Oh, that's right.
Dogs can't see green, can they?
I guess not?

Never fear! Birds have *great* color vision.

Humans have three types of *cone cells* in their eyes—these are cells that receive light, which the brain translates into color.

But birds have four, letting us see into the ultraviolet spectrum.

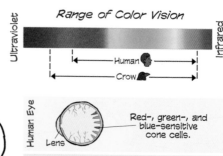

Range of Color Vision

Ultraviolet

Infrared

Human

Crow

Human Eye

Lens

Red-, green-, and blue-sensitive cone cells.

Crow Eye

Lens

Red-, green-, blue-, and violet-sensitive cone cells.

Oil droplets on each cone cell enhance color vision!

Since dogs only have two receptors, it may look different to you. You'll just have to trust me that these trashcans are different colors.

Buddy Vision

The trouble is, I'm not sure which one has the food in it.

Huh?

I thought you were super smart!

I'm smart, not psychic! This is my first time doing this!

Yeesh.

Hmm...

Arrgh!

Just knock them all over!

All of them?

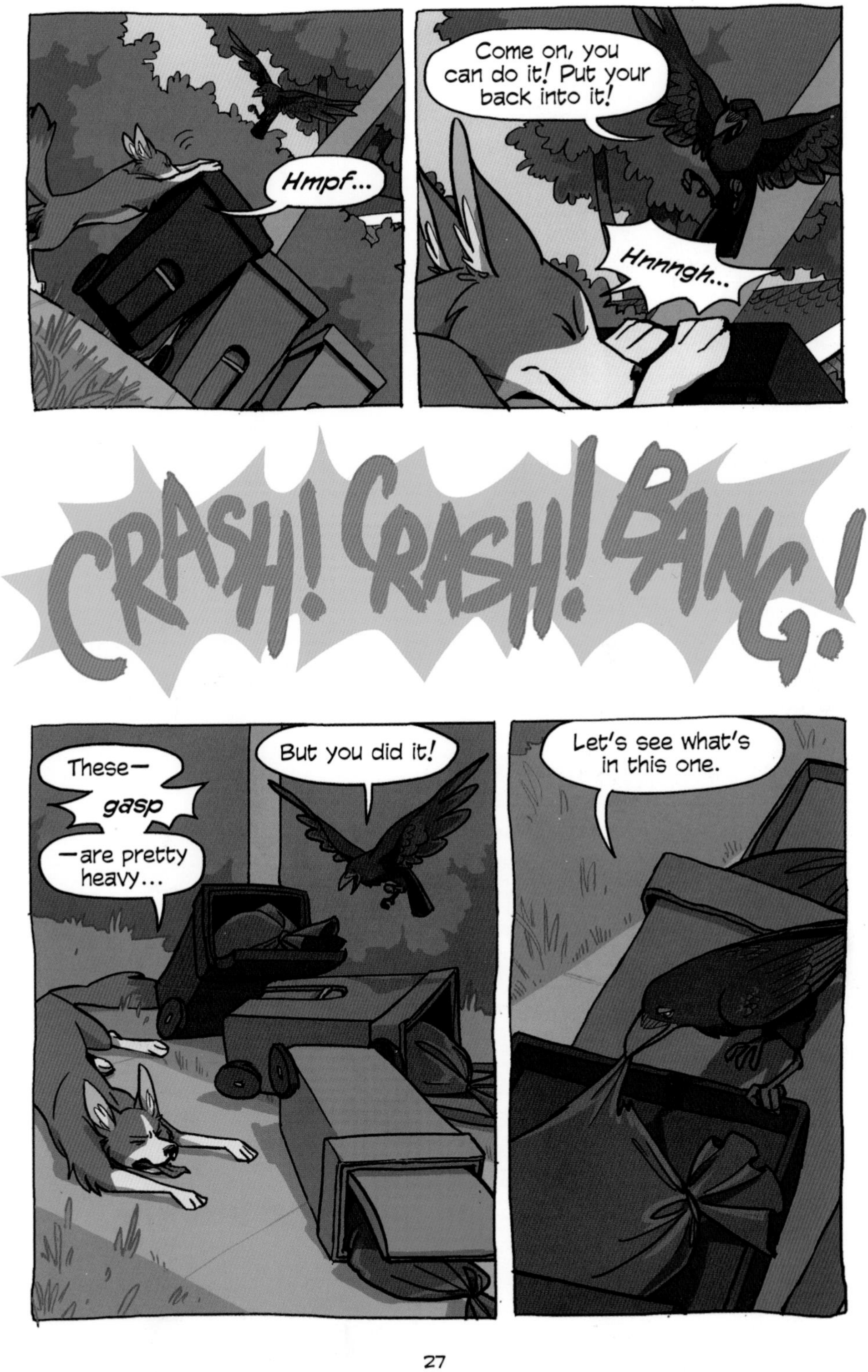
Hmpf...
Come on, you can do it! Put your back into it!
Hnnngh...
CRASH! CRASH! BANG!
These—
gasp
—are pretty heavy...
But you did it!
Let's see what's in this one.

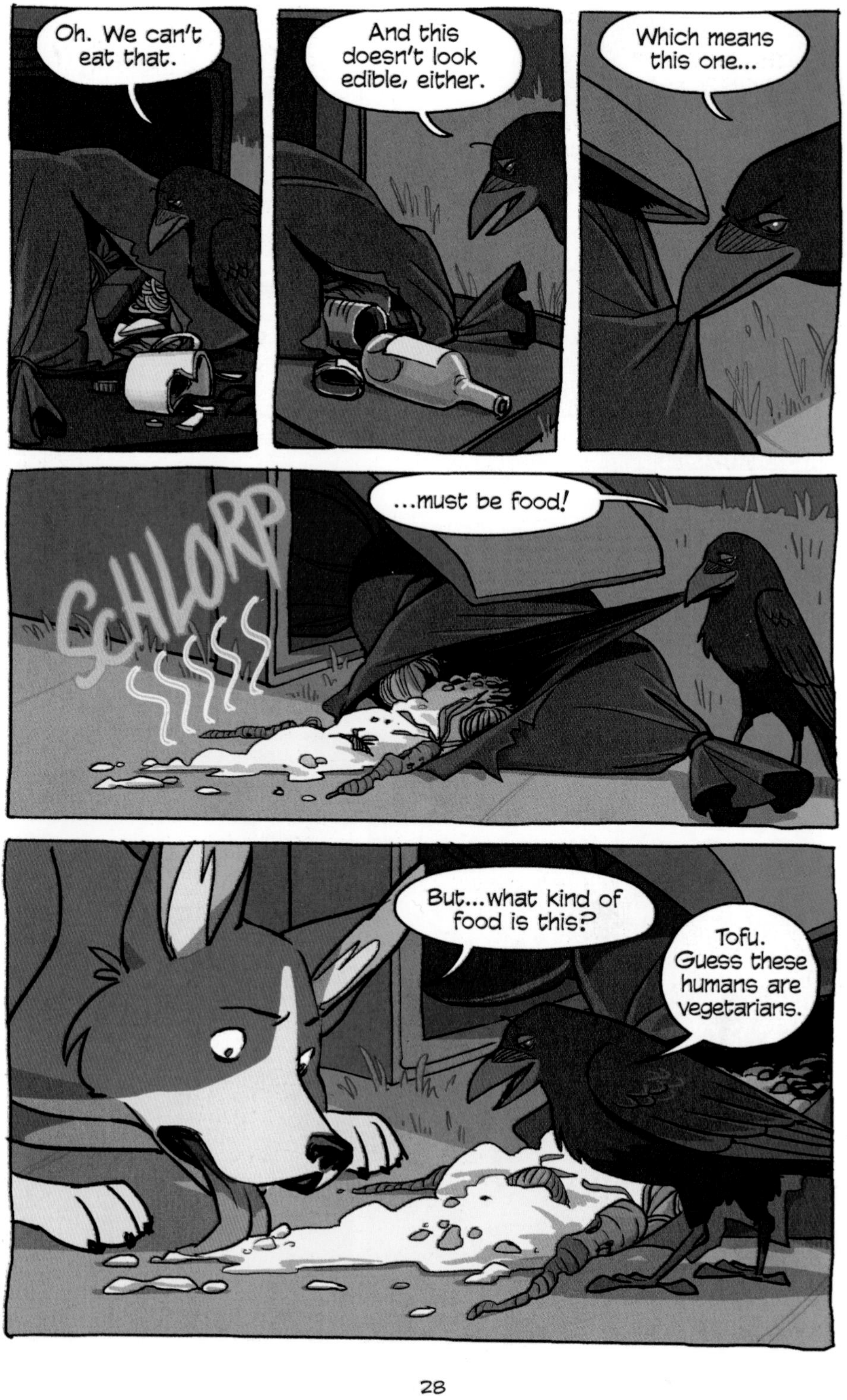
Oh. We can't eat that.
And this doesn't look edible, either.
Which means this one...
SCHLORP
...must be food!
But...what kind of food is this?
Tofu. Guess these humans are vegetarians.

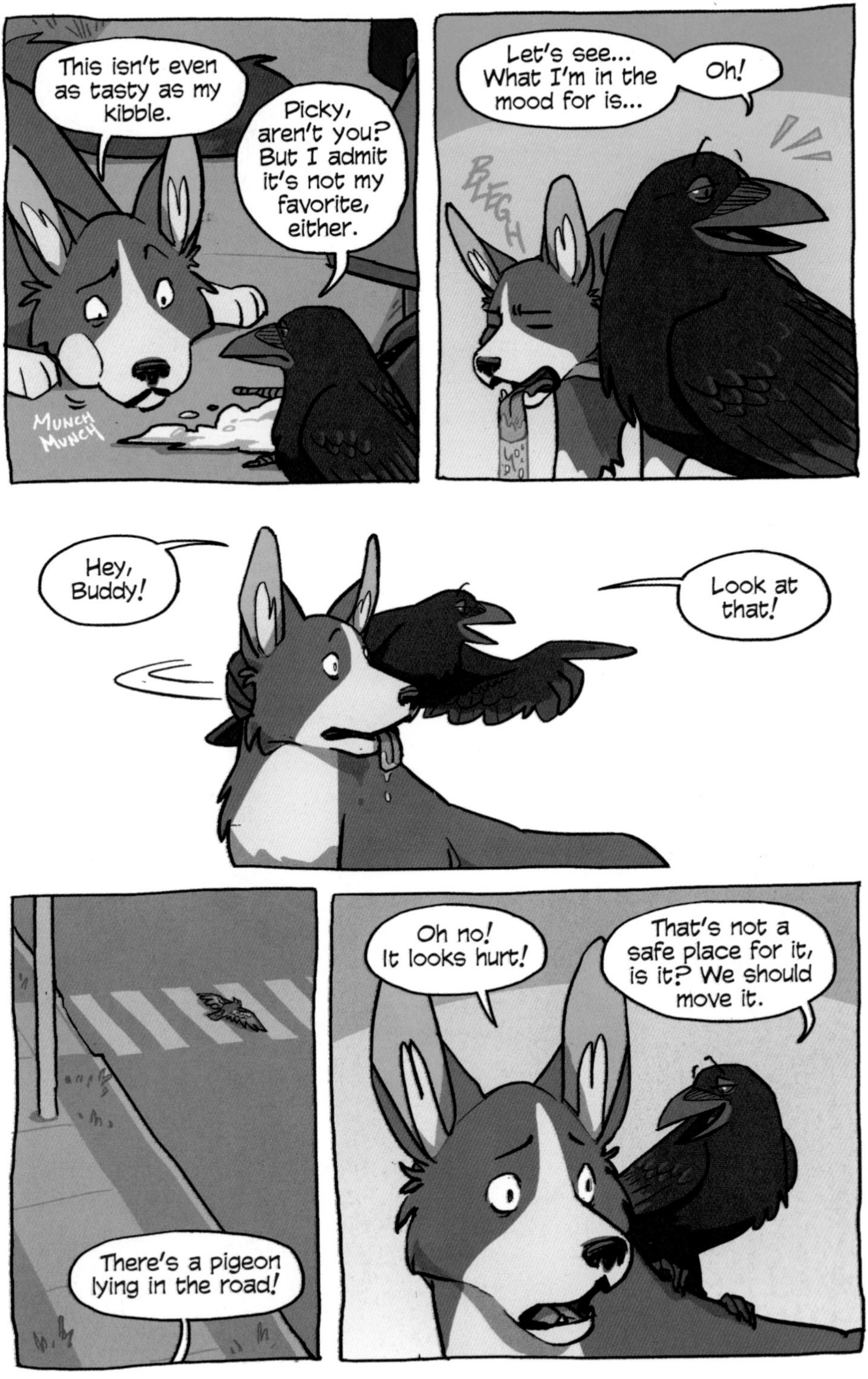
This isn't even as tasty as my kibble.
Picky, aren't you? But I admit it's not my favorite, either.
MUNCH MUNCH
Let's see... What I'm in the mood for is...
Oh!
BLEGH
Hey, Buddy!
Look at that!
There's a pigeon lying in the road!
Oh no! It looks hurt!
That's not a safe place for it, is it? We should move it.

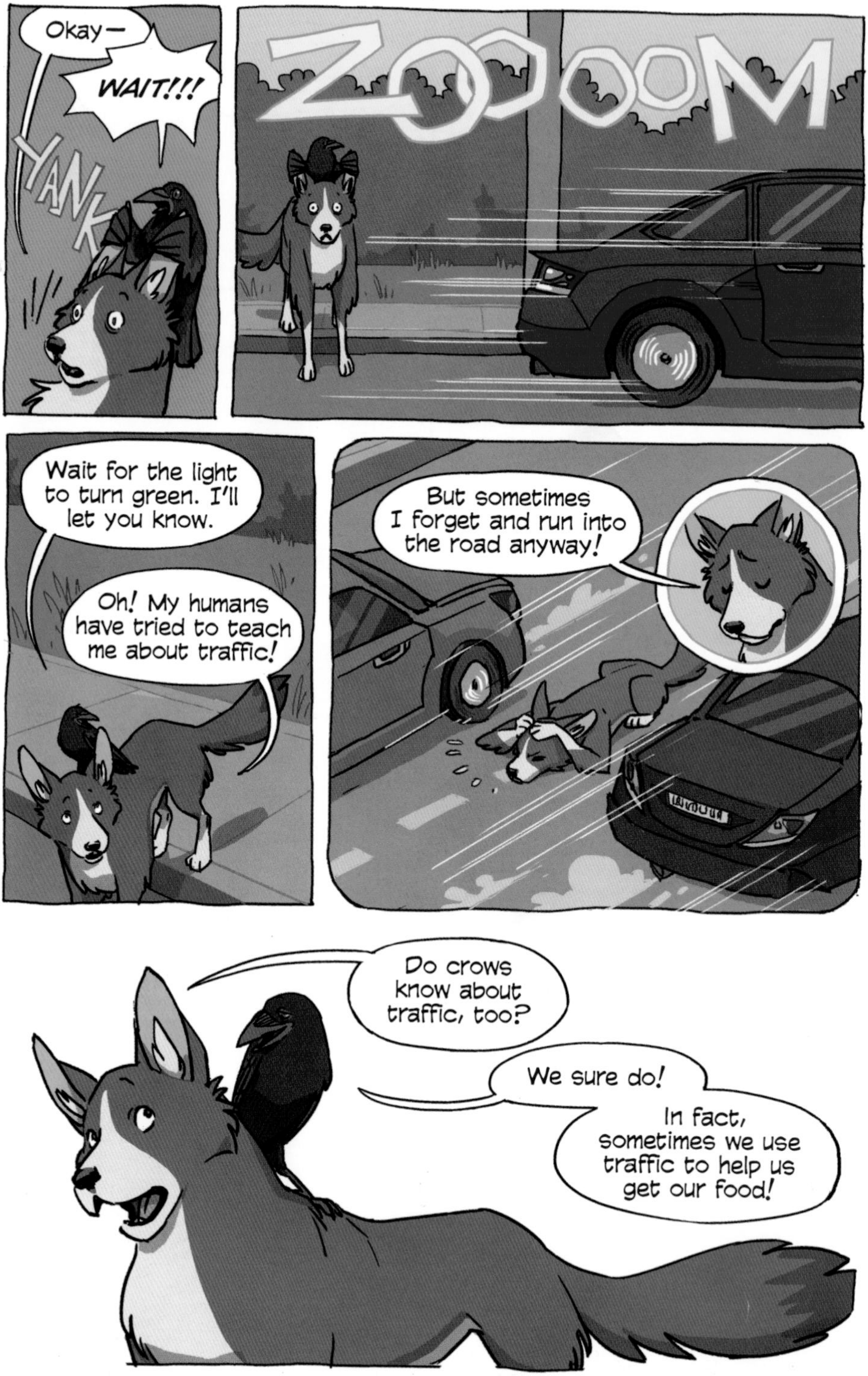
Okay—
WAIT!!!
YANK
ZOOOOM
Wait for the light to turn green. I'll let you know.
Oh! My humans have tried to teach me about traffic!
But sometimes I forget and run into the road anyway!
Do crows know about traffic, too?
We sure do!
In fact, sometimes we use traffic to help us get our food!

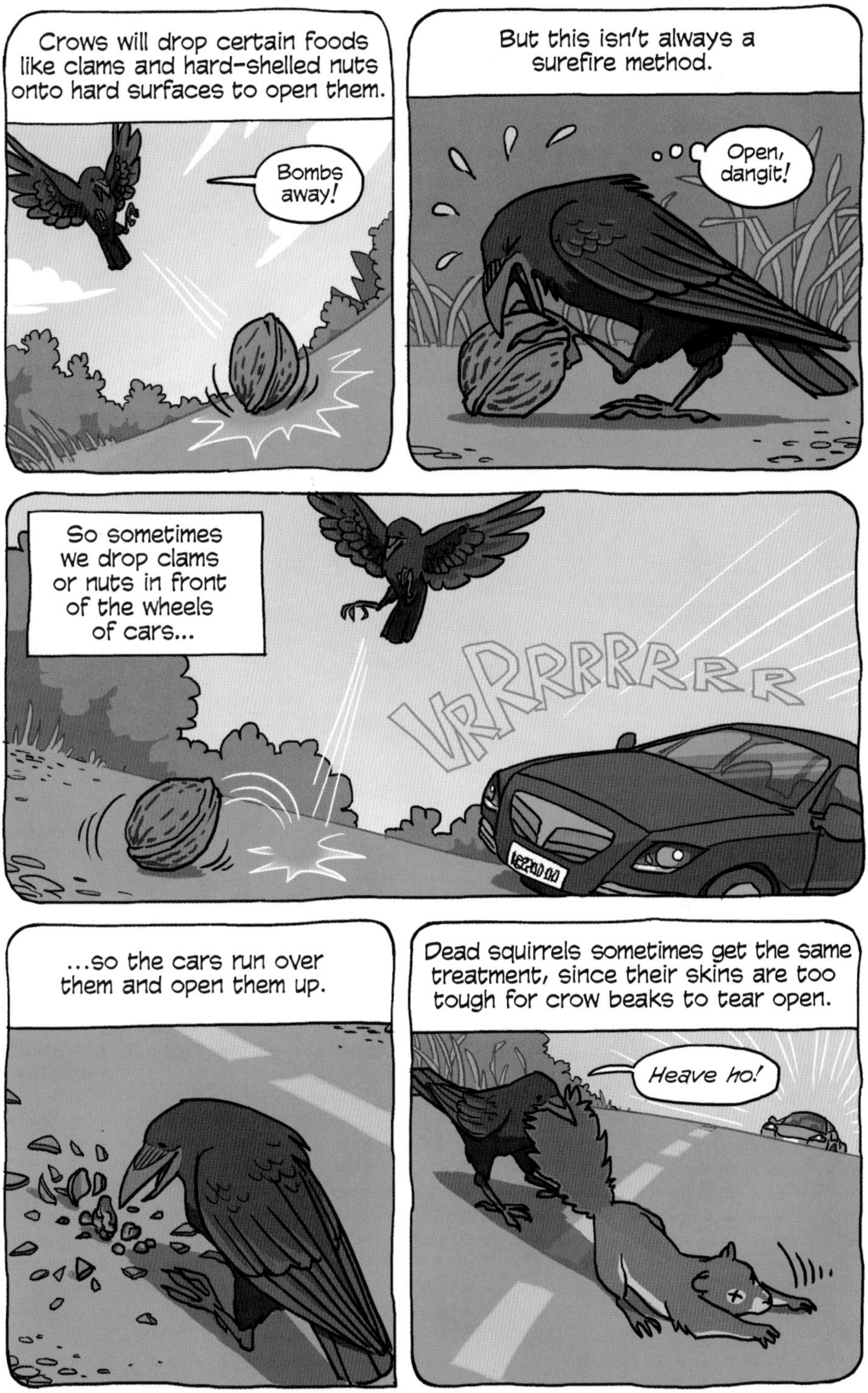
Crows will drop certain foods like clams and hard-shelled nuts onto hard surfaces to open them.
Bombs away!
But this isn't always a surefire method.
Open, dangit!
So sometimes we drop clams or nuts in front of the wheels of cars...
VRRRRRRRR
...so the cars run over them and open them up.
Dead squirrels sometimes get the same treatment, since their skins are too tough for crow beaks to tear open.
Heave ho!

Some crows have perfected this technique.

They position themselves on wires above crosswalks to drop their walnuts.

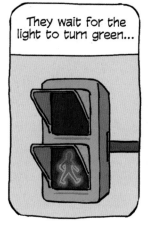

They wait for the light to turn green...

...then collect their opened nuts when it's safe.

Safety first!

Impressive, eh?

Nuts aren't as tasty as kibble, either.

Well, *you're* a tough nut to crack, aren't you? The light's green now, by the way.

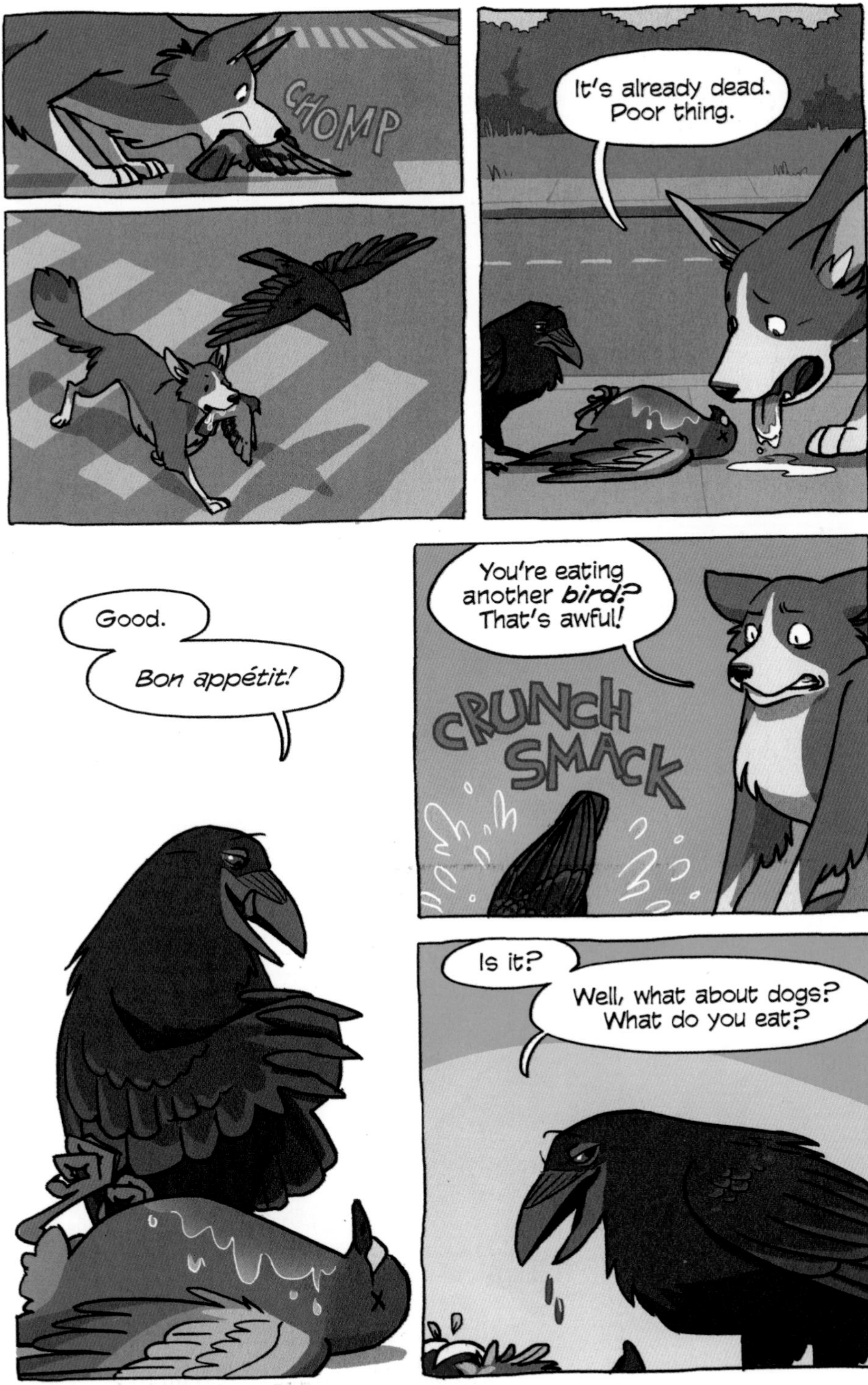
CHOMP
It's already dead. Poor thing.
Good.
Bon appétit!
You're eating another bird? That's awful!
CRUNCH
SMACK
Is it?
Well, what about dogs? What do you eat?

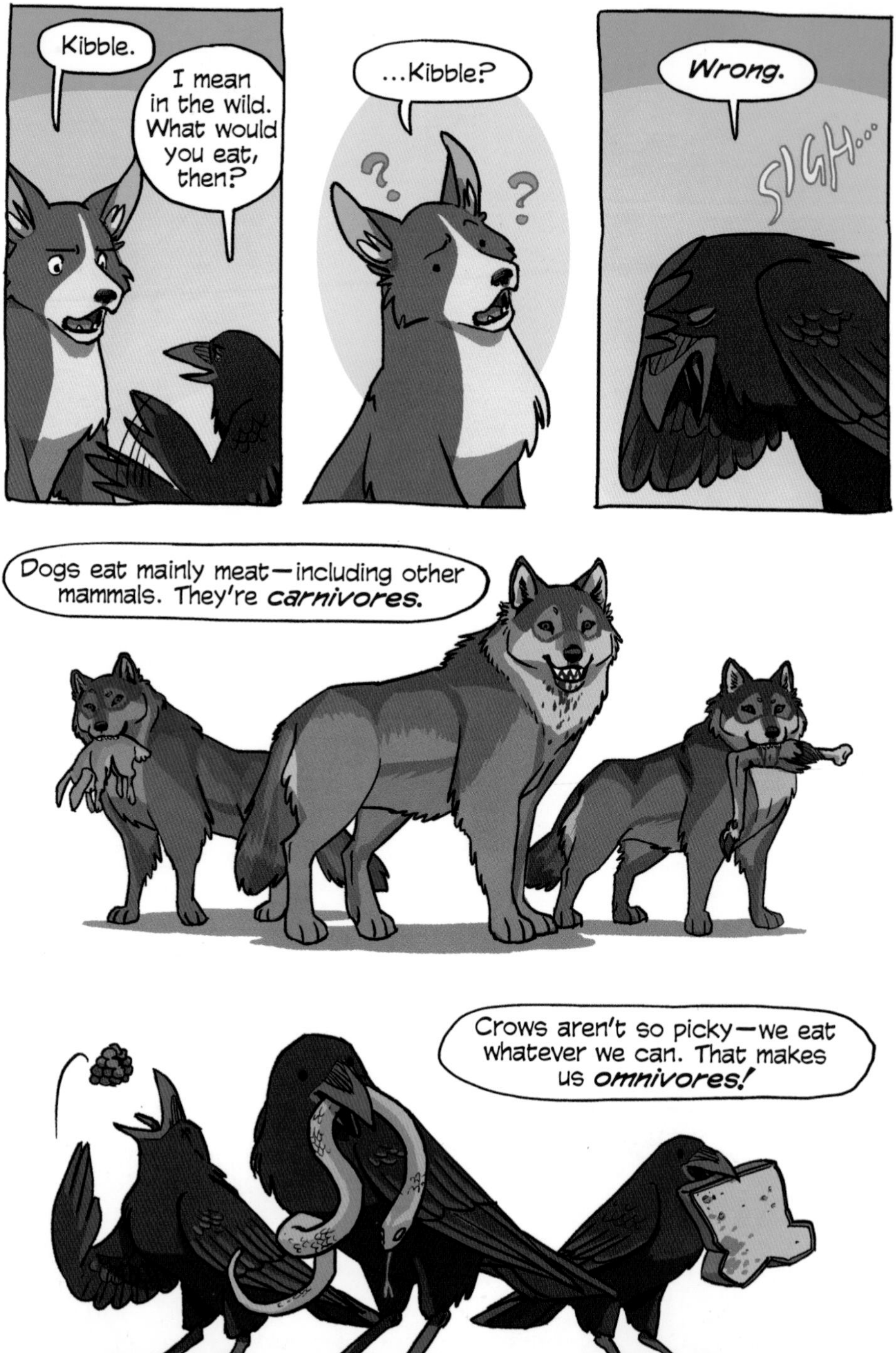
Kibble.
I mean in the wild. What would you eat, then?
...Kibble?
Wrong.
SIGH...
Dogs eat mainly meat—including other mammals. They're carnivores.
Crows aren't so picky—we eat whatever we can. That makes us omnivores!

A Crow's Diet

What a crow eats partly depends on where it lives. In urban areas, human garbage is a perennial favorite for crows and usually makes up most of our diet.

But we still keep up a more traditional diet as well!

| Some common foods are nuts and seeds, | fruits, | grains, | and eggs. |

| We get meat from invertebrates, | fish, | frogs and snakes, | and nestlings... |

...and, of course, carrion!

Which, in settled areas, usually means roadkill.

Ahem. Not that roadkill is a huge part of our diet.

We're pretty conspicuous when we're eating at the roadside, so some humans think that's *all we eat.*

But even in cities, roadkill makes up about only 5% of our diet.

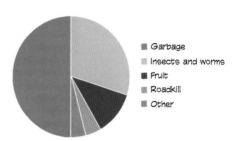

SSSLURP

Researchers recorded what crows in an urban area ate over the course of two seasons. Garbage and bugs won out big time.

- ■ Garbage
- ■ Insects and worms
- ■ Fruit
- ■ Roadkill
- ■ Other

Still, roadkill is *sooo* tasty. Want a bite?

Hmm... I'm not sure.

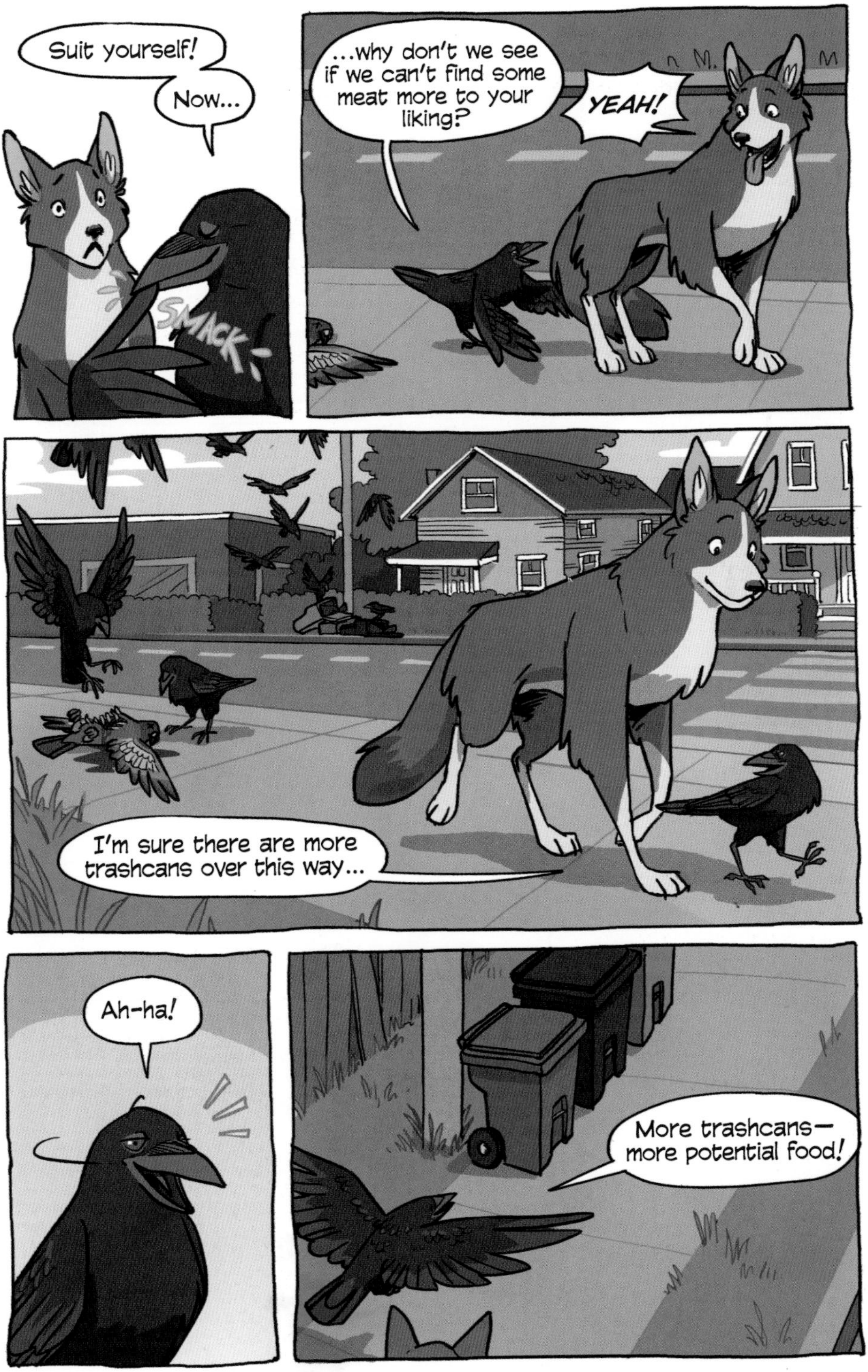
Suit yourself!
Now...
SMACK
...why don't we see if we can't find some meat more to your liking?
YEAH!
I'm sure there are more trashcans over this way...
Ah-ha!
More trashcans— more potential food!

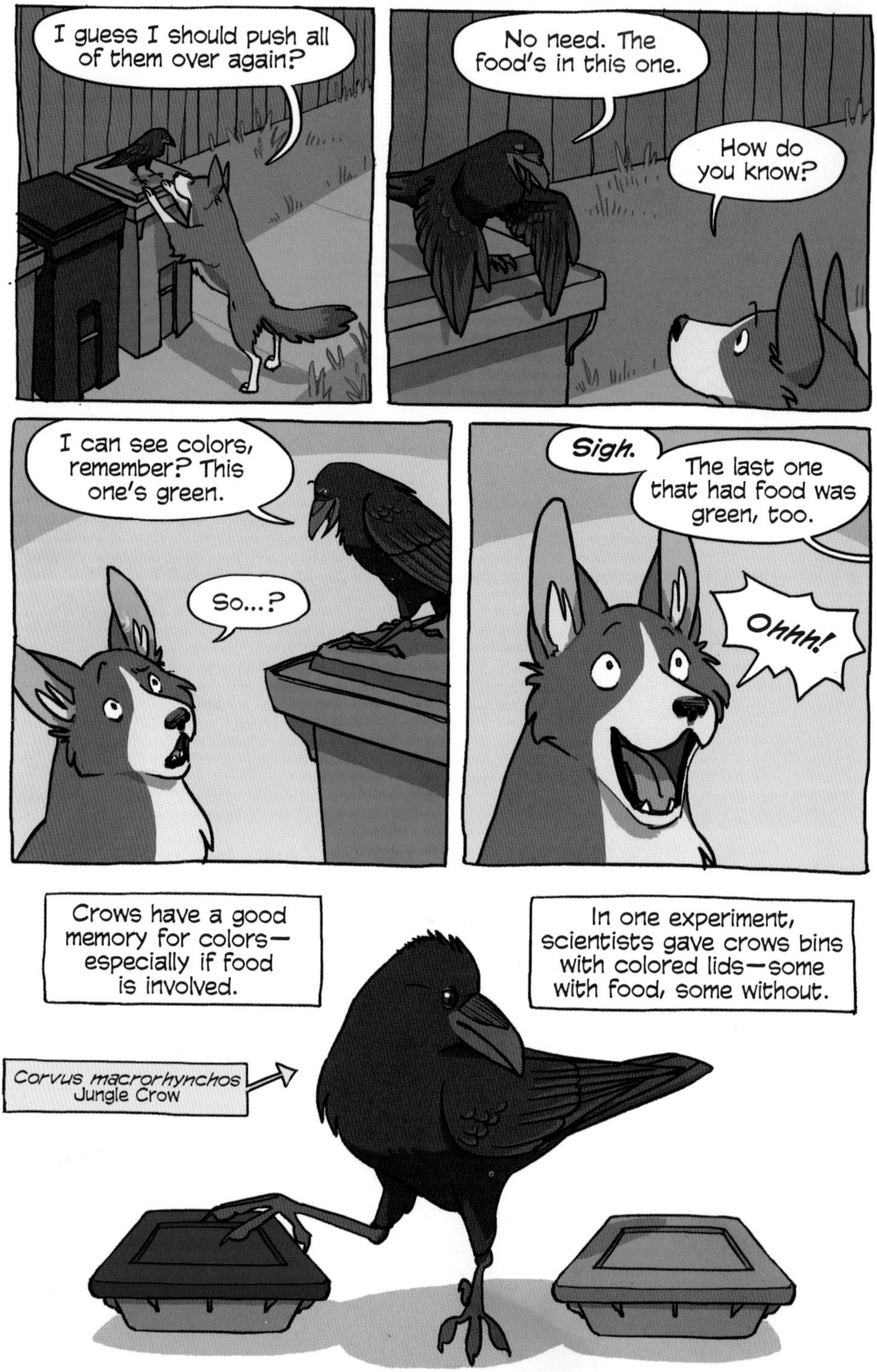
I guess I should push all of them over again?
No need. The food's in this one.
How do you know?
I can see colors, remember? This one's green.
So...?
Sigh.
The last one that had food was green, too.
Ohhh!
Crows have a good memory for colors—especially if food is involved.
In one experiment, scientists gave crows bins with colored lids—some with food, some without.
Corvus macrorhynchos
Jungle Crow

The crows quickly learned which colors had food in them.

Nearly a year passed...

...and the crows still remembered which colors of bin held the food.

Too easy!

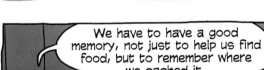

We have to have a good memory, not just to help us find food, but to remember where we cached it.

Cached it?

When an animal *caches* food, that means it's hiding it away to eat later.

Oh! I know this trick!

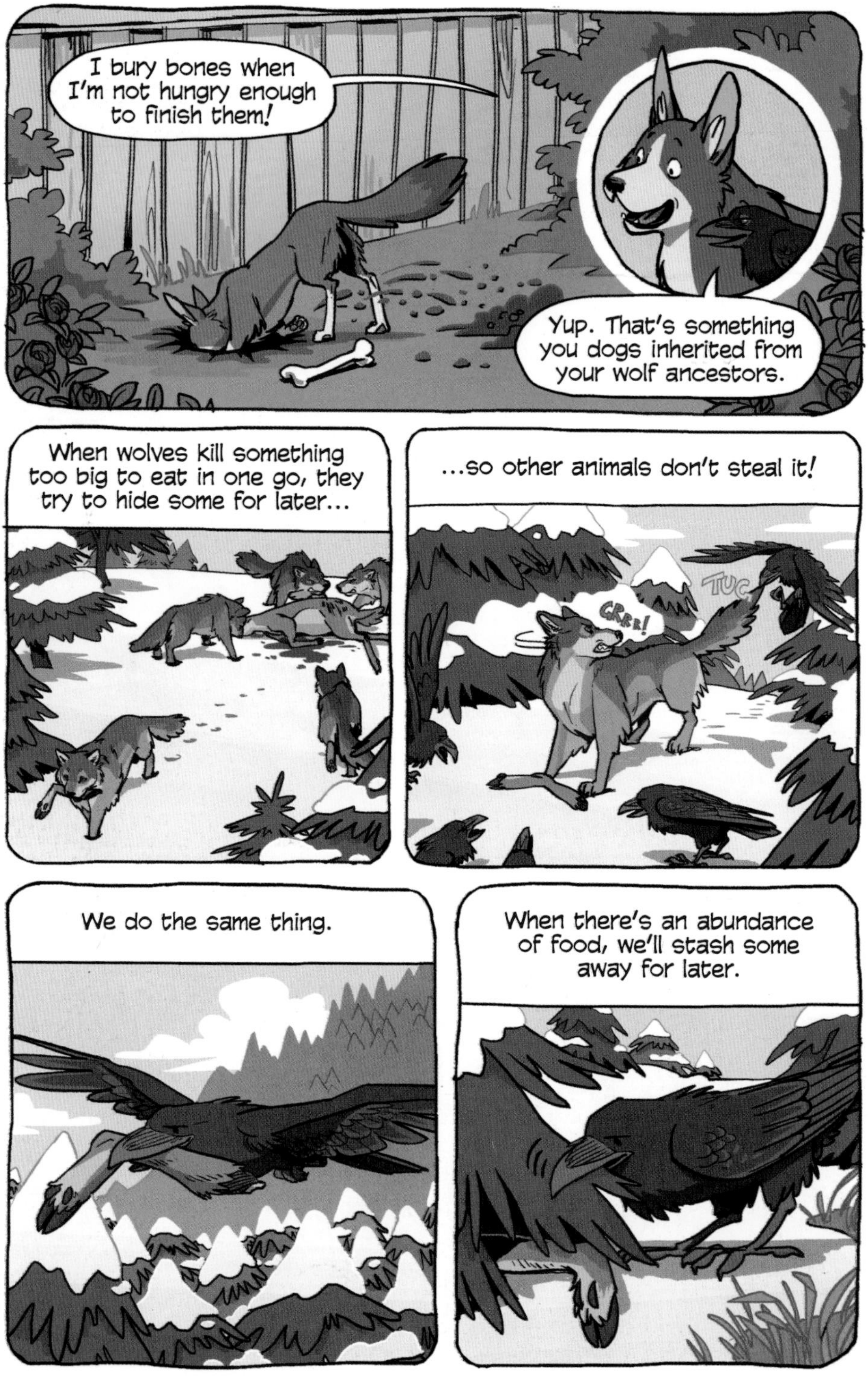
I bury bones when I'm not hungry enough to finish them!
Yup. That's something you dogs inherited from your wolf ancestors.
When wolves kill something too big to eat in one go, they try to hide some for later...
...so other animals don't steal it!
GRRR!
TUG
We do the same thing.
When there's an abundance of food, we'll stash some away for later.

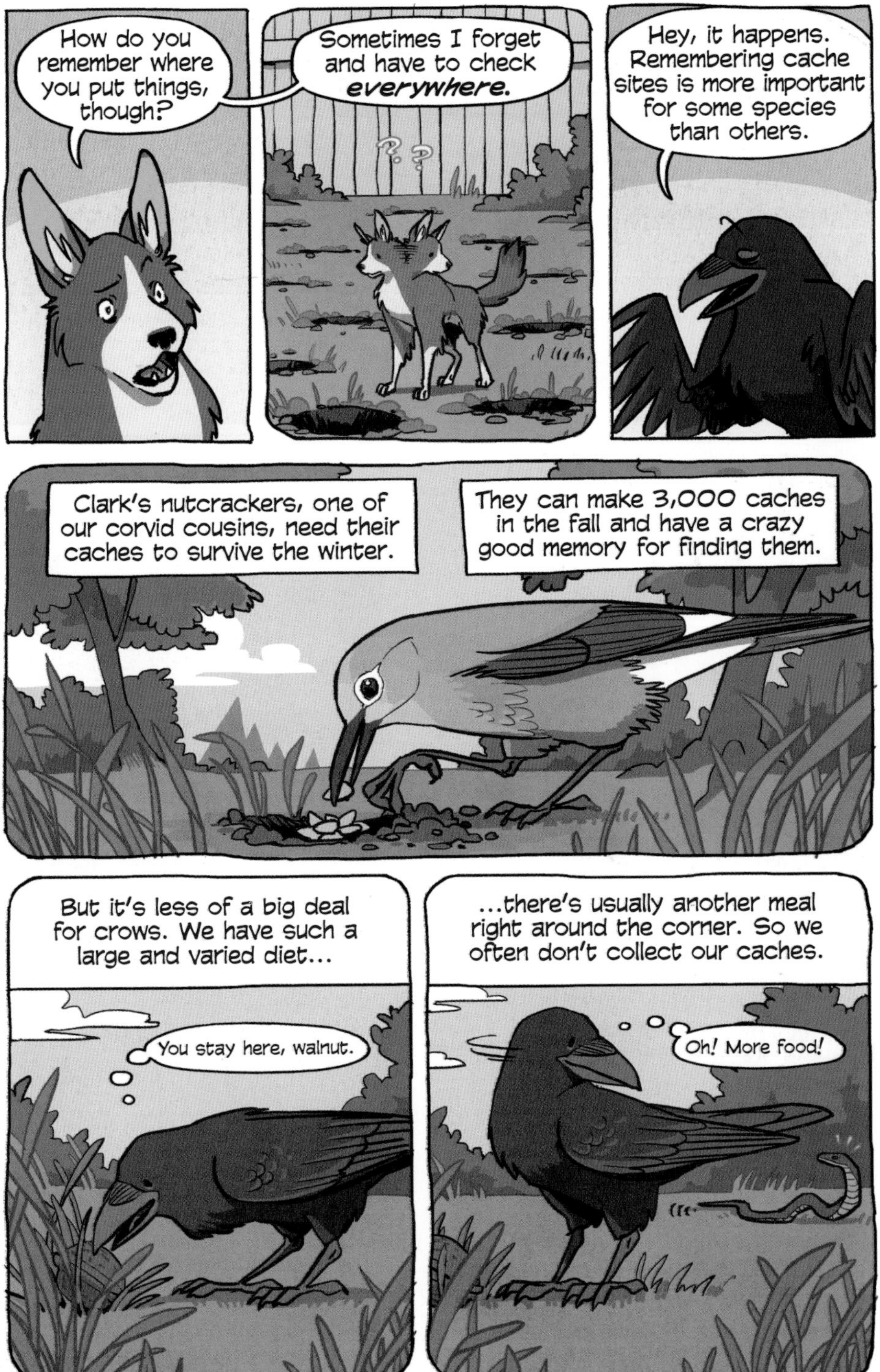
How do you remember where you put things, though?
Sometimes I forget and have to check *everywhere.*
? ?
Hey, it happens. Remembering cache sites is more important for some species than others.
Clark's nutcrackers, one of our corvid cousins, need their caches to survive the winter.
They can make 3,000 caches in the fall and have a crazy good memory for finding them.
But it's less of a big deal for crows. We have such a large and varied diet...
You stay here, walnut.
...there's usually another meal right around the corner. So we often don't collect our caches.
Oh! More food!

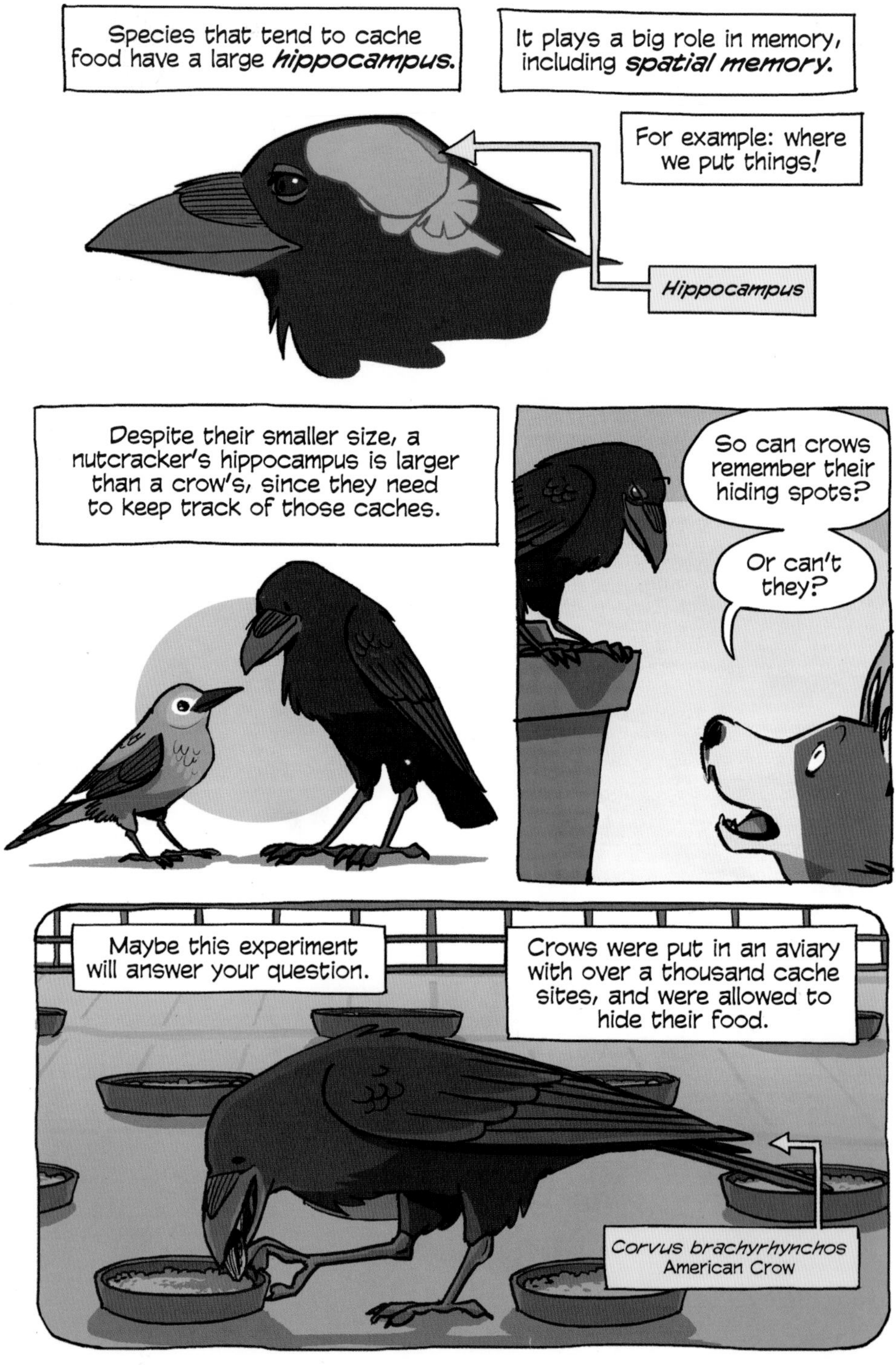

Species that tend to cache food have a large *hippocampus.*
It plays a big role in memory, including ***spatial memory.***
For example: where we put things!
Hippocampus
Despite their smaller size, a nutcracker's hippocampus is larger than a crow's, since they need to keep track of those caches.
So can crows remember their hiding spots?
Or can't they?
Maybe this experiment will answer your question.
Crows were put in an aviary with over a thousand cache sites, and were allowed to hide their food.
Corvus brachyrhynchos
American Crow

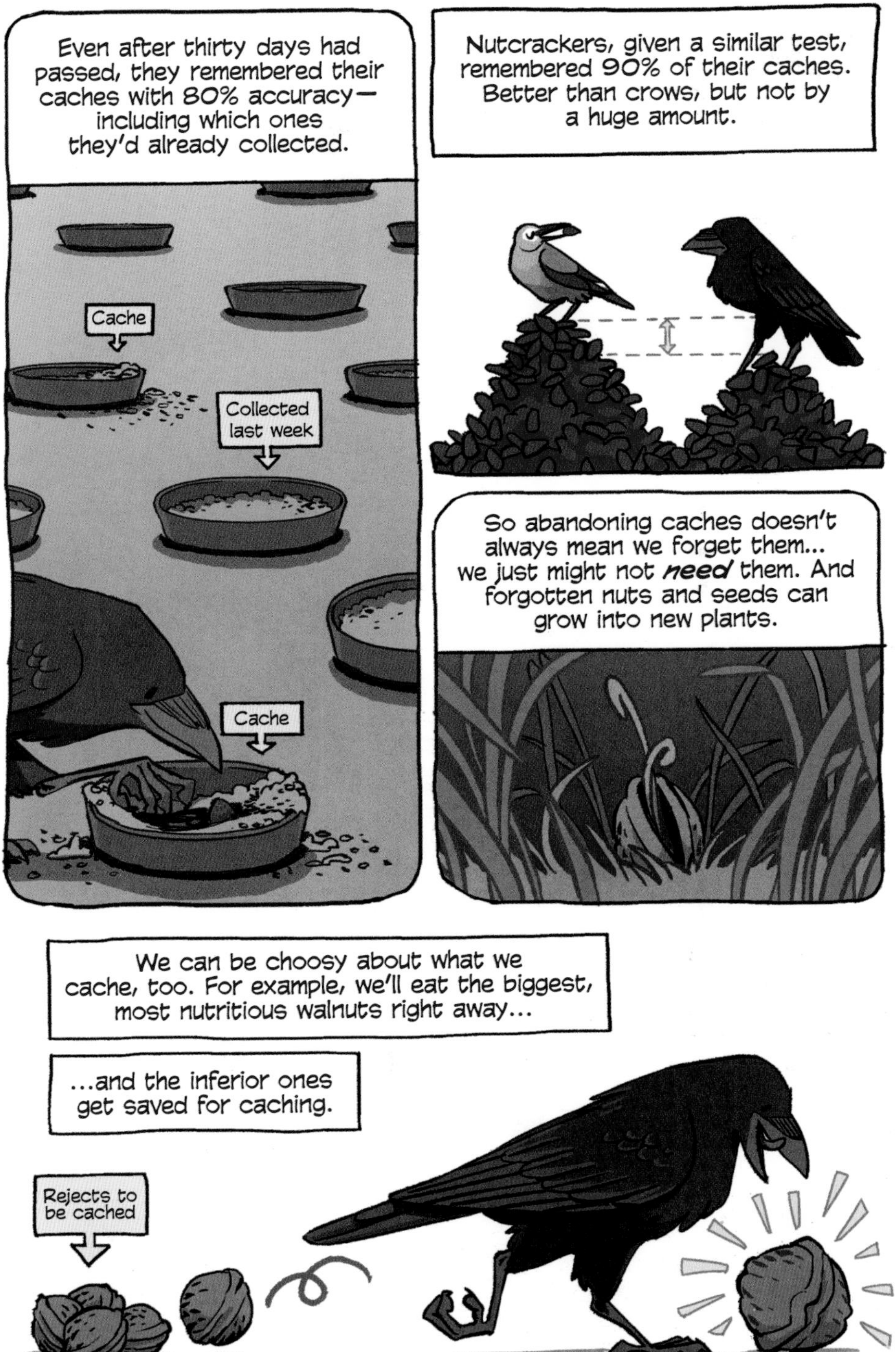

Even after thirty days had passed, they remembered their caches with 80% accuracy—including which ones they'd already collected.
Cache
Collected last week
Cache
Nutcrackers, given a similar test, remembered 90% of their caches. Better than crows, but not by a huge amount.
So abandoning caches doesn't always mean we forget them... we just might not *need* them. And forgotten nuts and seeds can grow into new plants.
We can be choosy about what we cache, too. For example, we'll eat the biggest, most nutritious walnuts right away...
...and the inferior ones get saved for caching.
Rejects to be cached

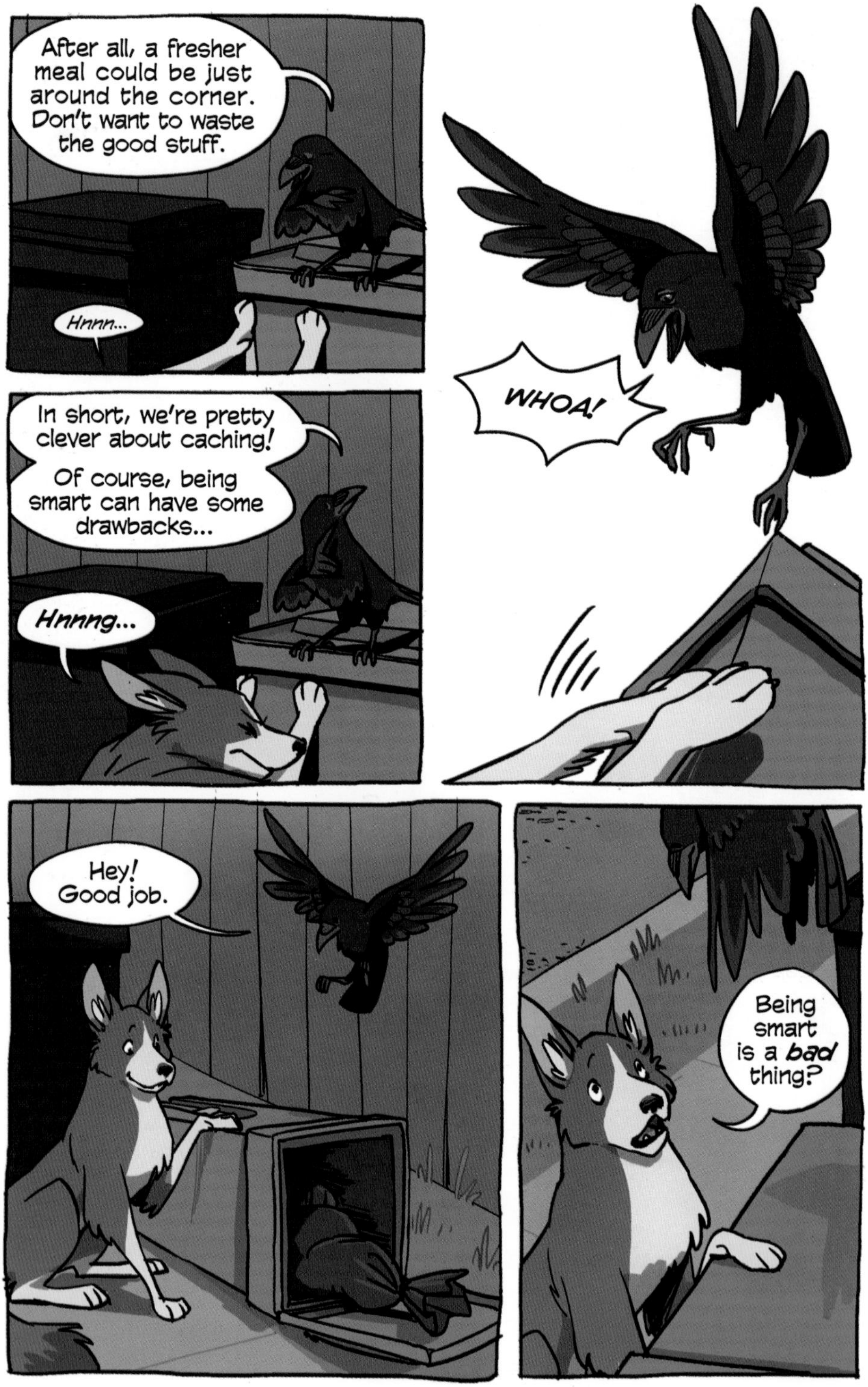
After all, a fresher meal could be just around the corner. Don't want to waste the good stuff.
Hnnn...
In short, we're pretty clever about caching!
Of course, being smart can have some drawbacks...
Hnnng...
WHOA!
Hey! Good job.
Being smart is a *bad* thing?

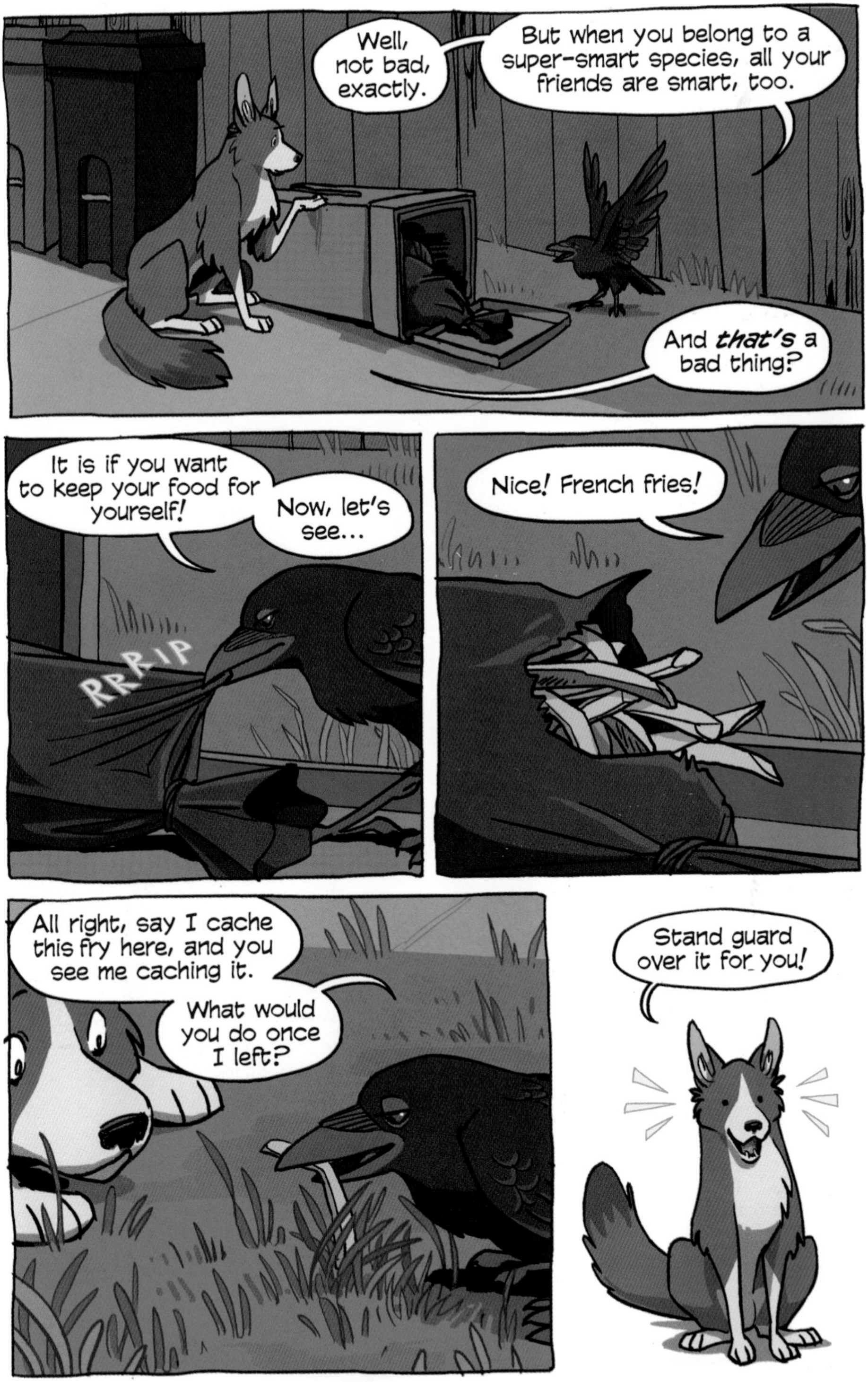
Well, not bad, exactly.
But when you belong to a super-smart species, all your friends are smart, too.
And *that's* a bad thing?
It is if you want to keep your food for yourself!
Now, let's see...
RRRIP
Nice! French fries!
All right, say I cache this fry here, and you see me caching it.
What would you do once I left?
Stand guard over it for you!

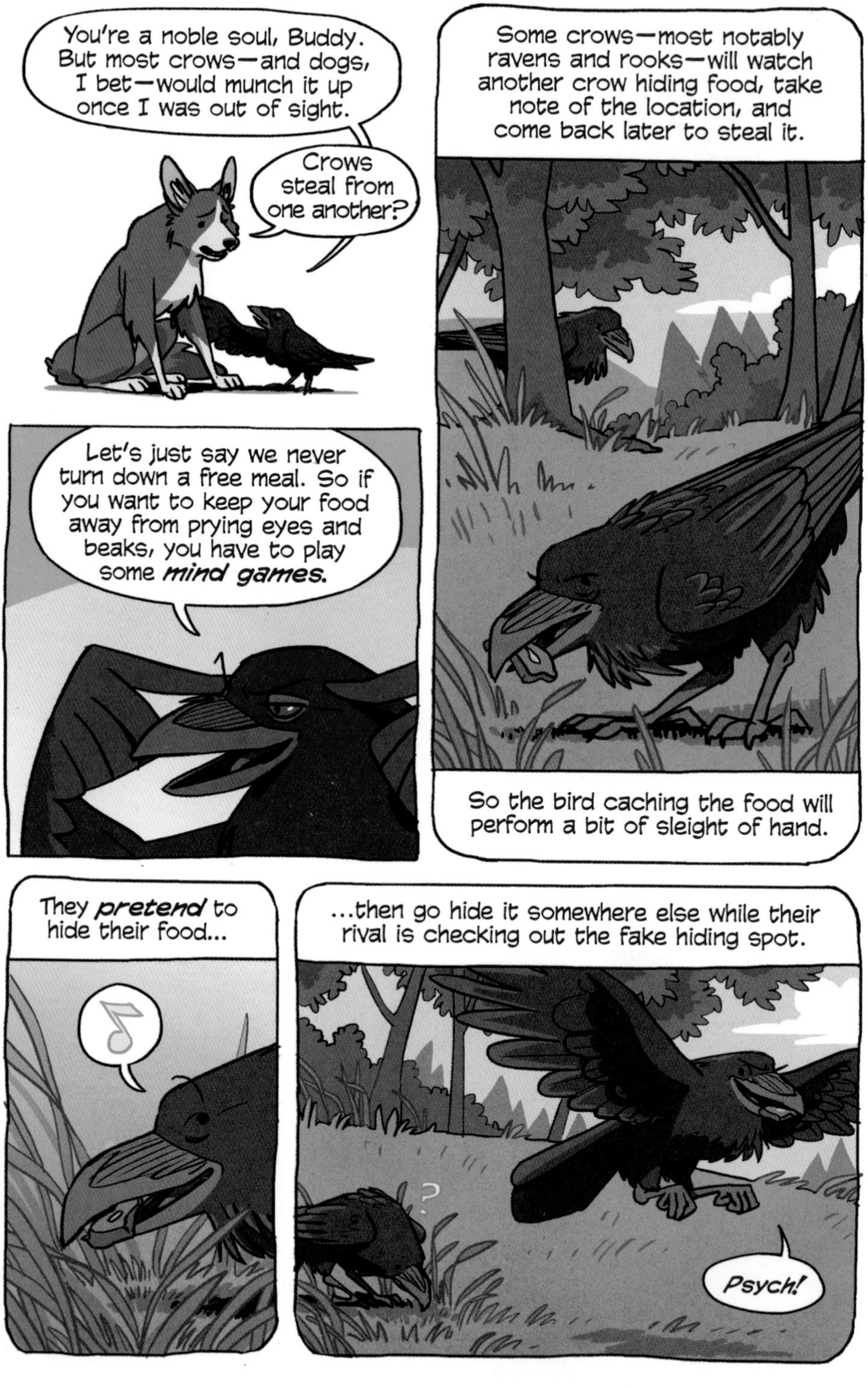
You're a noble soul, Buddy. But most crows—and dogs, I bet—would munch it up once I was out of sight.
Crows steal from one another?
Let's just say we never turn down a free meal. So if you want to keep your food away from prying eyes and beaks, you have to play some *mind games.*
Some crows—most notably ravens and rooks—will watch another crow hiding food, take note of the location, and come back later to steal it.
So the bird caching the food will perform a bit of sleight of hand.
They *pretend* to hide their food...
...then go hide it somewhere else while their rival is checking out the fake hiding spot.
?
Psych!

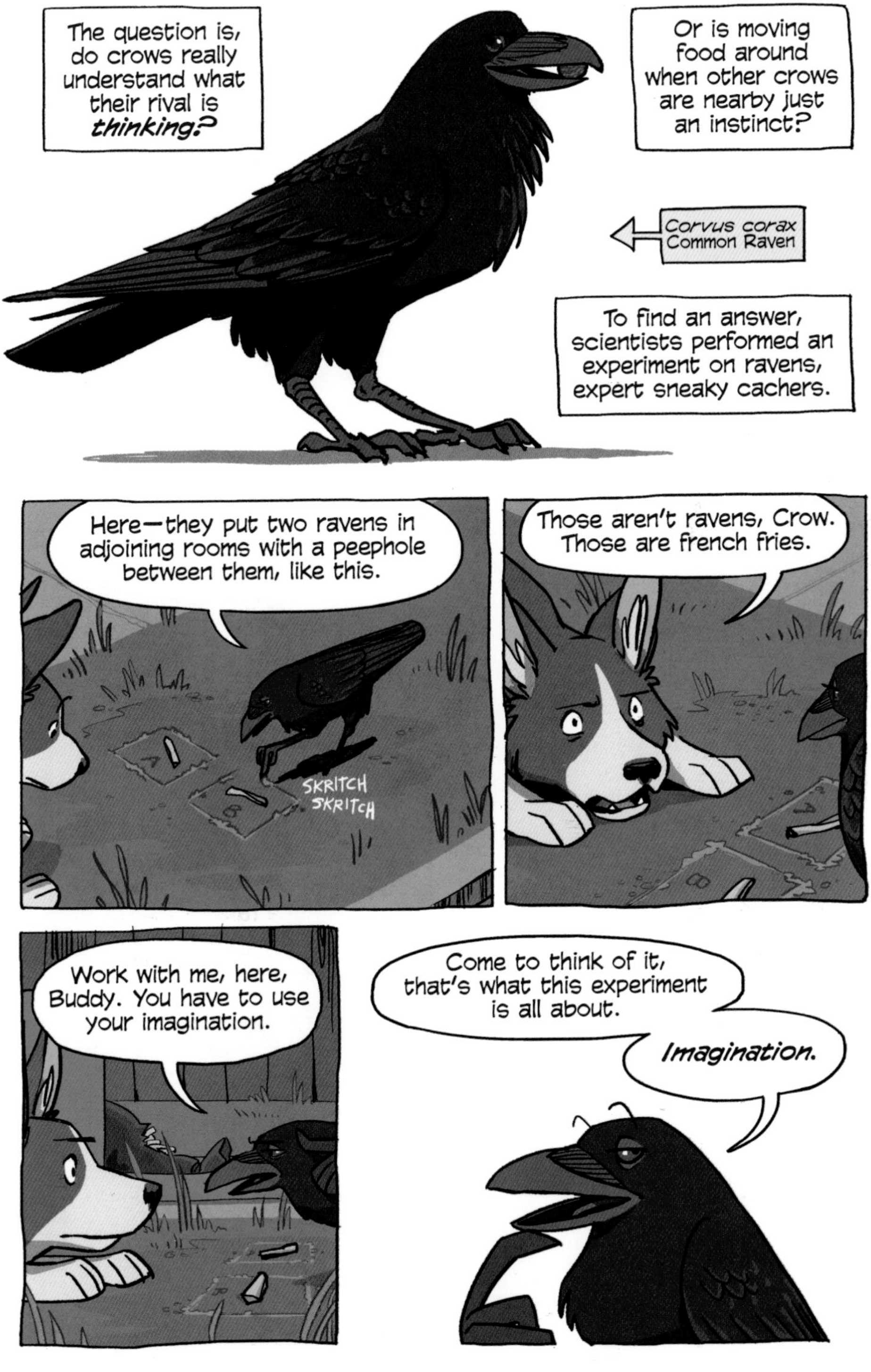
The question is, do crows really understand what their rival is *thinking?*
Or is moving food around when other crows are nearby just an instinct?
Corvus corax
Common Raven
To find an answer, scientists performed an experiment on ravens, expert sneaky cachers.
Here—they put two ravens in adjoining rooms with a peephole between them, like this.
SKRITCH SKRITCH
Those aren't ravens, Crow. Those are french fries.
Work with me, here, Buddy. You have to use your imagination.
Come to think of it, that's what this experiment is all about.
Imagination.

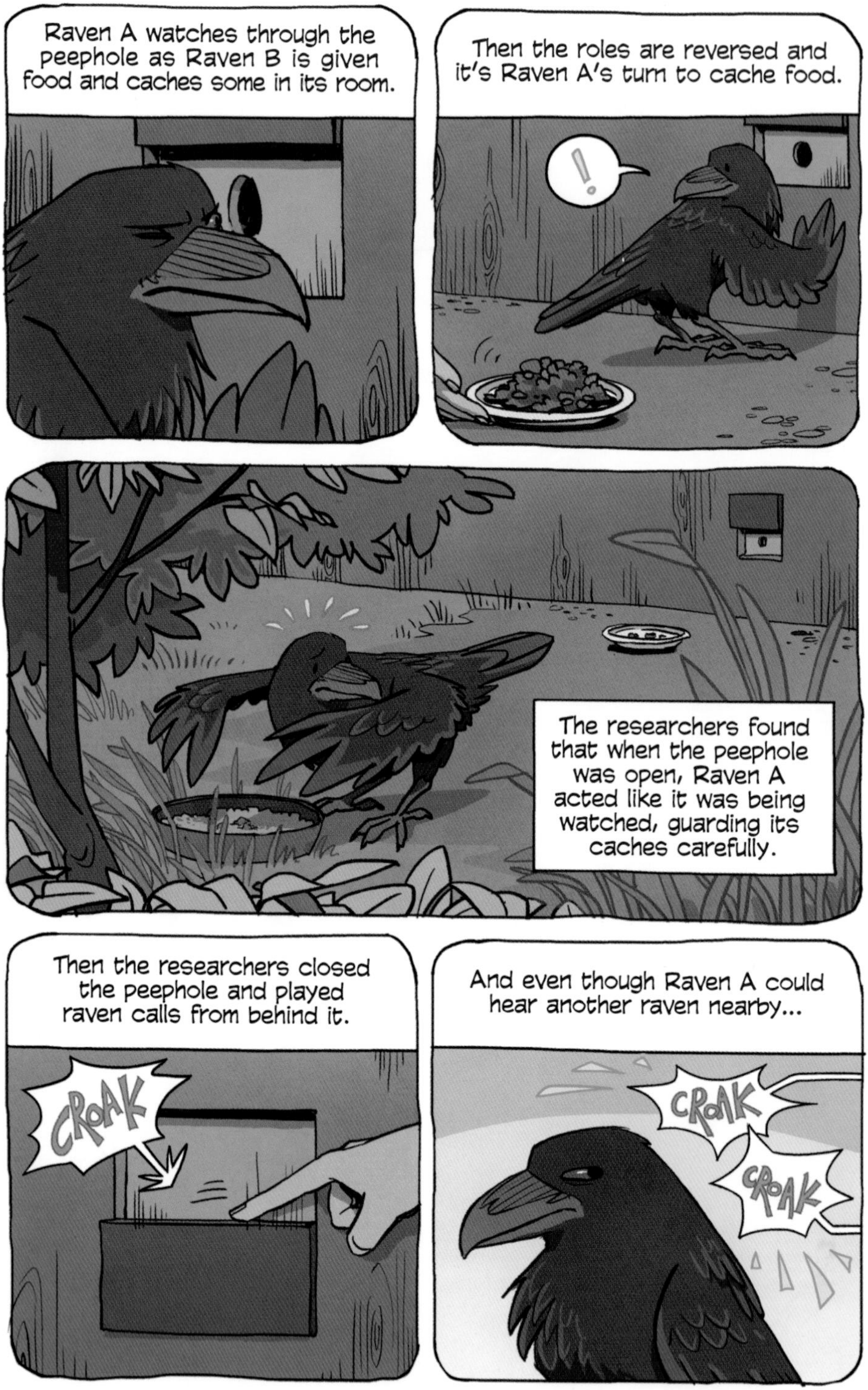
Raven A watches through the peephole as Raven B is given food and caches some in its room.
Then the roles are reversed and it's Raven A's turn to cache food.
!
The researchers found that when the peephole was open, Raven A acted like it was being watched, guarding its caches carefully.
Then the researchers closed the peephole and played raven calls from behind it.
CROAK
And even though Raven A could hear another raven nearby...
CROAK
CROAK

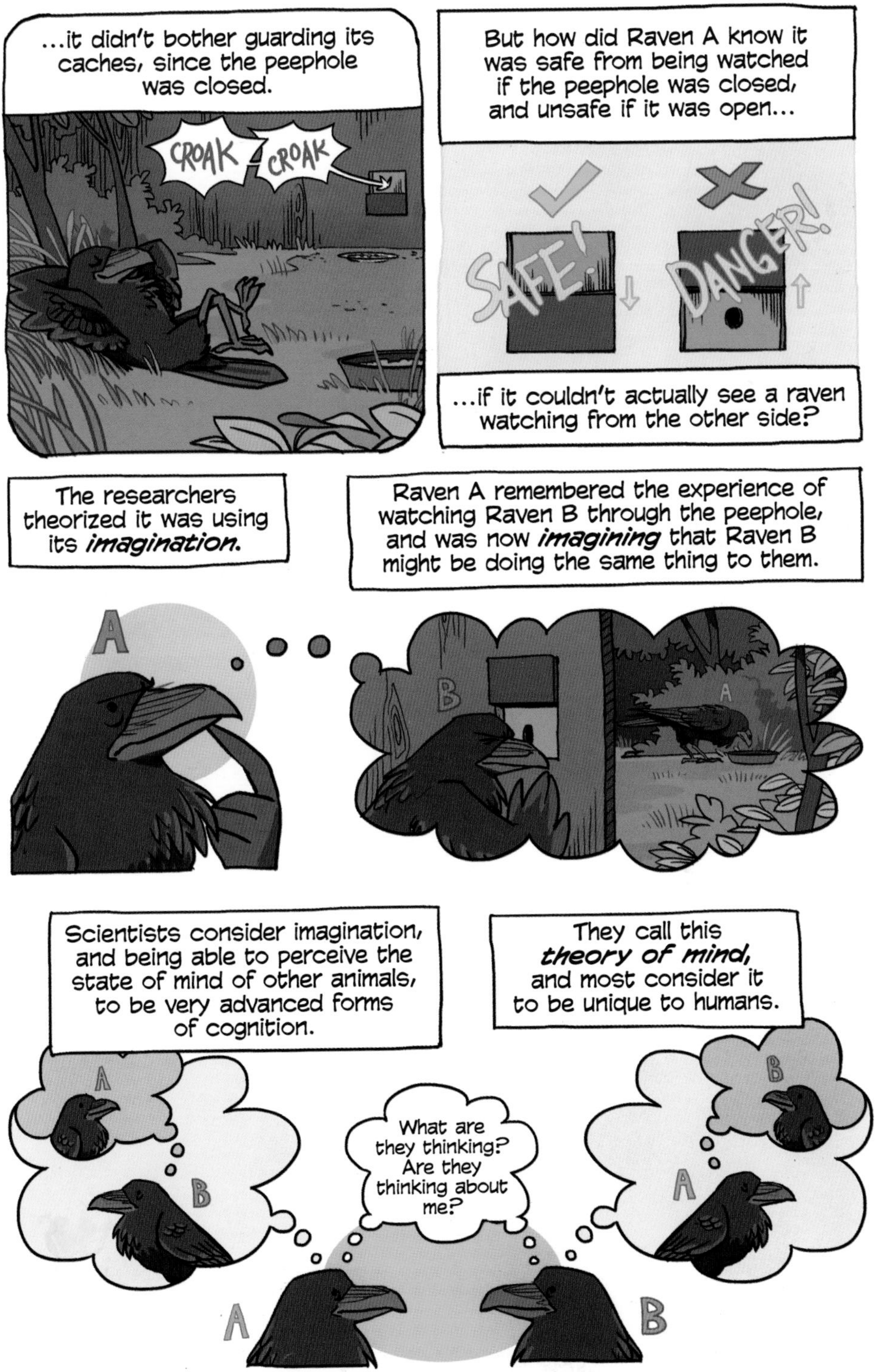

...it didn't bother guarding its caches, since the peephole was closed.
CROAK
CROAK
But how did Raven A know it was safe from being watched if the peephole was closed, and unsafe if it was open...
SAFE!
DANGER!
...if it couldn't actually see a raven watching from the other side?
The researchers theorized it was using its *imagination.*
Raven A remembered the experience of watching Raven B through the peephole, and was now *imagining* that Raven B might be doing the same thing to them.
A
B
A
Scientists consider imagination, and being able to perceive the state of mind of other animals, to be very advanced forms of cognition.
They call this ***theory of mind,*** and most consider it to be unique to humans.
A
B
What are they thinking? Are they thinking about me?
B
A
A
B

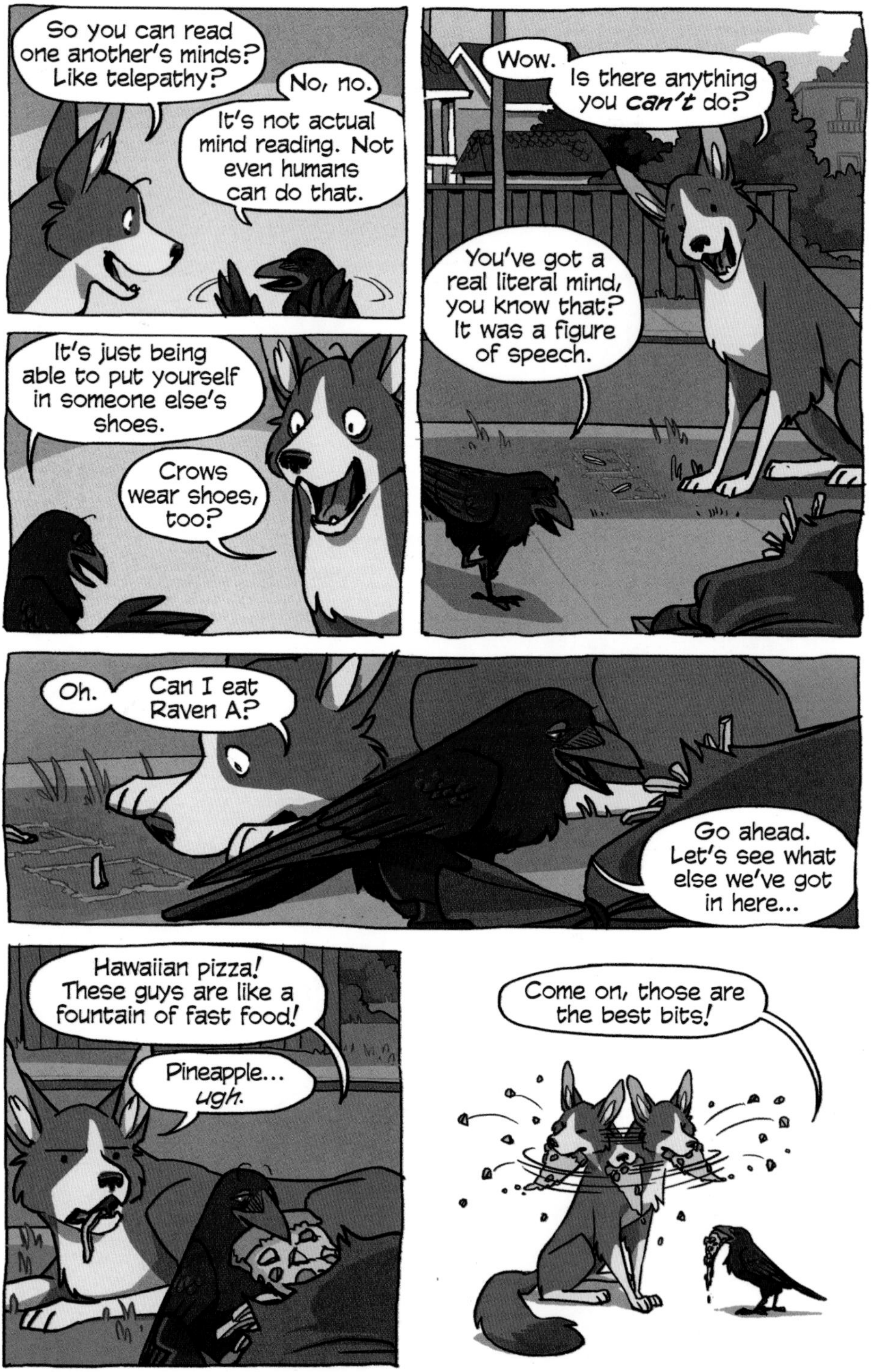
So you can read one another's minds? Like telepathy?
No, no.
It's not actual mind reading. Not even humans can do that.
Wow.
Is there anything you *can't* do?
It's just being able to put yourself in someone else's shoes.
Crows wear shoes, too?
You've got a real literal mind, you know that? It was a figure of speech.
Oh.
Can I eat Raven A?
Go ahead. Let's see what else we've got in here...
Hawaiian pizza! These guys are like a fountain of fast food!
Pineapple... *ugh*.
Come on, those are the best bits!

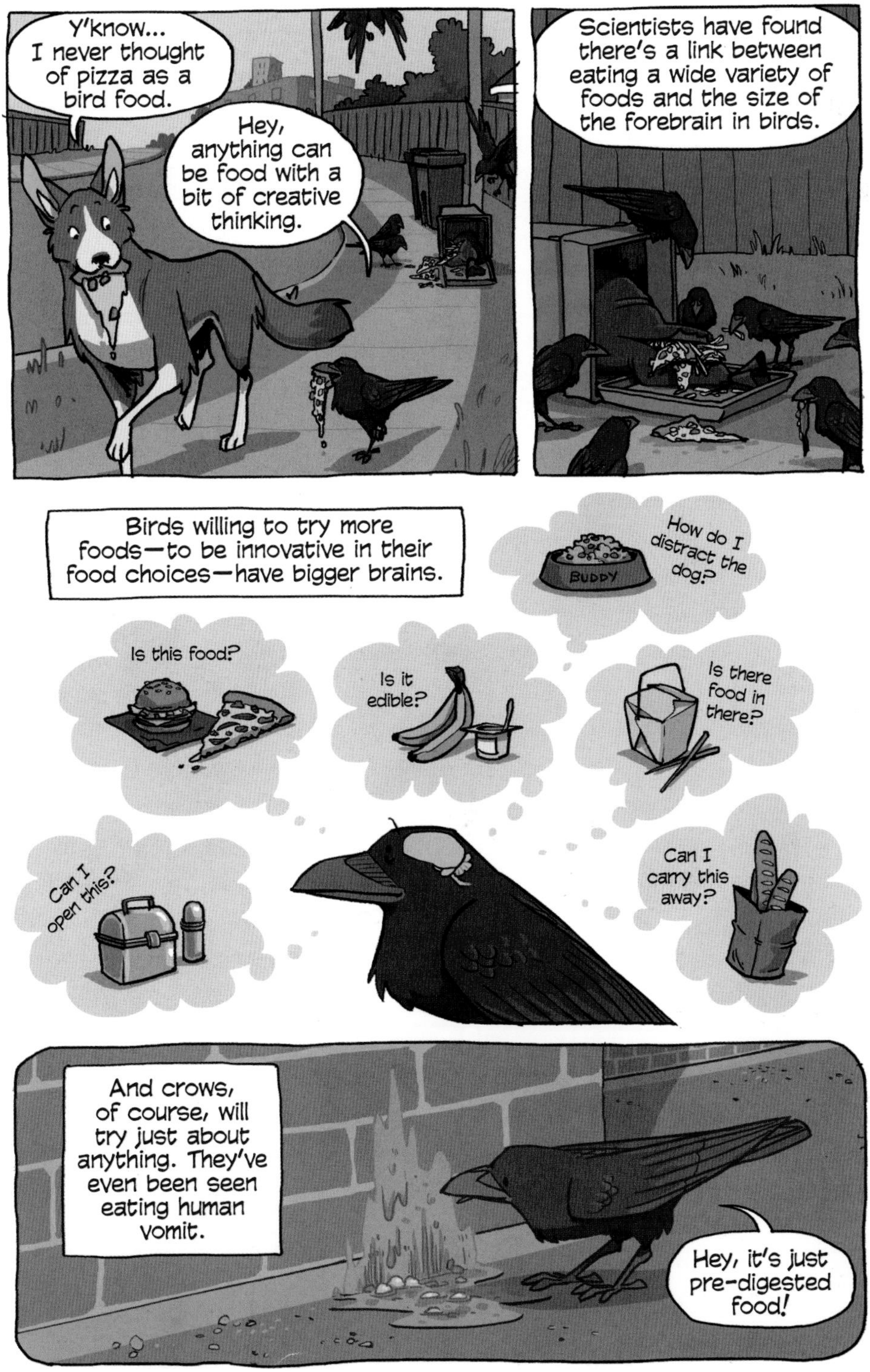
Y'know... I never thought of pizza as a bird food.
Hey, anything can be food with a bit of creative thinking.
Scientists have found there's a link between eating a wide variety of foods and the size of the forebrain in birds.
Birds willing to try more foods—to be innovative in their food choices—have bigger brains.
How do I distract the dog?
BUDDY
Is this food?
Is it edible?
Is there food in there?
Can I open this?
Can I carry this away?
And crows, of course, will try just about anything. They've even been seen eating human vomit.
Hey, it's just pre-digested food!

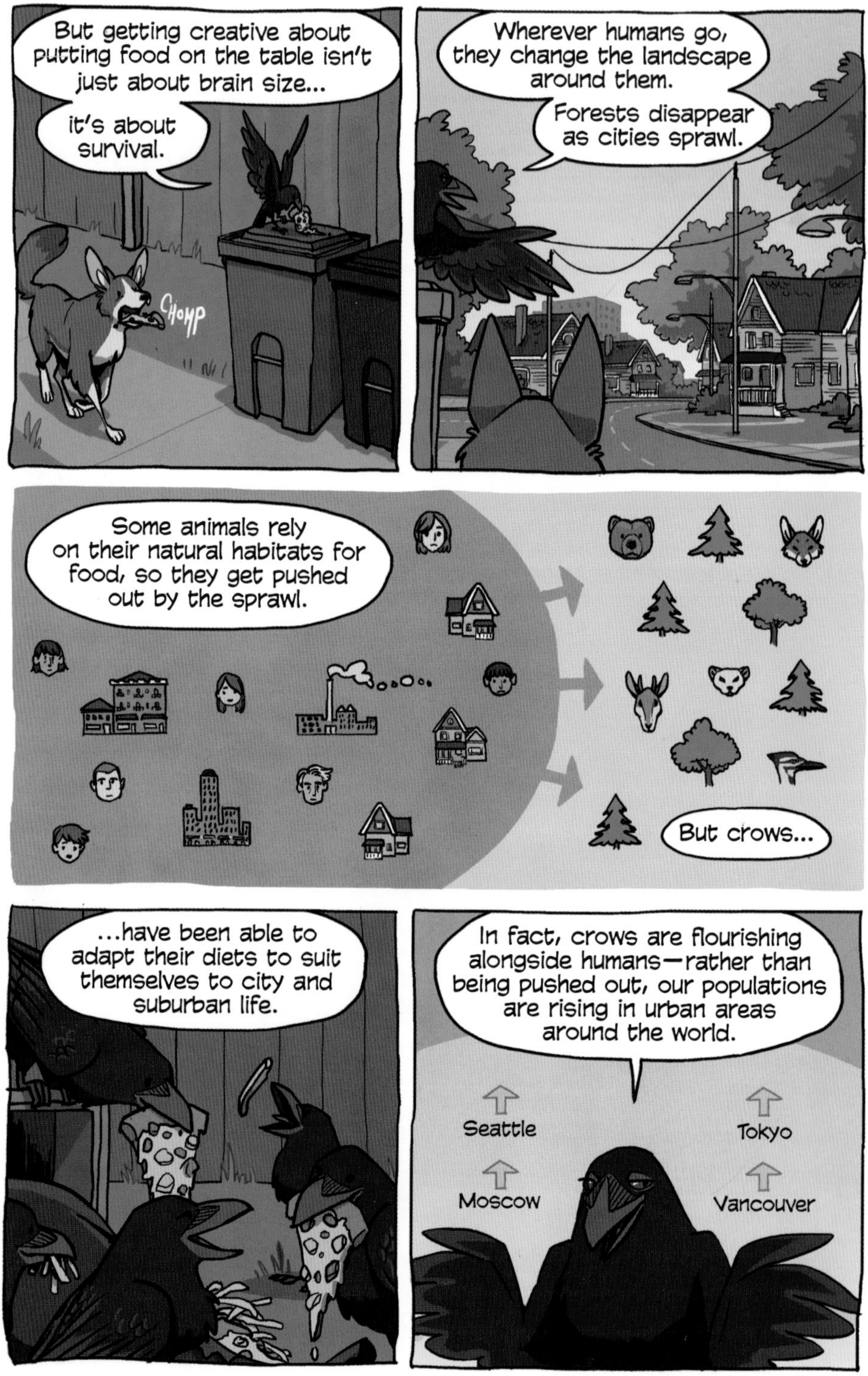
But getting creative about putting food on the table isn't just about brain size...
it's about survival.
CHOMP
Wherever humans go, they change the landscape around them.
Forests disappear as cities sprawl.
Some animals rely on their natural habitats for food, so they get pushed out by the sprawl.
But crows...
...have been able to adapt their diets to suit themselves to city and suburban life.
In fact, crows are flourishing alongside humans—rather than being pushed out, our populations are rising in urban areas around the world.
Seattle
Tokyo
Moscow
Vancouver

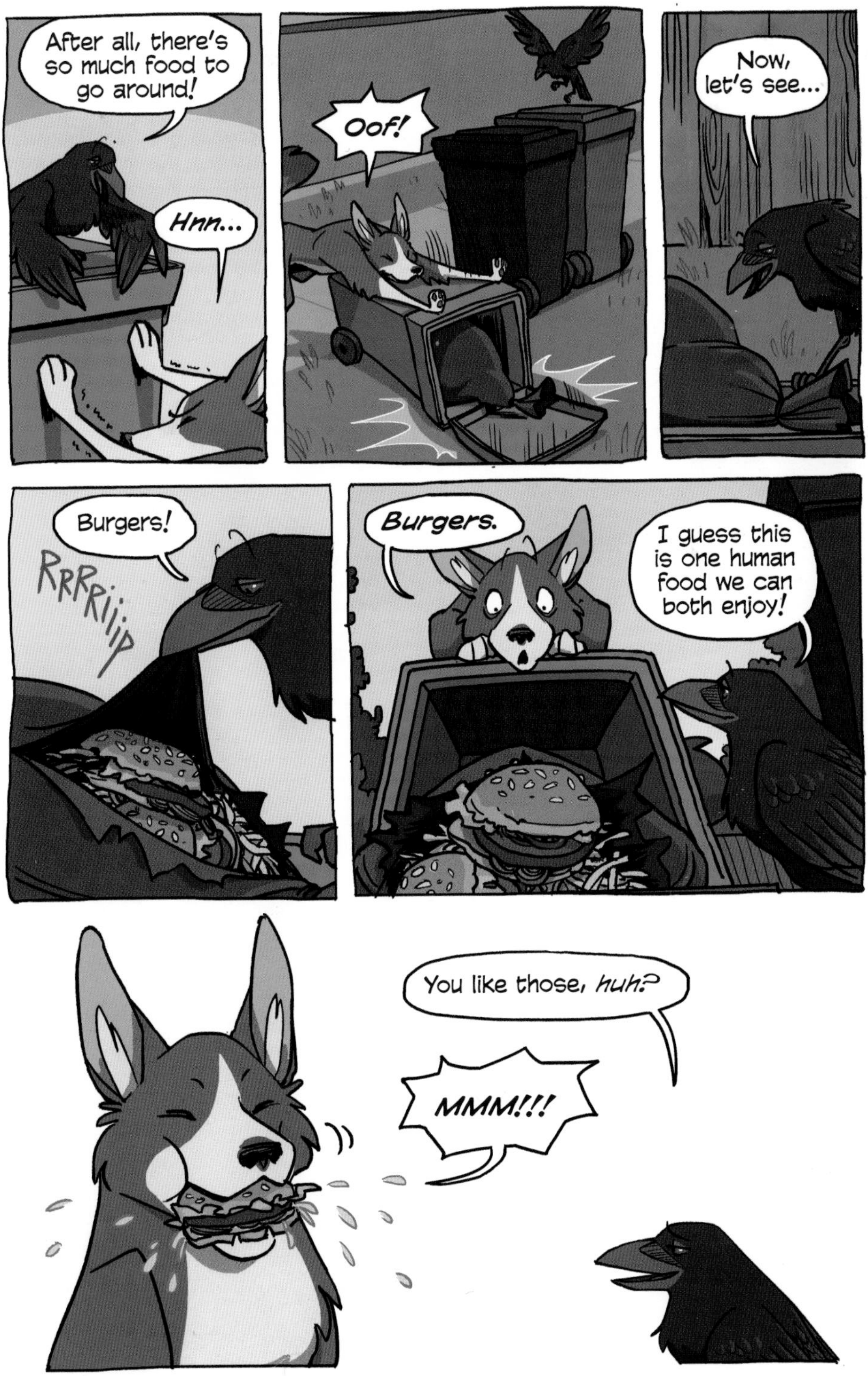
After all, there's so much food to go around!
Hnn...
Oof!
Now, let's see...
Burgers!
RRRRiiiip
Burgers.
I guess this is one human food we can both enjoy!
You like those, huh?
MMM!!!

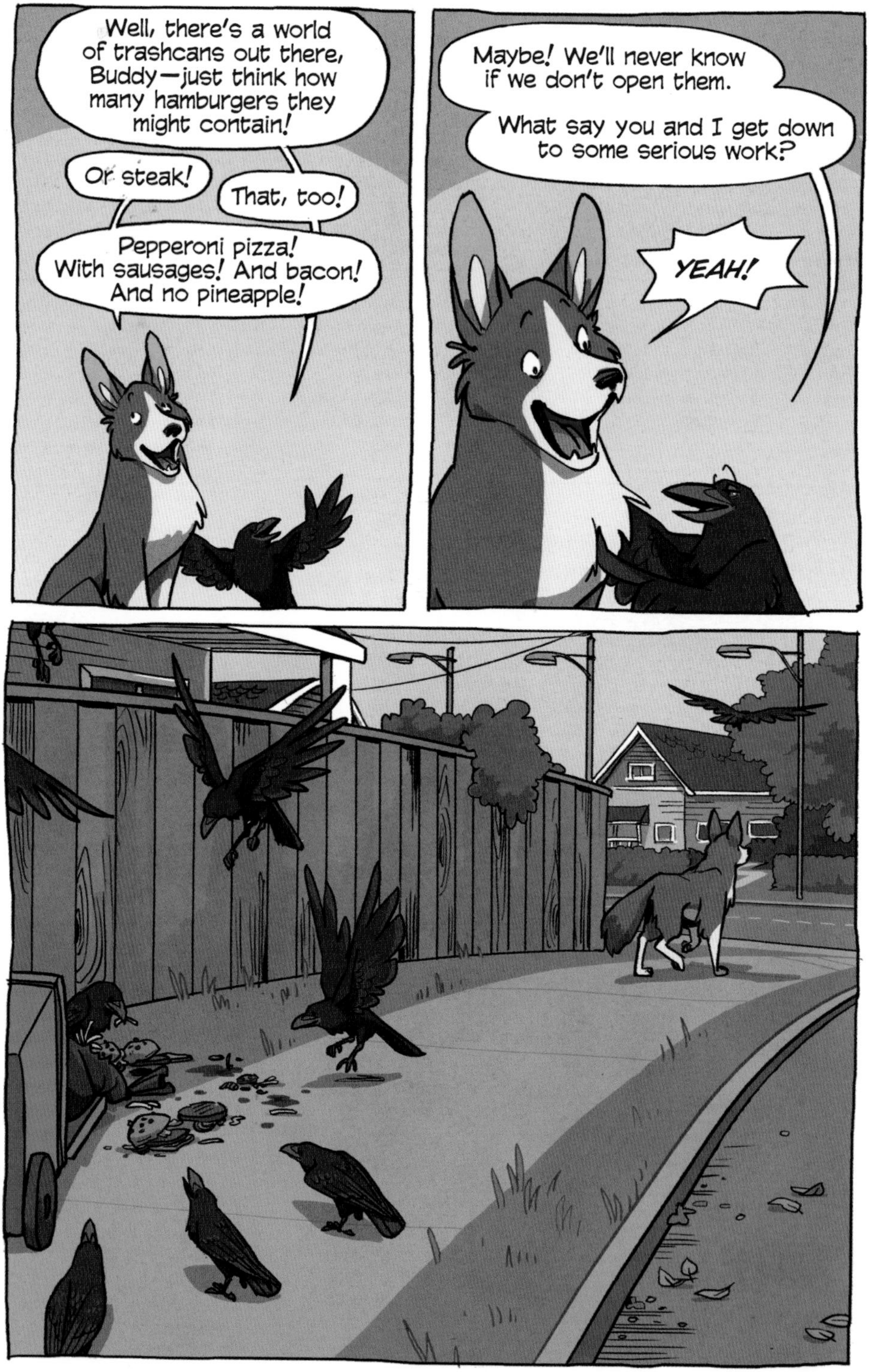
Well, there's a world of trashcans out there, Buddy—just think how many hamburgers they might contain!
Or steak!
That, too!
Pepperoni pizza! With sausages! And bacon! And no pineapple!
Maybe! We'll never know if we don't open them.
What say you and I get down to some serious work?
YEAH!

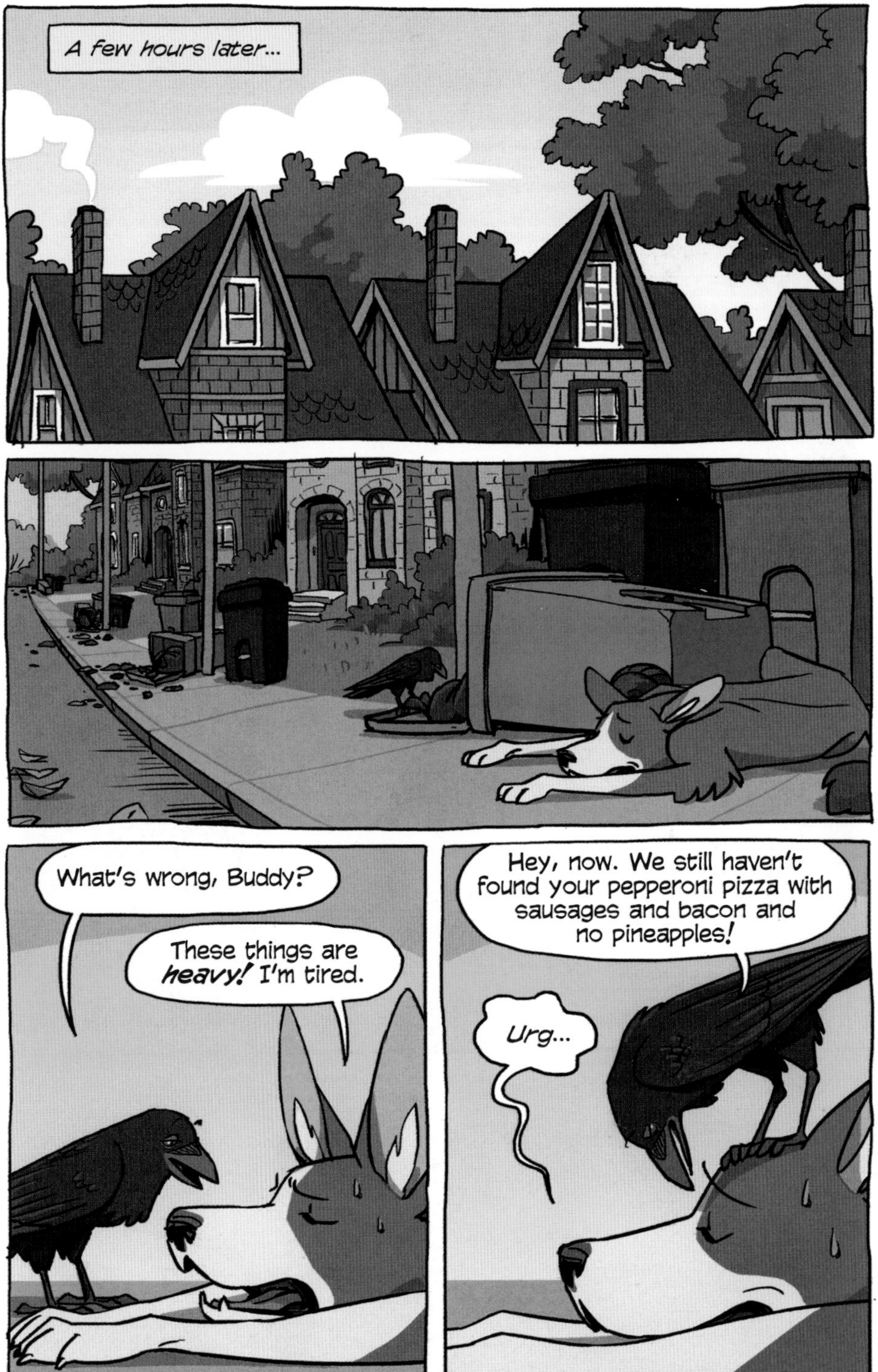
A few hours later...
What's wrong, Buddy?
These things are *heavy!* I'm tired.
Hey, now. We still haven't found your pepperoni pizza with sausages and bacon and no pineapples!
Urg...

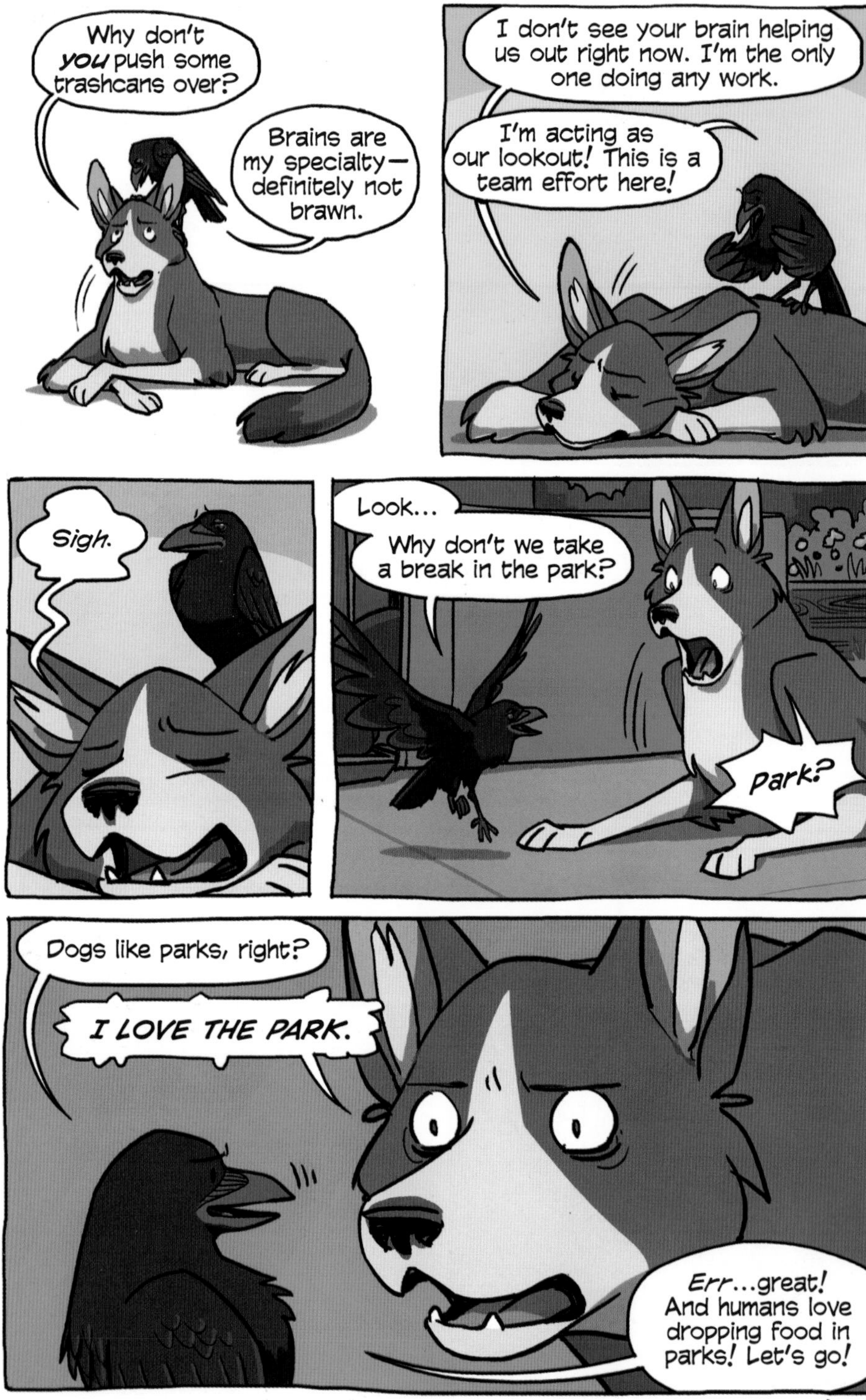

Why don't *you* push some trashcans over?
Brains are my specialty—definitely not brawn.
I don't see your brain helping us out right now. I'm the only one doing any work.
I'm acting as our lookout! This is a team effort here!
Sigh.
Look...
Why don't we take a break in the park?
Park?
Dogs like parks, right?
I LOVE THE PARK.
Err...great! And humans love dropping food in parks! Let's go!

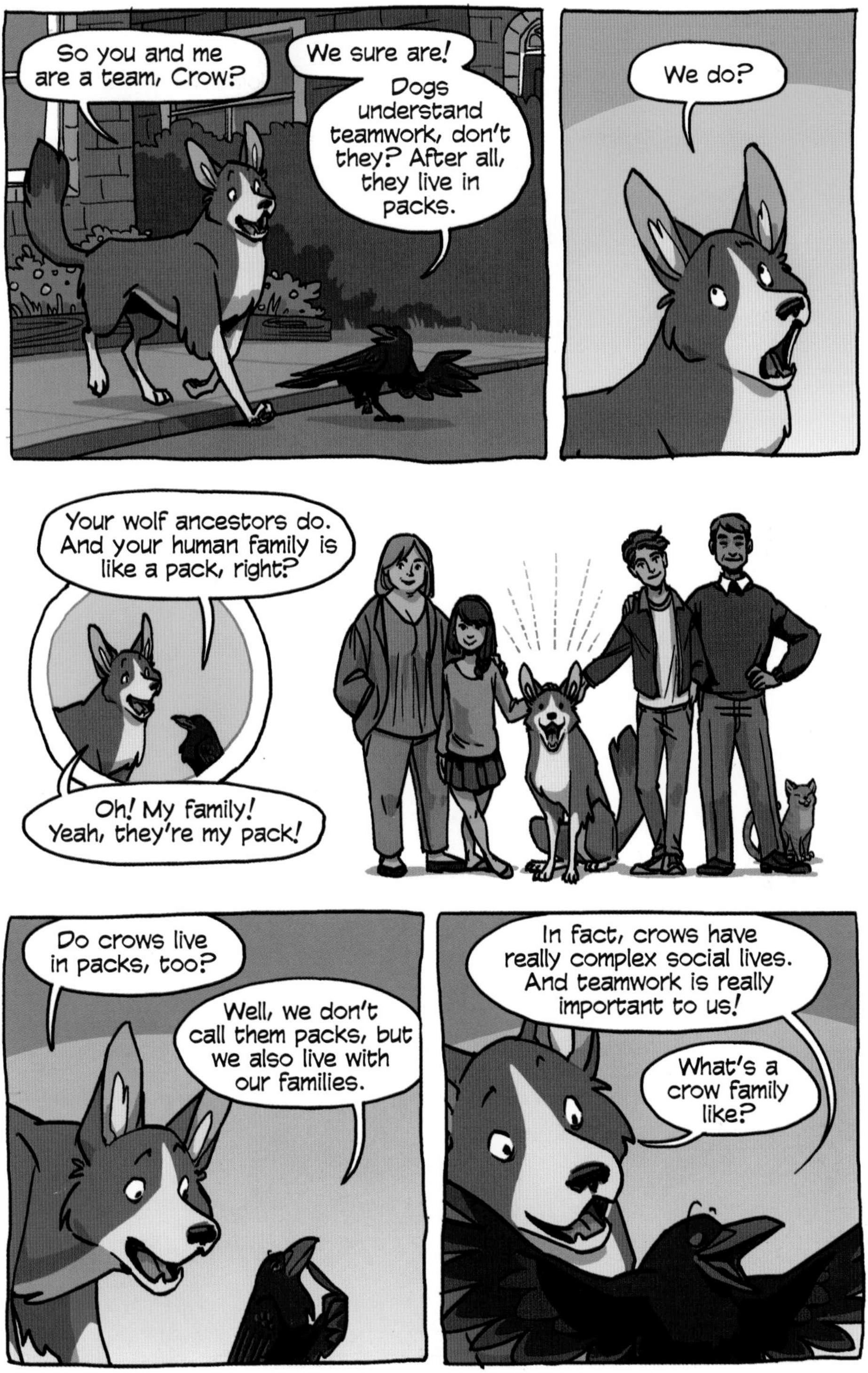
So you and me are a team, Crow?
We sure are!
Dogs understand teamwork, don't they? After all, they live in packs.
We do?
Your wolf ancestors do. And your human family is like a pack, right?
Oh! My family! Yeah, they're my pack!
Do crows live in packs, too?
Well, we don't call them packs, but we also live with our families.
In fact, crows have really complex social lives. And teamwork is really important to us!
What's a crow family like?

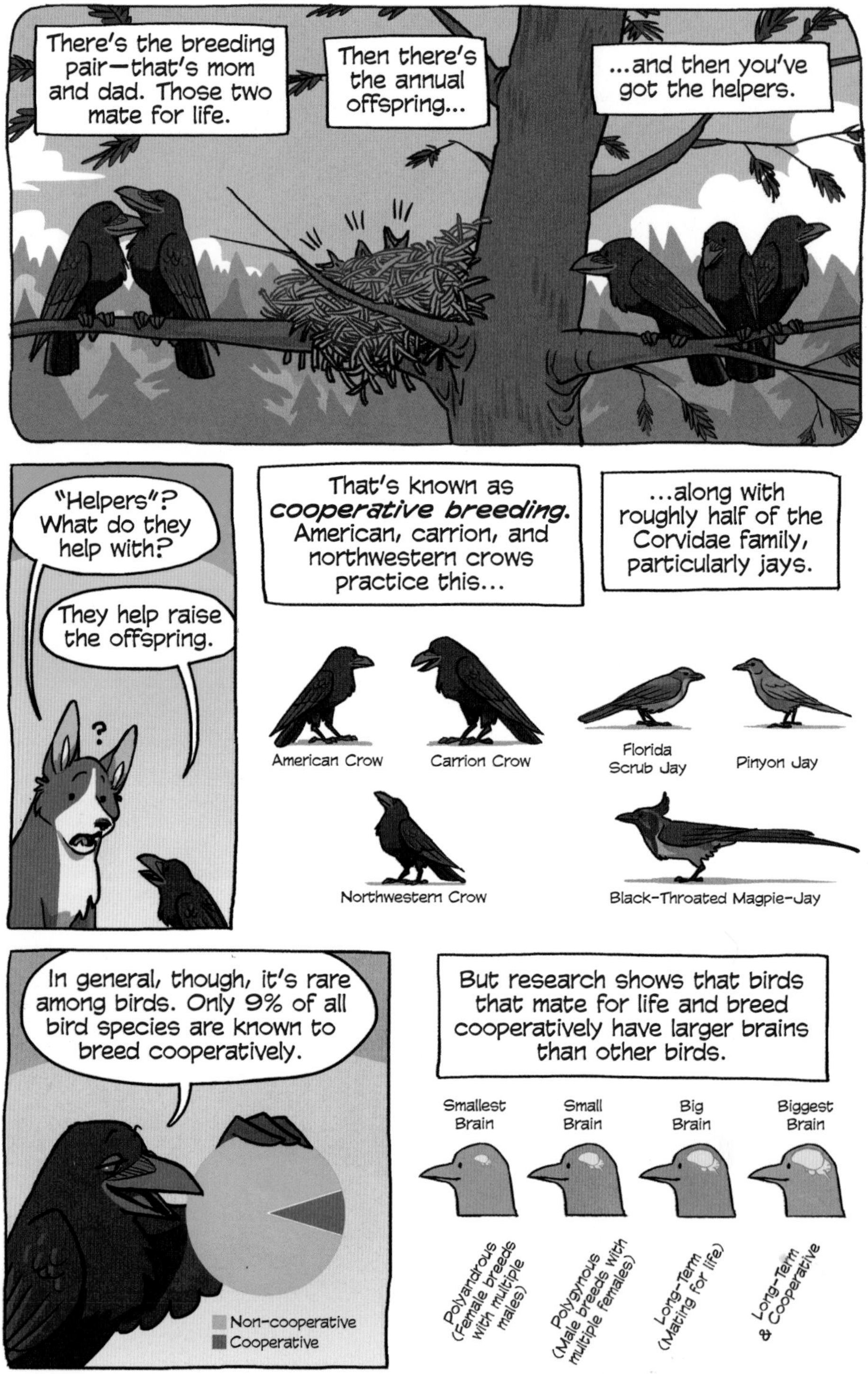

There's the breeding pair—that's mom and dad. Those two mate for life.
Then there's the annual offspring...
...and then you've got the helpers.
"Helpers"? What do they help with?
They help raise the offspring.
That's known as *cooperative breeding*. American, carrion, and northwestern crows practice this...
...along with roughly half of the Corvidae family, particularly jays.
American Crow
Carrion Crow
Florida Scrub Jay
Pinyon Jay
Northwestern Crow
Black-Throated Magpie-Jay
In general, though, it's rare among birds. Only 9% of all bird species are known to breed cooperatively.
Non-cooperative
Cooperative
But research shows that birds that mate for life and breed cooperatively have larger brains than other birds.
Smallest Brain
Small Brain
Big Brain
Biggest Brain
Polyandrous (Female breeds with multiple males)
Polygynous (Male breeds with multiple females)
Long-Term (Mating for life)
Long-Term & Cooperative

Helpers are the breeding pair's offspring from previous years.

Crows are usually at least two years old before they move out—but they might stay at home as long as six years.

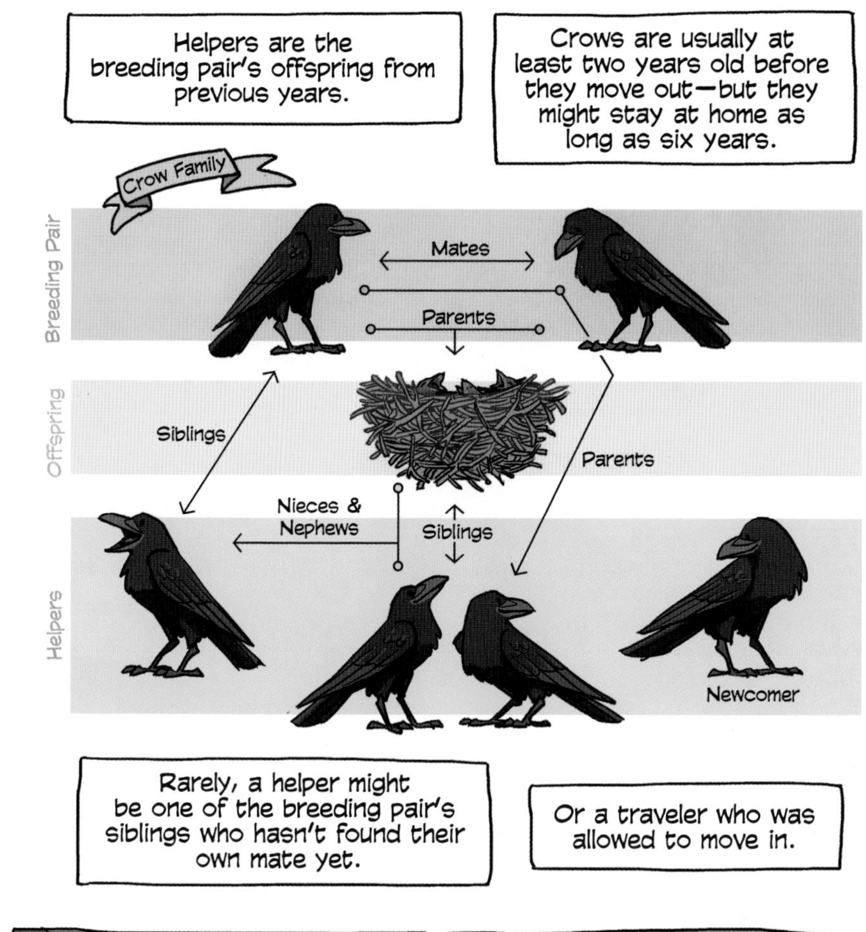
Crow Family
Breeding Pair
Offspring
Helpers
Mates
Parents
Siblings
Parents
Nieces & Nephews
Siblings
Newcomer

Rarely, a helper might be one of the breeding pair's siblings who hasn't found their own mate yet.

Or a traveler who was allowed to move in.

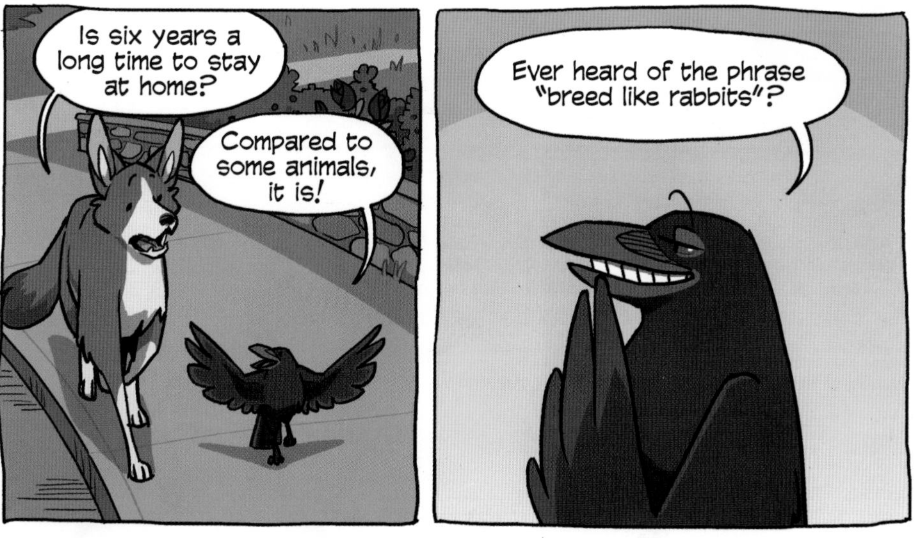
Is six years a long time to stay at home?
Compared to some animals, it is!
Ever heard of the phrase "breed like rabbits"?

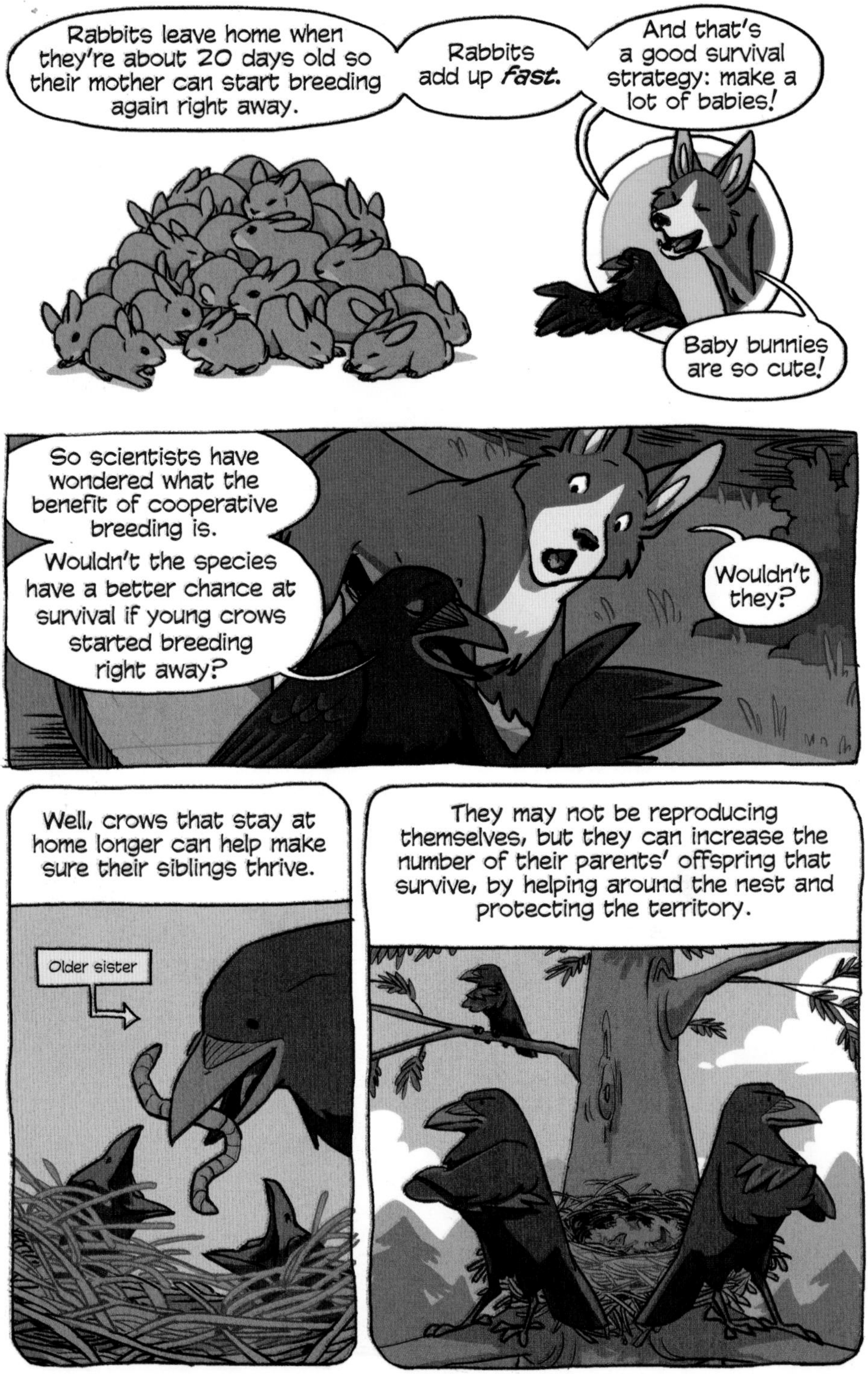

Rabbits leave home when they're about 20 days old so their mother can start breeding again right away.
Rabbits add up *fast.*
And that's a good survival strategy: make a lot of babies!
Baby bunnies are so cute!
So scientists have wondered what the benefit of cooperative breeding is.
Wouldn't the species have a better chance at survival if young crows started breeding right away?
Wouldn't they?
Well, crows that stay at home longer can help make sure their siblings thrive.
Older sister
They may not be reproducing themselves, but they can increase the number of their parents' offspring that survive, by helping around the nest and protecting the territory.

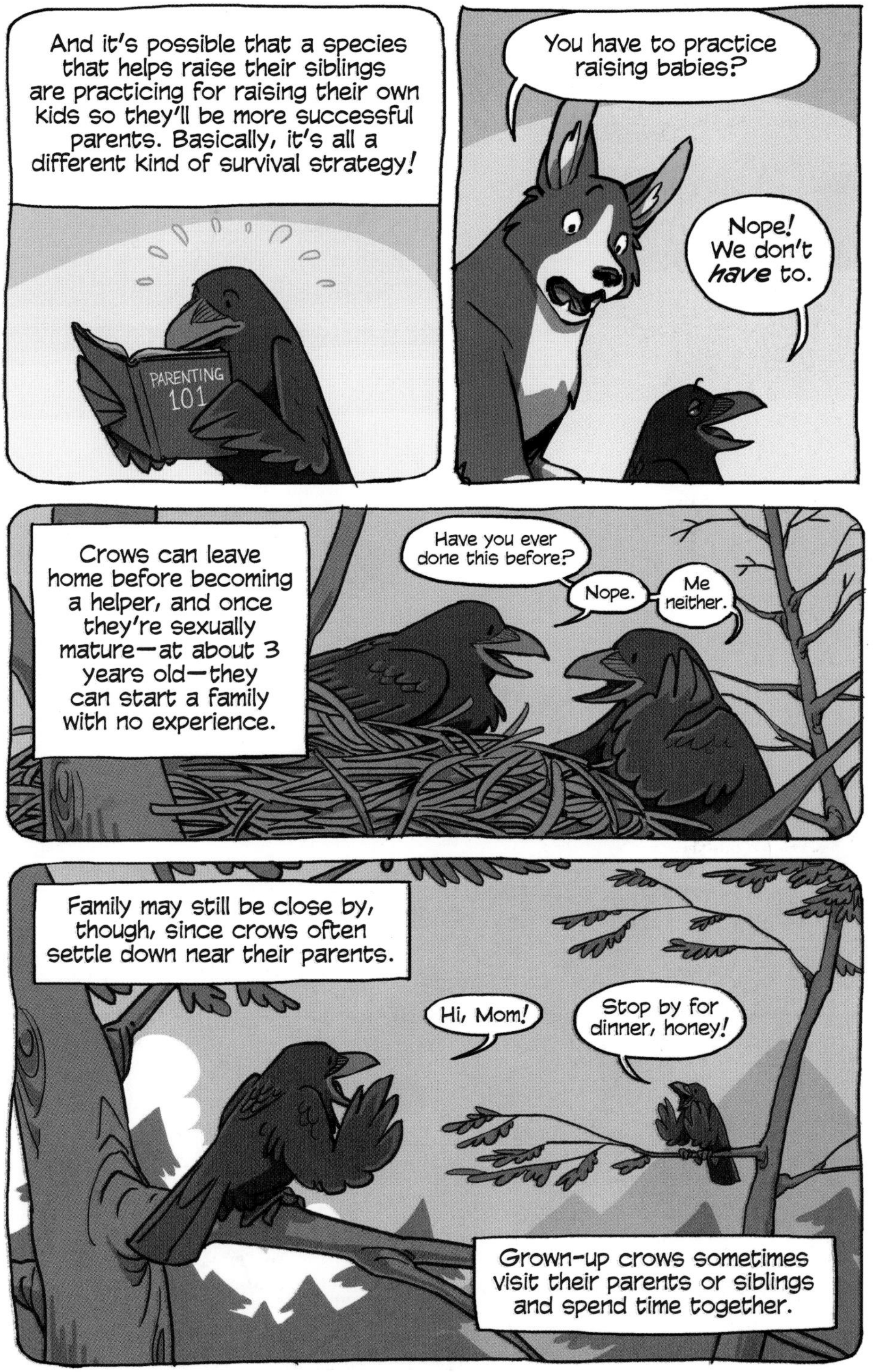

And it's possible that a species that helps raise their siblings are practicing for raising their own kids so they'll be more successful parents. Basically, it's all a different kind of survival strategy!
PARENTING 101
You have to practice raising babies?
Nope! We don't *have* to.
Crows can leave home before becoming a helper, and once they're sexually mature—at about 3 years old—they can start a family with no experience.
Have you ever done this before?
Nope.
Me neither.
Family may still be close by, though, since crows often settle down near their parents.
Hi, Mom!
Stop by for dinner, honey!
Grown-up crows sometimes visit their parents or siblings and spend time together.

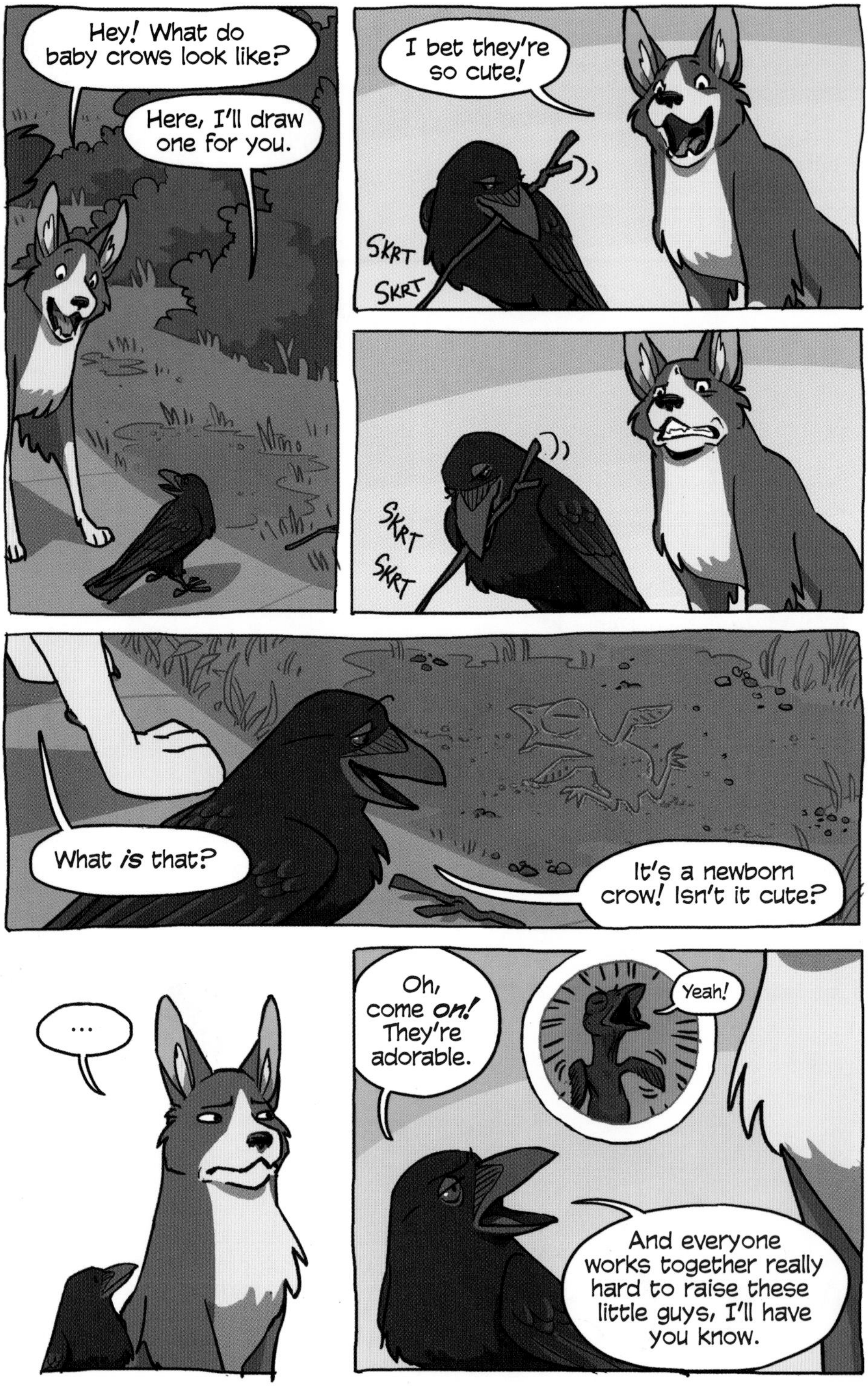
Hey! What do baby crows look like?
Here, I'll draw one for you.
I bet they're so cute!
SKRT
SKRT
SKRT
SKRT
What *is* that?
It's a newborn crow! Isn't it cute?
...
Oh, come *on*! They're adorable.
Yeah!
And everyone works together really hard to raise these little guys, I'll have you know.

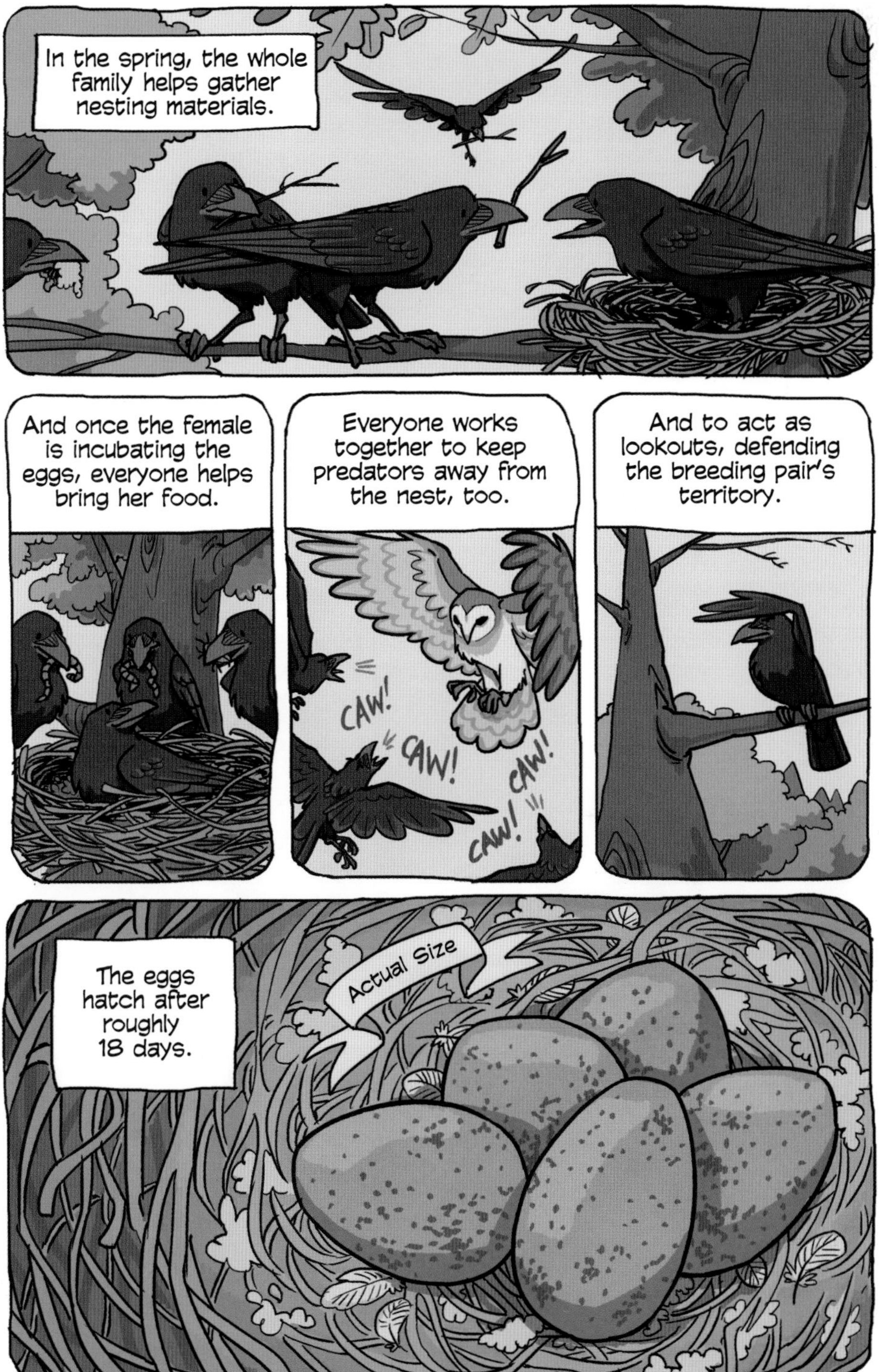
In the spring, the whole family helps gather nesting materials.
And once the female is incubating the eggs, everyone helps bring her food.
Everyone works together to keep predators away from the nest, too.
CAW!
CAW!
CAW!
CAW!
And to act as lookouts, defending the breeding pair's territory.
The eggs hatch after roughly 18 days.
Actual Size

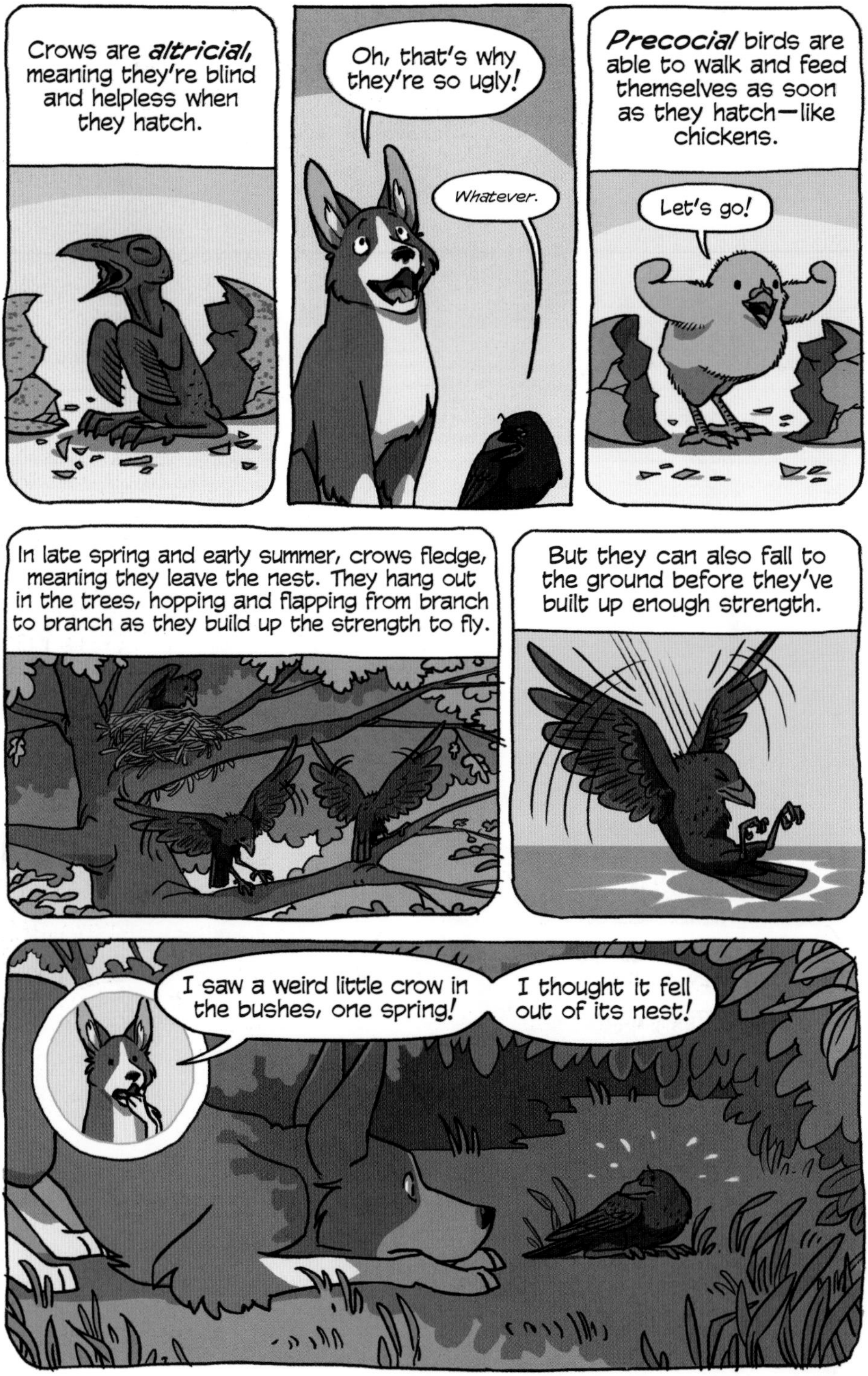
Crows are *altricial,* meaning they're blind and helpless when they hatch.
Oh, that's why they're so ugly!
Whatever.
Precocial birds are able to walk and feed themselves as soon as they hatch—like chickens.
Let's go!
In late spring and early summer, crows fledge, meaning they leave the nest. They hang out in the trees, hopping and flapping from branch to branch as they build up the strength to fly.
But they can also fall to the ground before they've built up enough strength.
I saw a weird little crow in the bushes, one spring!
I thought it fell out of its nest!

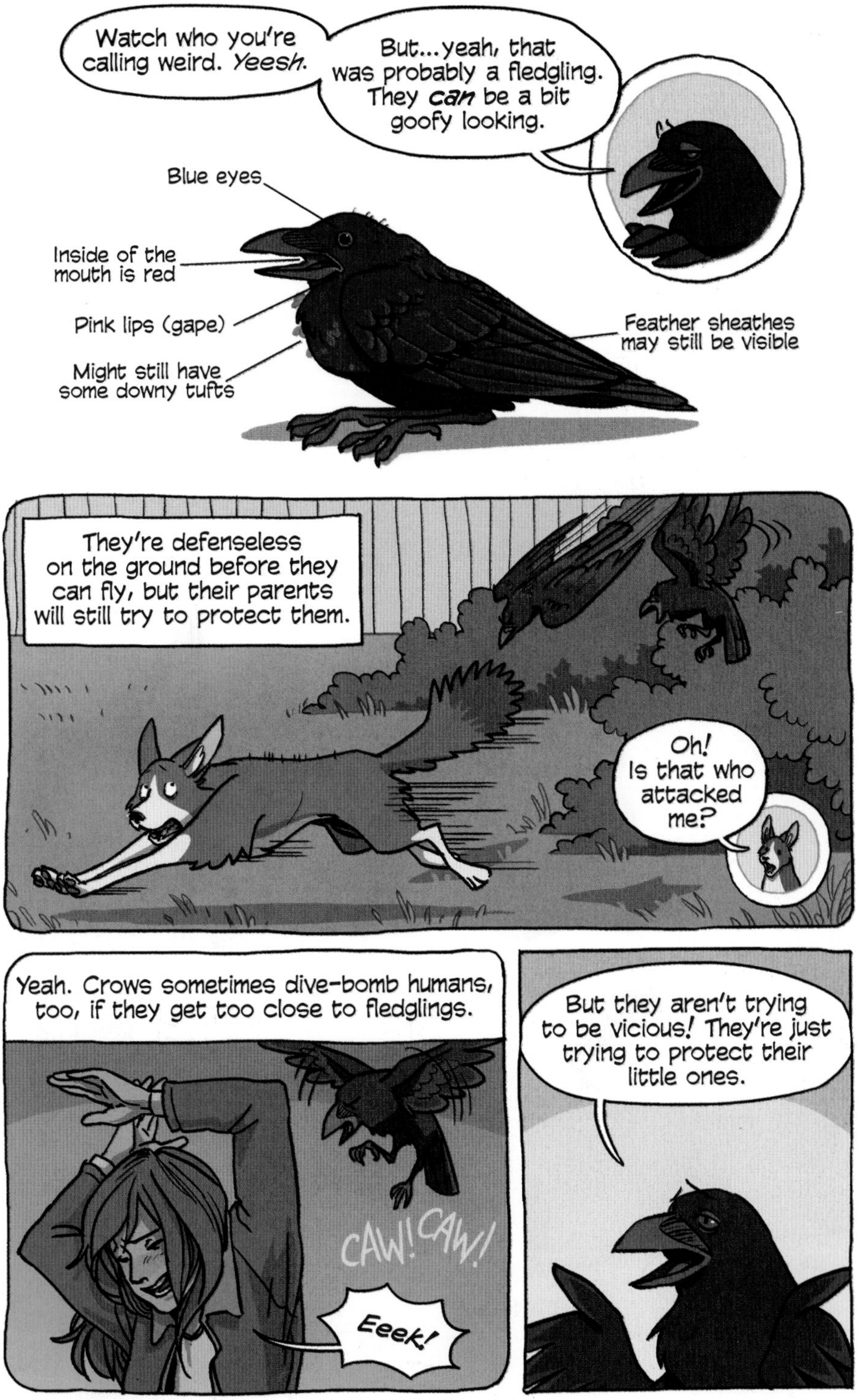
Watch who you're calling weird. *Yeesh.*
But...yeah, that was probably a fledgling. They ***can*** be a bit goofy looking.
Blue eyes
Inside of the mouth is red
Pink lips (gape)
Might still have some downy tufts
Feather sheathes may still be visible
They're defenseless on the ground before they can fly, but their parents will still try to protect them.
Oh! Is that who attacked me?
Yeah. Crows sometimes dive-bomb humans, too, if they get too close to fledglings.
CAW! CAW!
Eeek!
But they aren't trying to be vicious! They're just trying to protect their little ones.

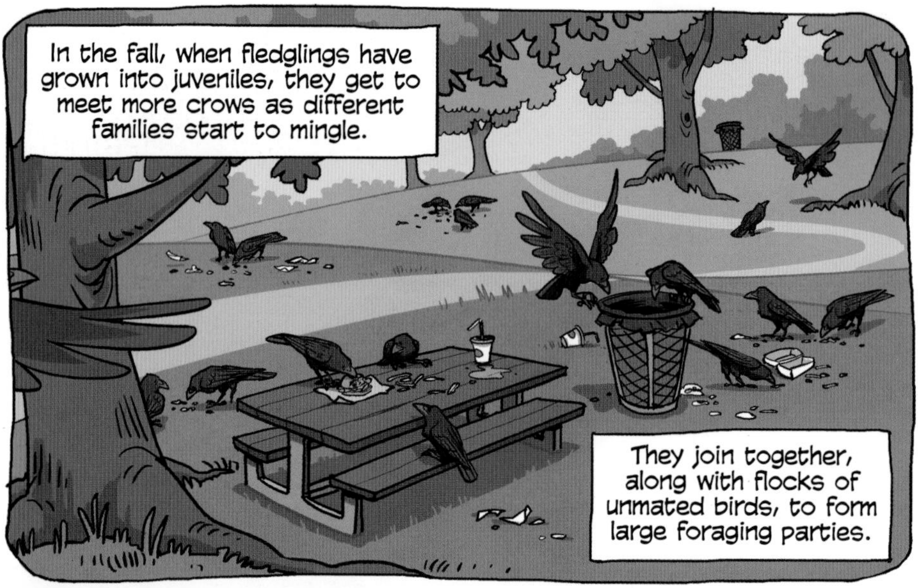
In the fall, when fledglings have grown into juveniles, they get to meet more crows as different families start to mingle.
They join together, along with flocks of unmated birds, to form large foraging parties.

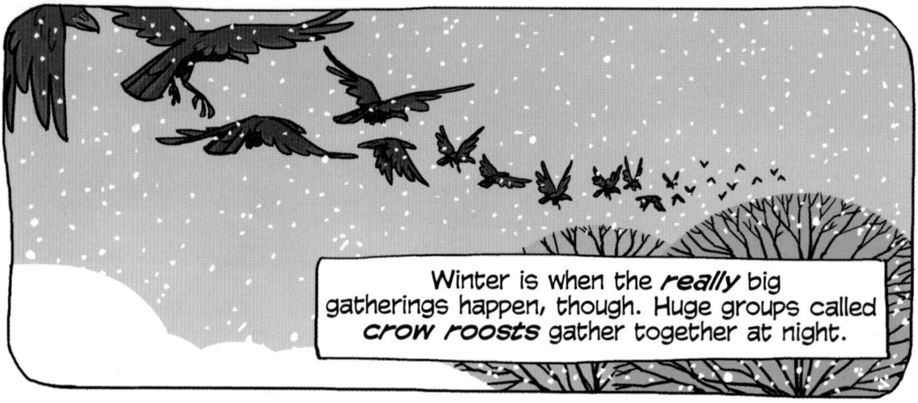
Winter is when the ***really*** big gatherings happen, though. Huge groups called ***crow roosts*** gather together at night.

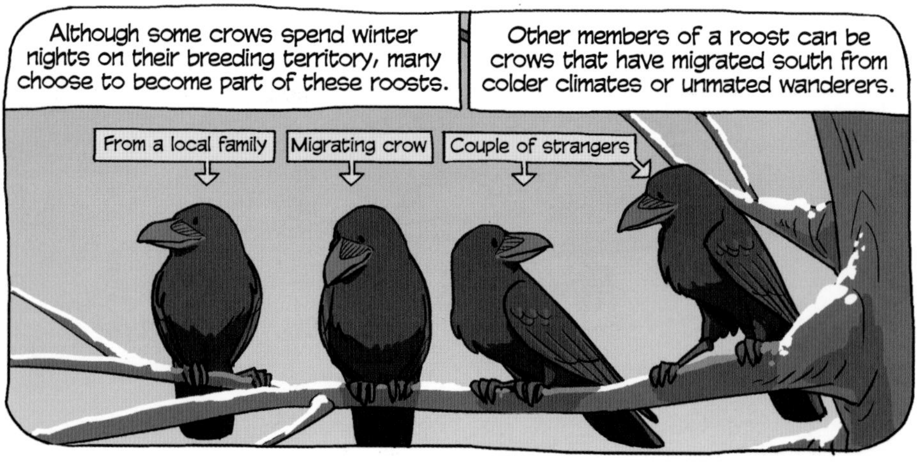
Although some crows spend winter nights on their breeding territory, many choose to become part of these roosts.
Other members of a roost can be crows that have migrated south from colder climates or unmated wanderers.
From a local family
Migrating crow
Couple of strangers

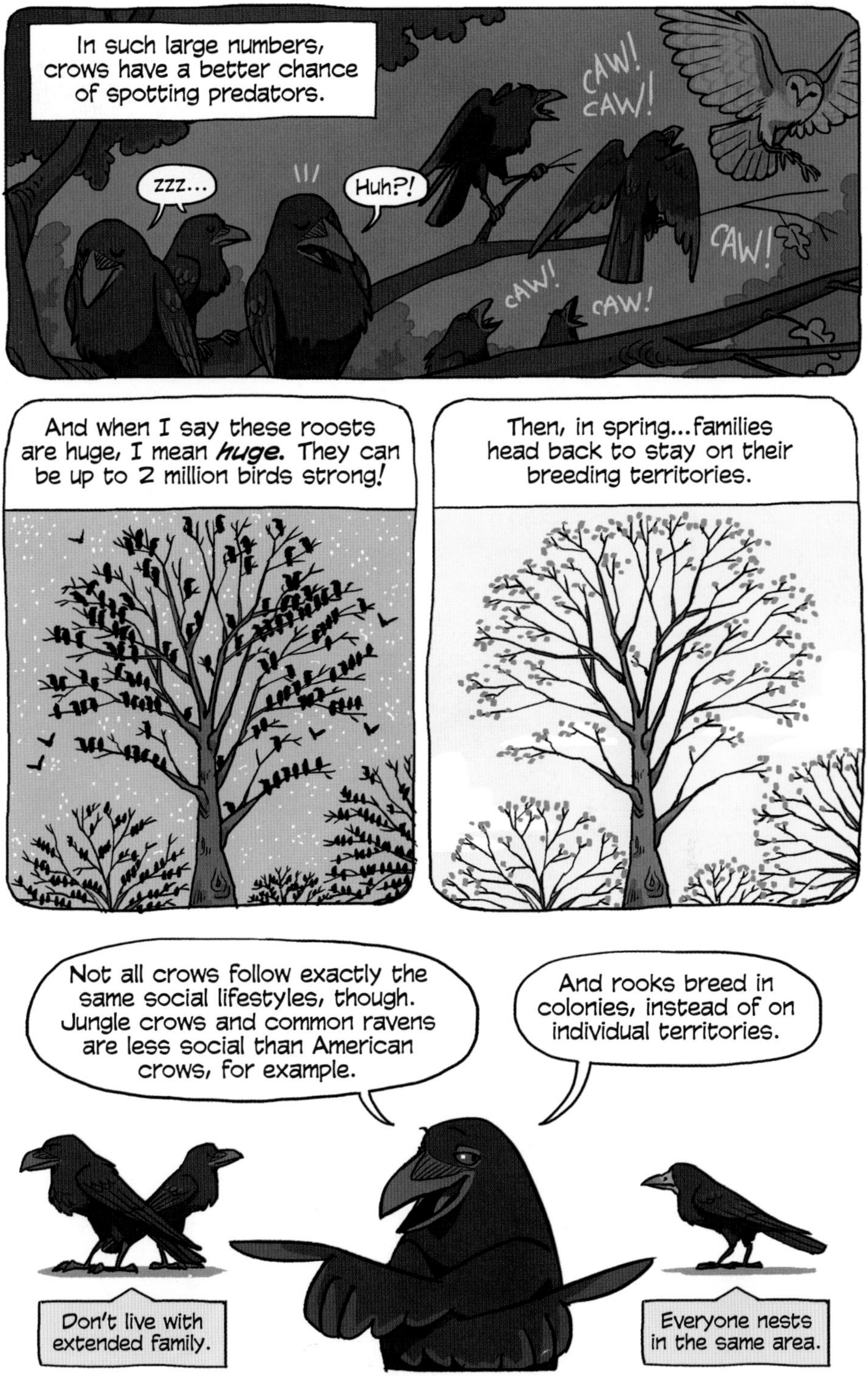
In such large numbers, crows have a better chance of spotting predators.
ZZZ...
Huh?!
CAW! CAW!
CAW!
CAW!
CAW!
And when I say these roosts are huge, I mean ***huge.*** They can be up to 2 million birds strong!
Then, in spring...families head back to stay on their breeding territories.
Not all crows follow exactly the same social lifestyles, though. Jungle crows and common ravens are less social than American crows, for example.
And rooks breed in colonies, instead of on individual territories.
Don't live with extended family.
Everyone nests in the same area.

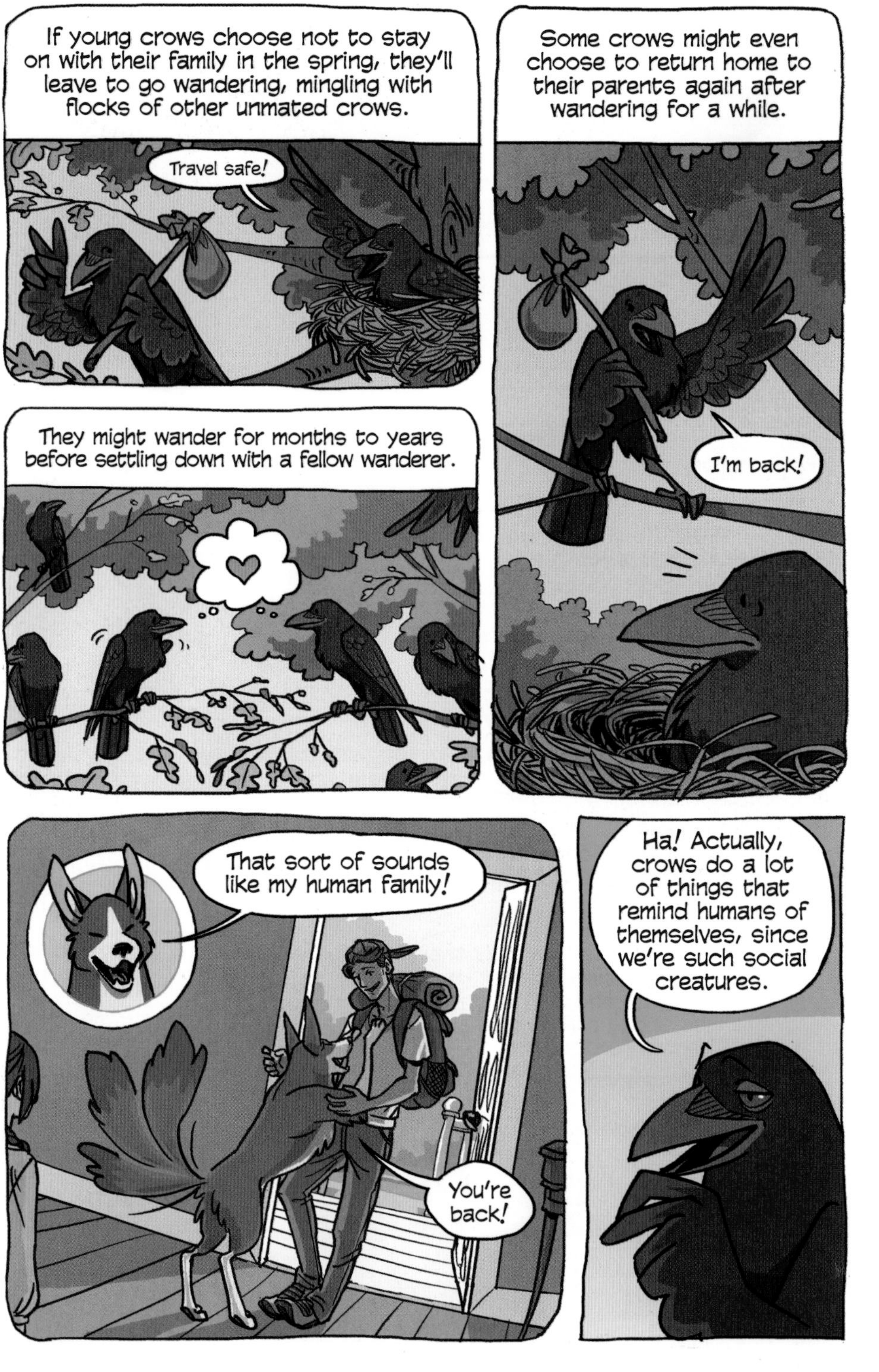
If young crows choose not to stay on with their family in the spring, they'll leave to go wandering, mingling with flocks of other unmated crows.
Travel safe!
Some crows might even choose to return home to their parents again after wandering for a while.
I'm back!
They might wander for months to years before settling down with a fellow wanderer.
That sort of sounds like my human family!
You're back!
Ha! Actually, crows do a lot of things that remind humans of themselves, since we're such social creatures.

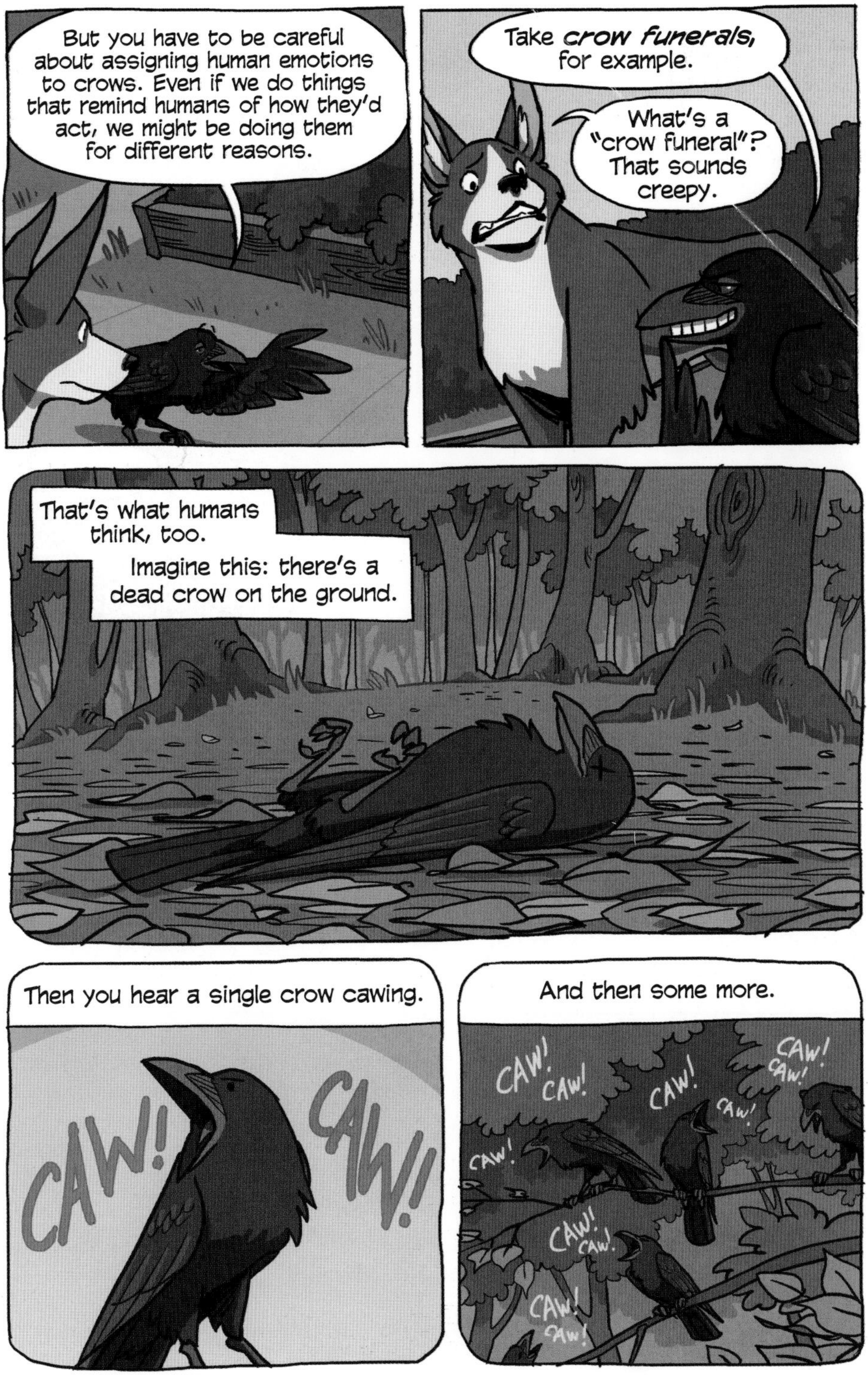
But you have to be careful about assigning human emotions to crows. Even if we do things that remind humans of how they'd act, we might be doing them for different reasons.
Take *crow funerals,* for example.
What's a "crow funeral"? That sounds creepy.
That's what humans think, too.
Imagine this: there's a dead crow on the ground.
Then you hear a single crow cawing.
CAW! CAW!
And then some more.
CAW! CAW! CAW! CAW! CAW! CAW! CAW! CAW! CAW! CAW! CAW!

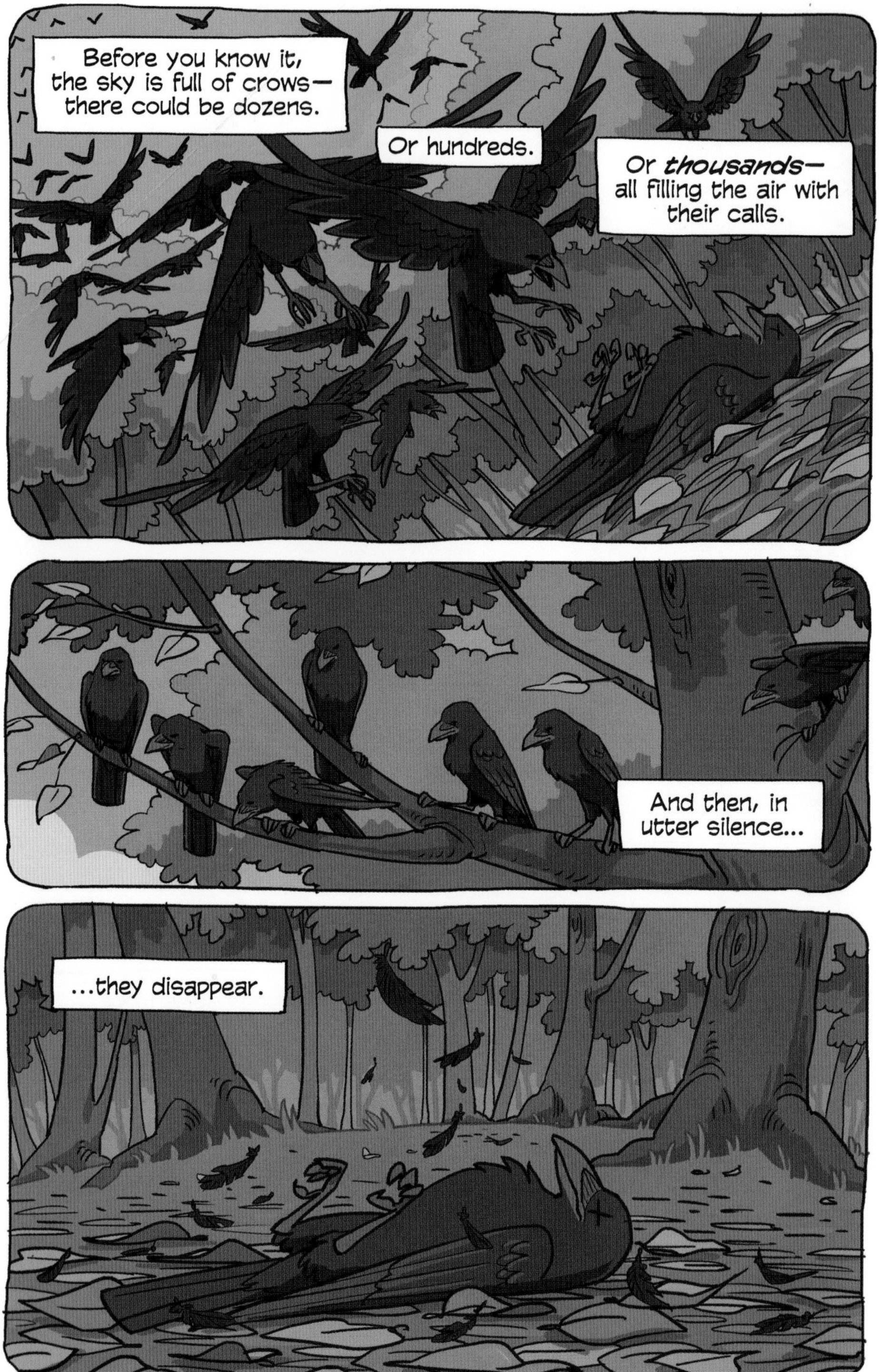
Before you know it, the sky is full of crows— there could be dozens.
Or hundreds.
Or *thousands*— all filling the air with their calls.
And then, in utter silence...
...they disappear.

That's definitely creepy.

Right.

So what does it remind humans of?

A funeral?

A funeral.

Because to them, it looks like the crows are gathering to pay their respects to a departed soul.

But that's not all there is to it. Scientists conducted an experiment where they measured crows' brain activity while showing them a dead crow.

Corvus brachyrhynchos
American Crow

That's kind of mean!

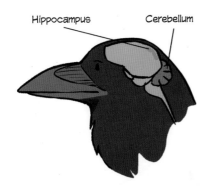

The areas of crow's brain activity showed that it was *learning* about danger and forming memories.

Hippocampus

Cerebellum

For crows, the death of another crow is a teachable moment.

I'm not forgetting this anytime soon!

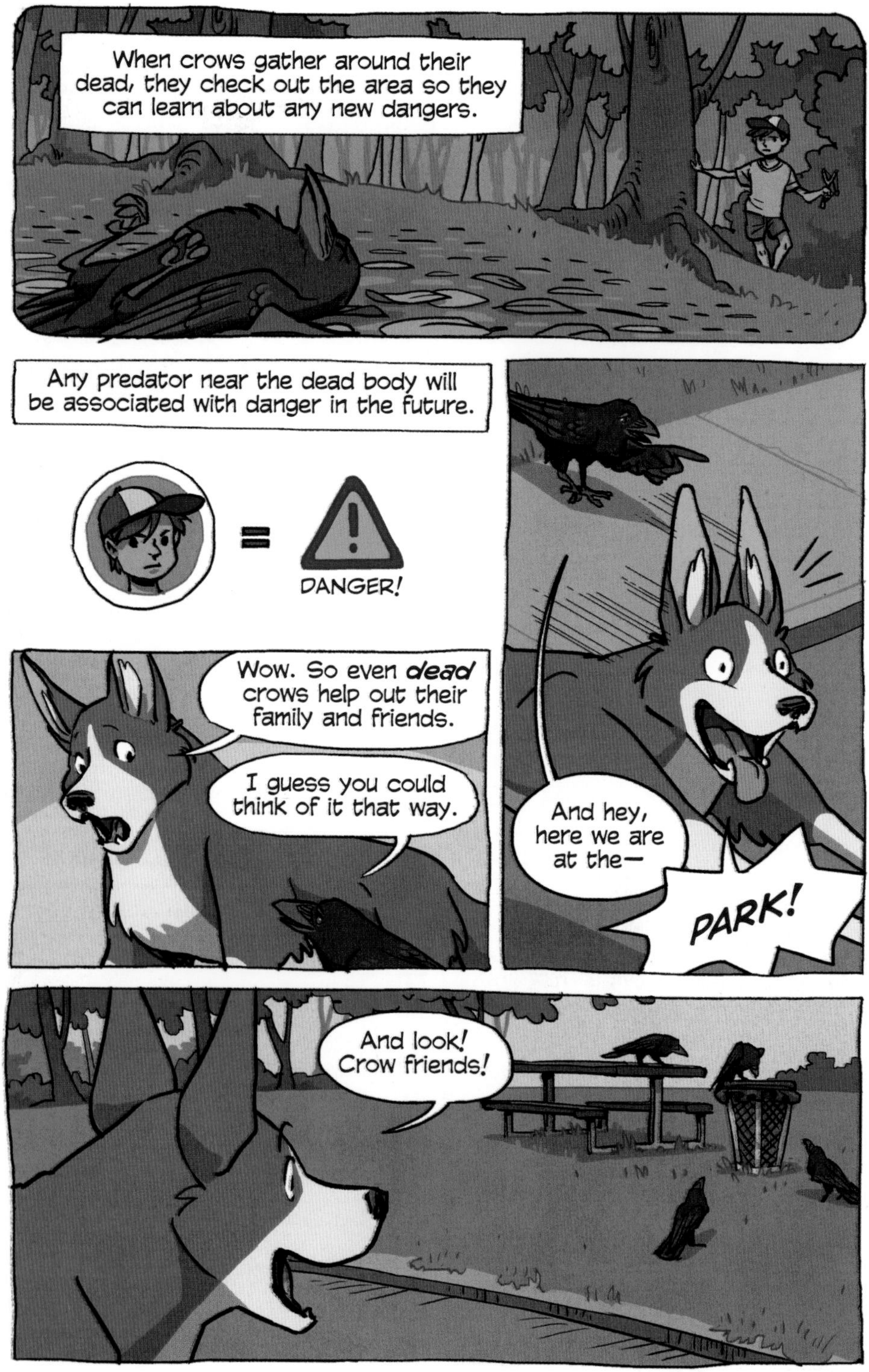
When crows gather around their dead, they check out the area so they can learn about any new dangers.
Any predator near the dead body will be associated with danger in the future.
DANGER!
Wow. So even ***dead*** crows help out their family and friends.
I guess you could think of it that way.
And hey, here we are at the—
PARK!
And look! Crow friends!

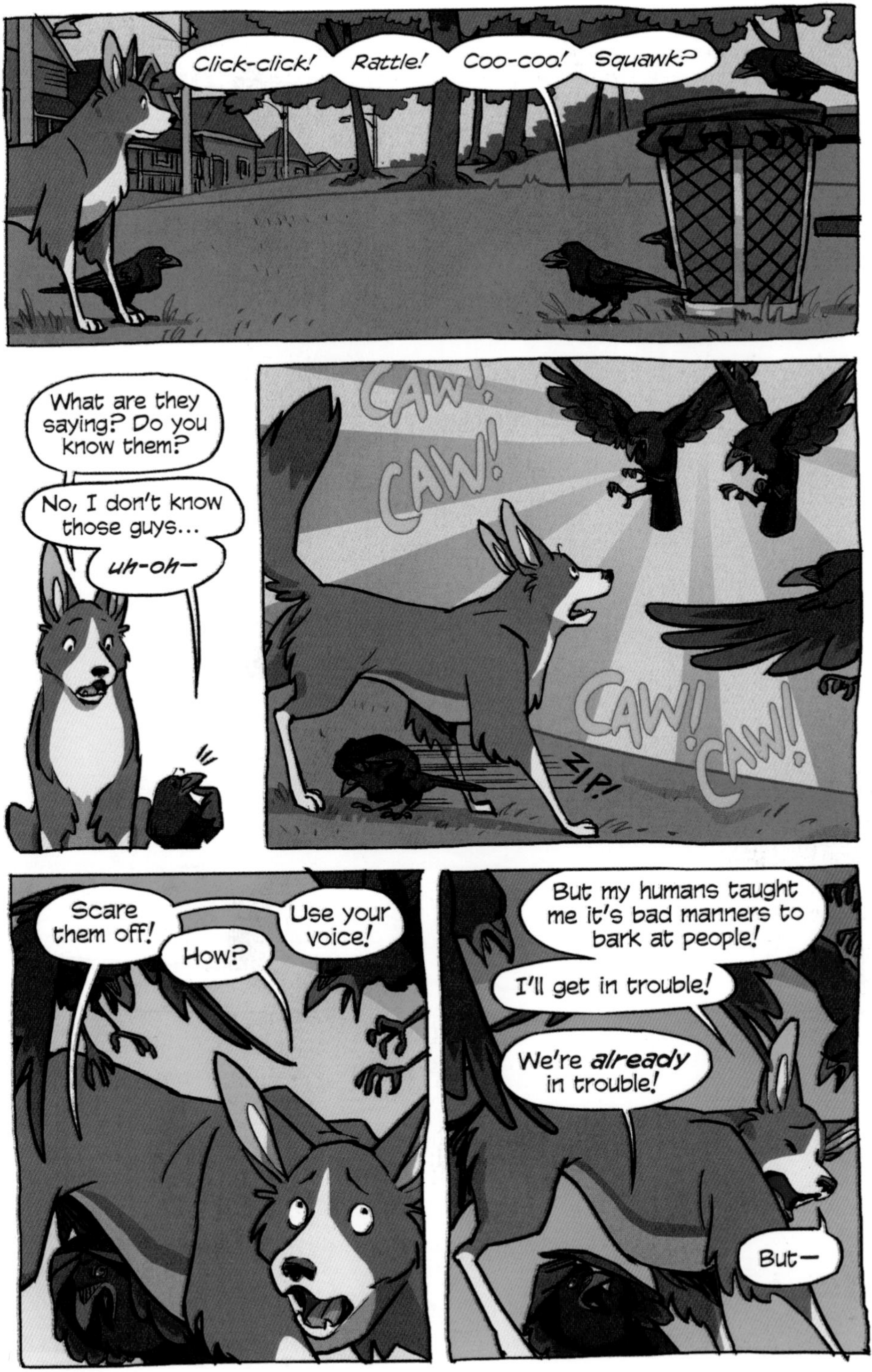

Click-click!
Rattle!
Coo-coo!
Squawk?
What are they saying? Do you know them?
No, I don't know those guys...
uh-oh—
CAW! CAW!
CAW! CAW!
ZIP!
Scare them off!
How?
Use your voice!
But my humans taught me it's bad manners to bark at people!
I'll get in trouble!
We're **already** in trouble!
But—

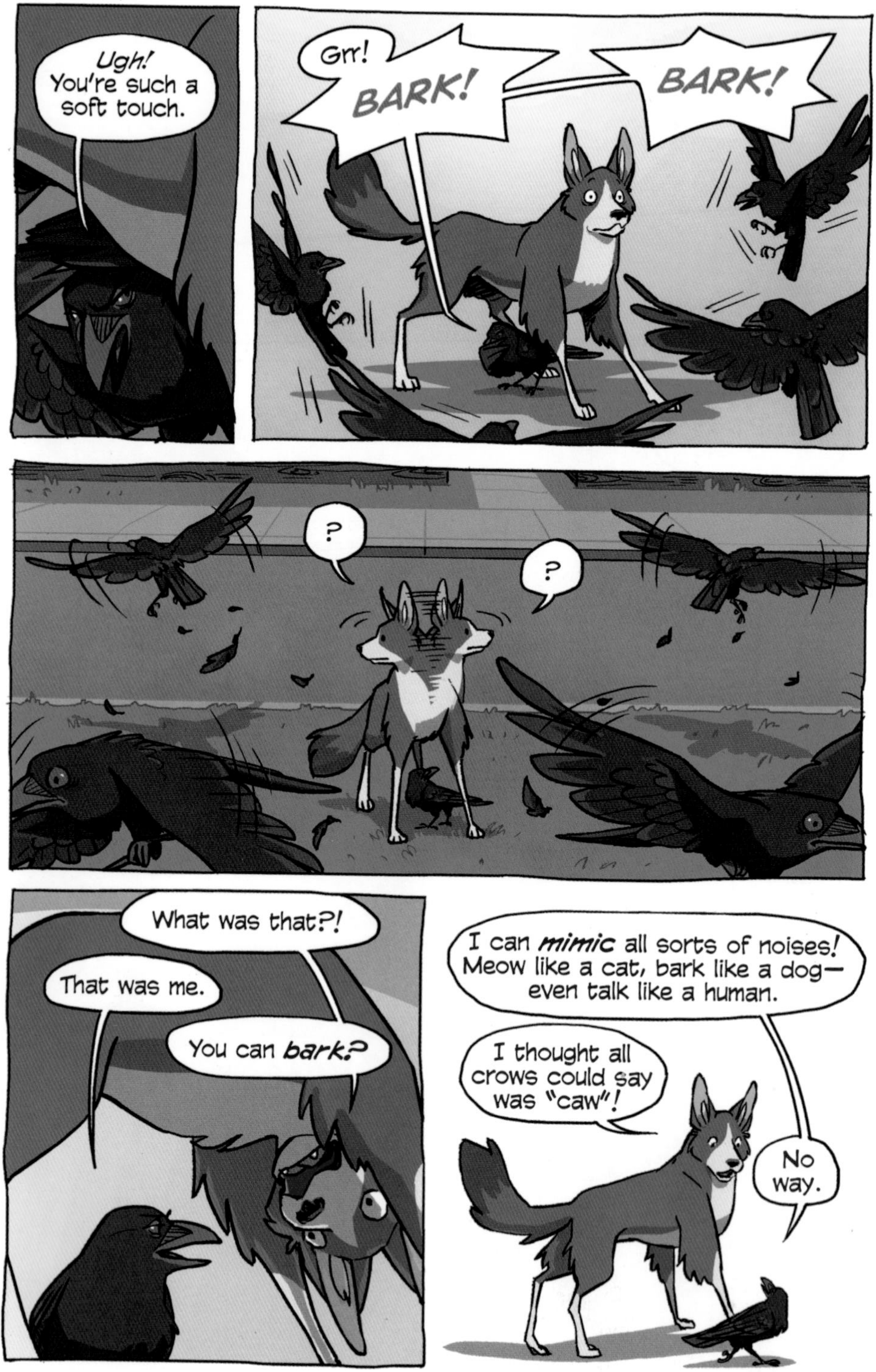
Ugh! You're such a soft touch.
Grr! BARK!
BARK!
?
?
What was that?!
That was me.
You can bark?
I can mimic all sorts of noises! Meow like a cat, bark like a dog— even talk like a human.
I thought all crows could say was "caw"!
No way.

Crows are *songbirds,* after all.

Really...?

Yup. We might not have the prettiest songs—but we do have a big repertoire!

Some birds have their calls hardwired into their brain. A chicken who never hears another chicken will still vocalize normally.

COCK-A-DOODLE-DOO!

But songbirds learn their calls. Most learn during childhood, but some songbirds can learn new songs throughout their lives.

Birds like mockingbirds, lyrebirds...and crows!

Mimus polyglottos / Northern Mockingbird

Menura novaehollandiae / Lyrebird

That's pretty important for social birds like crows, because different groups of crows have different *dialects*—unique songs.

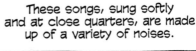

These songs, sung softly and at close quarters, are made up of a variety of noises.

Coo-coo.

Squawk.

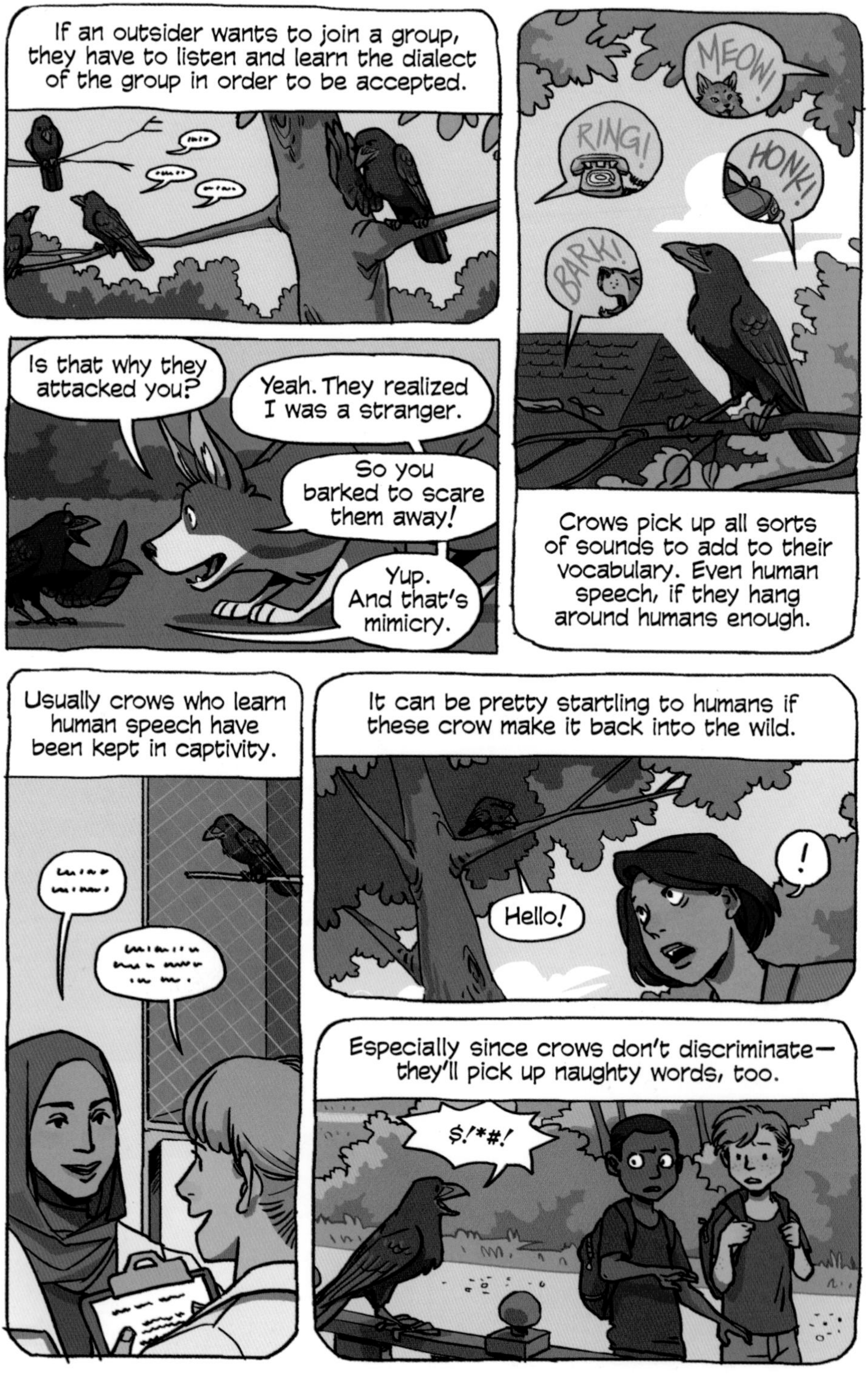
If an outsider wants to join a group, they have to listen and learn the dialect of the group in order to be accepted.
MEOW!
RING!
HONK!
BARK!
Is that why they attacked you?
Yeah. They realized I was a stranger.
So you barked to scare them away!
Yup. And that's mimicry.
Crows pick up all sorts of sounds to add to their vocabulary. Even human speech, if they hang around humans enough.
Usually crows who learn human speech have been kept in captivity.
It can be pretty startling to humans if these crow make it back into the wild.
Hello!
!
Especially since crows don't discriminate— they'll pick up naughty words, too.
$!*#!

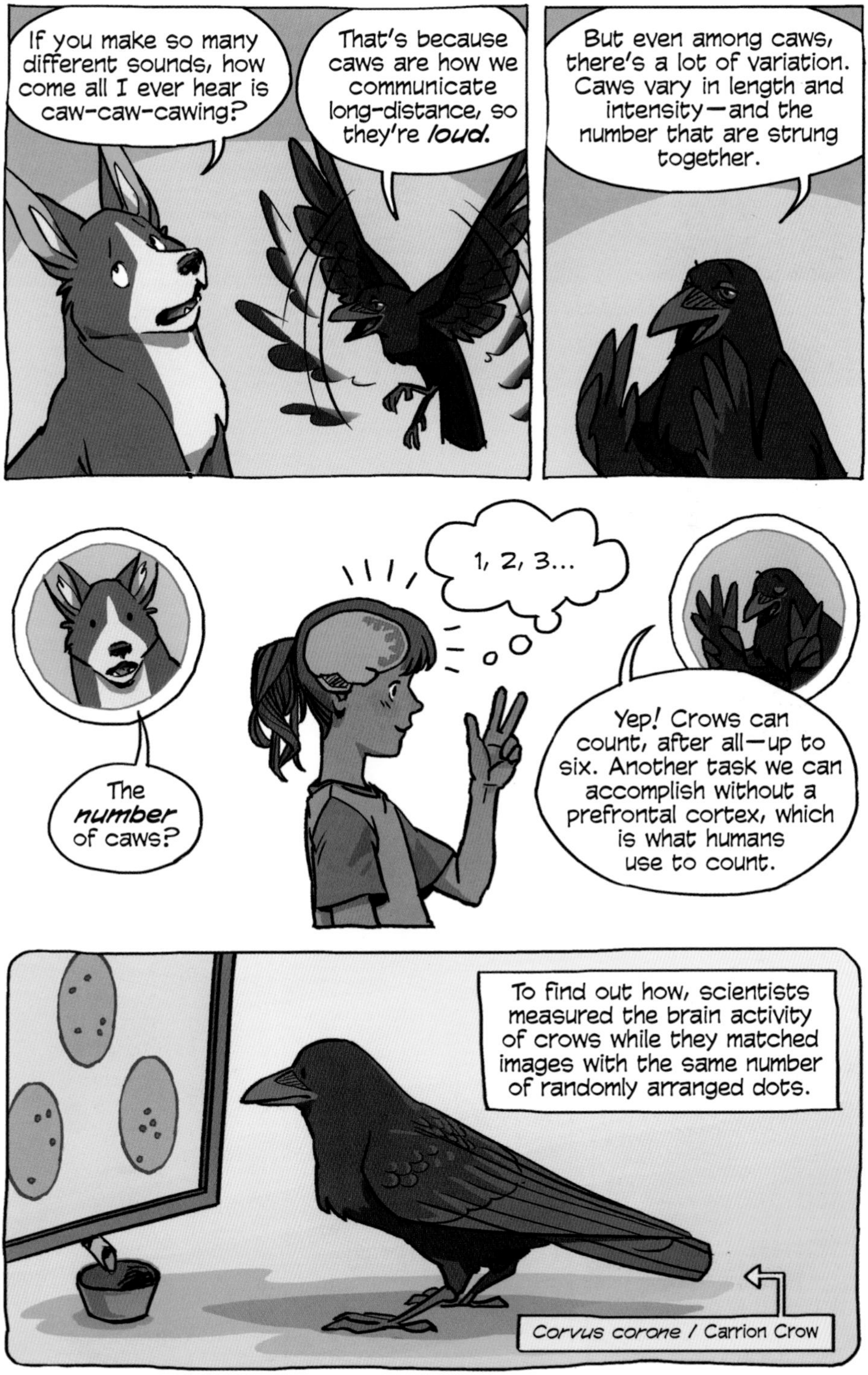
If you make so many different sounds, how come all I ever hear is caw-caw-cawing?
That's because caws are how we communicate long-distance, so they're *loud.*
But even among caws, there's a lot of variation. Caws vary in length and intensity—and the number that are strung together.
The *number* of caws?
1, 2, 3...
Yep! Crows can count, after all—up to six. Another task we can accomplish without a prefrontal cortex, which is what humans use to count.
To find out how, scientists measured the brain activity of crows while they matched images with the same number of randomly arranged dots.
Corvus corone / Carrion Crow

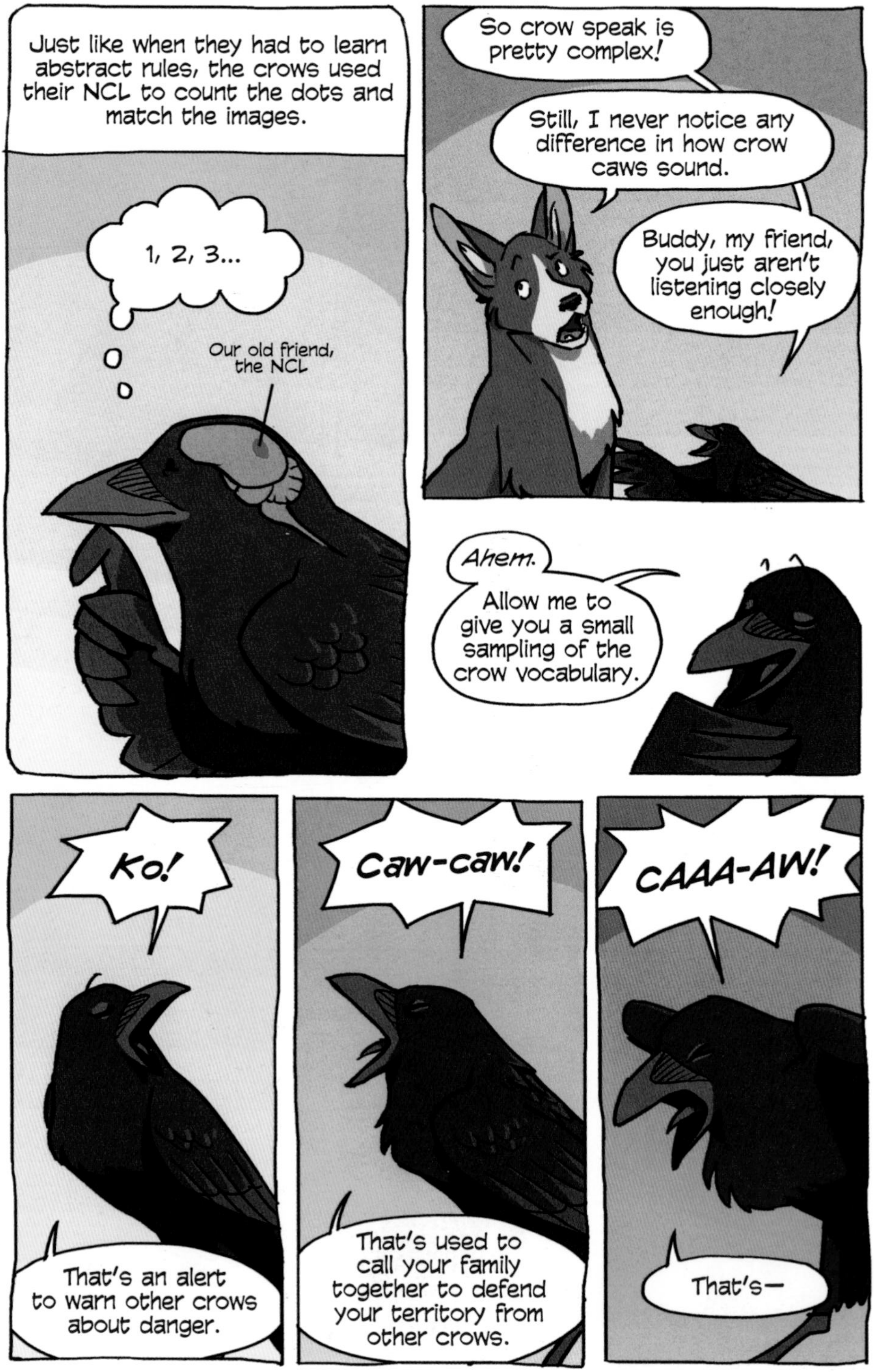
Just like when they had to learn abstract rules, the crows used their NCL to count the dots and match the images.
1, 2, 3...
Our old friend, the NCL
So crow speak is pretty complex!
Still, I never notice any difference in how crow caws sound.
Buddy, my friend, you just aren't listening closely enough!
Ahem.
Allow me to give you a small sampling of the crow vocabulary.
Ko!
That's an alert to warn other crows about danger.
Caw-caw!
That's used to call your family together to defend your territory from other crows.
CAAA-AW!
That's—

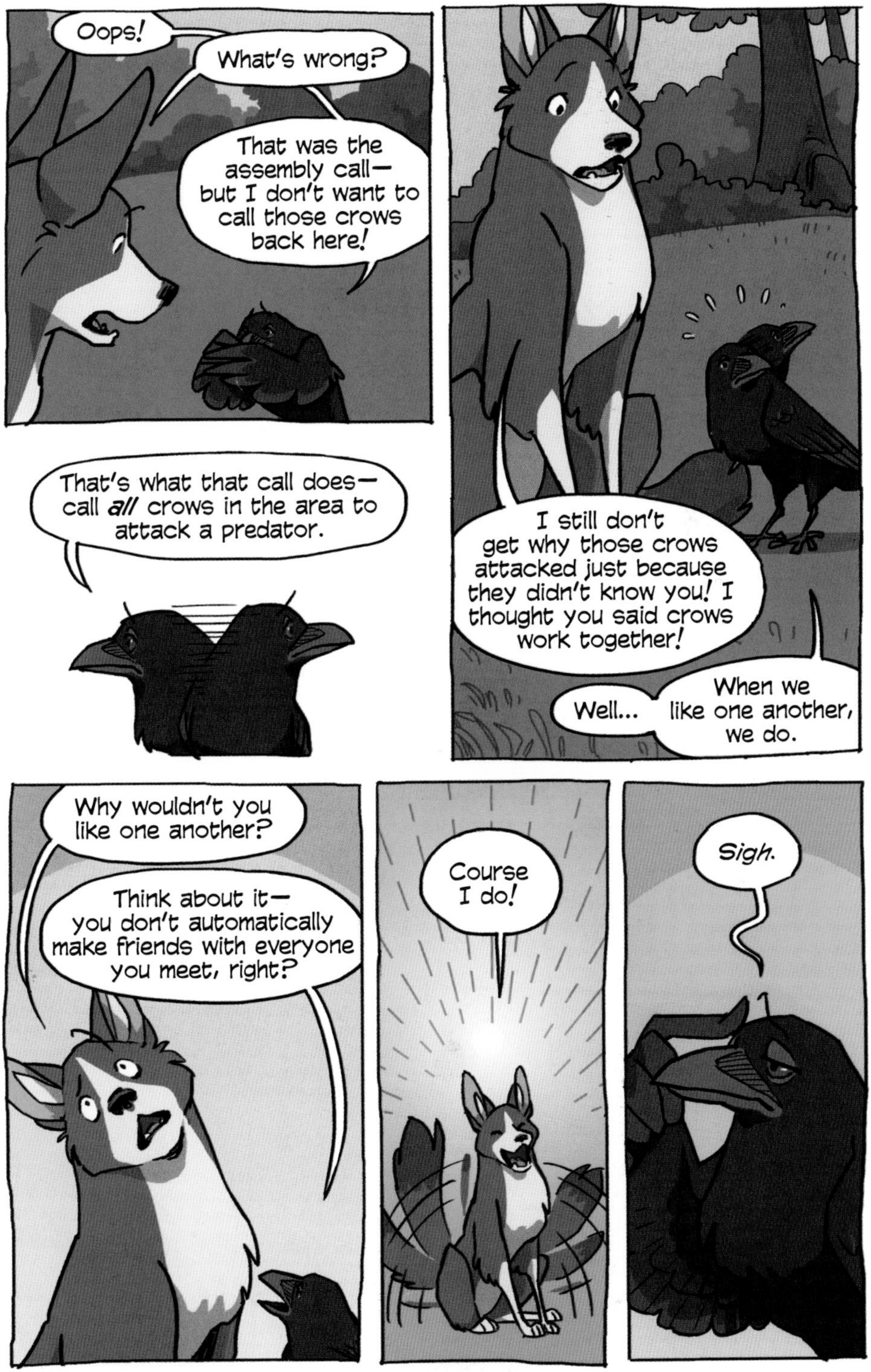
Oops!
What's wrong?
That was the assembly call—but I don't want to call those crows back here!
That's what that call does—call *all* crows in the area to attack a predator.
I still don't get why those crows attacked just because they didn't know you! I thought you said crows work together!
Well...
When we like one another, we do.
Why wouldn't you like one another?
Think about it—you don't automatically make friends with everyone you meet, right?
Course I do!
Sigh.

Well, generally, crows get along pretty swell, and most squabbles aren't serious. But we can get touchy about the boundaries of our territories.

Oh! That's what that "caw-caw" call is for!

You got it.

Even in winter, when crows roost communally, a breeding pair will check in on their territory during the day.

Territories can be a few square miles in the wild. But in cities, with so much food to go around, they can be much smaller.

But even a small territory is still a territory worth defending!

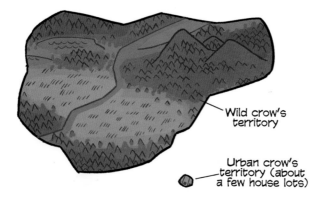

Wild crow's territory

Urban crow's territory (about a few house lots)

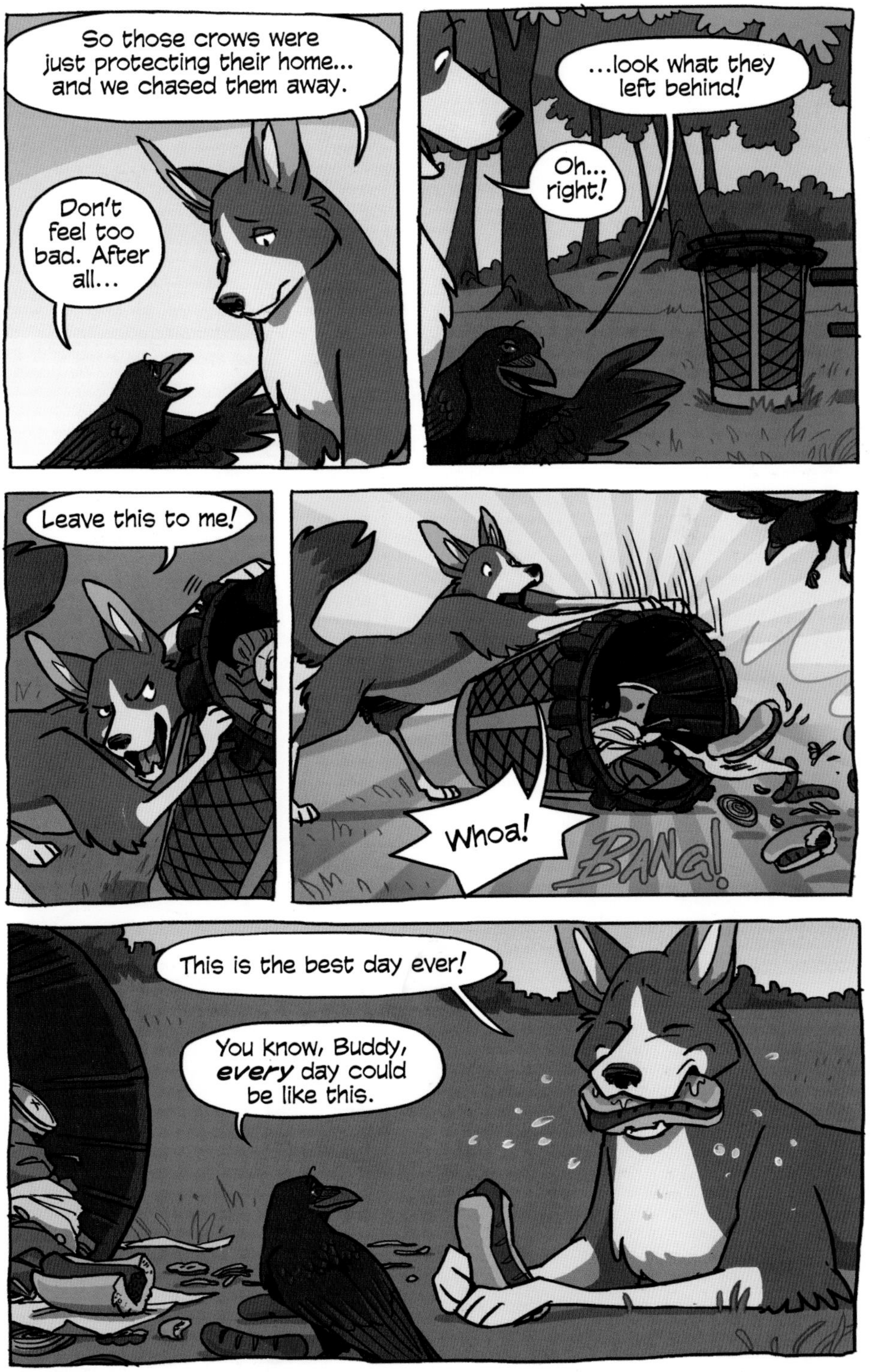
So those crows were just protecting their home... and we chased them away.
Don't feel too bad. After all...
...look what they left behind!
Oh... right!
Leave this to me!
Whoa!
BANG!
This is the best day ever!
You know, Buddy, every day could be like this.

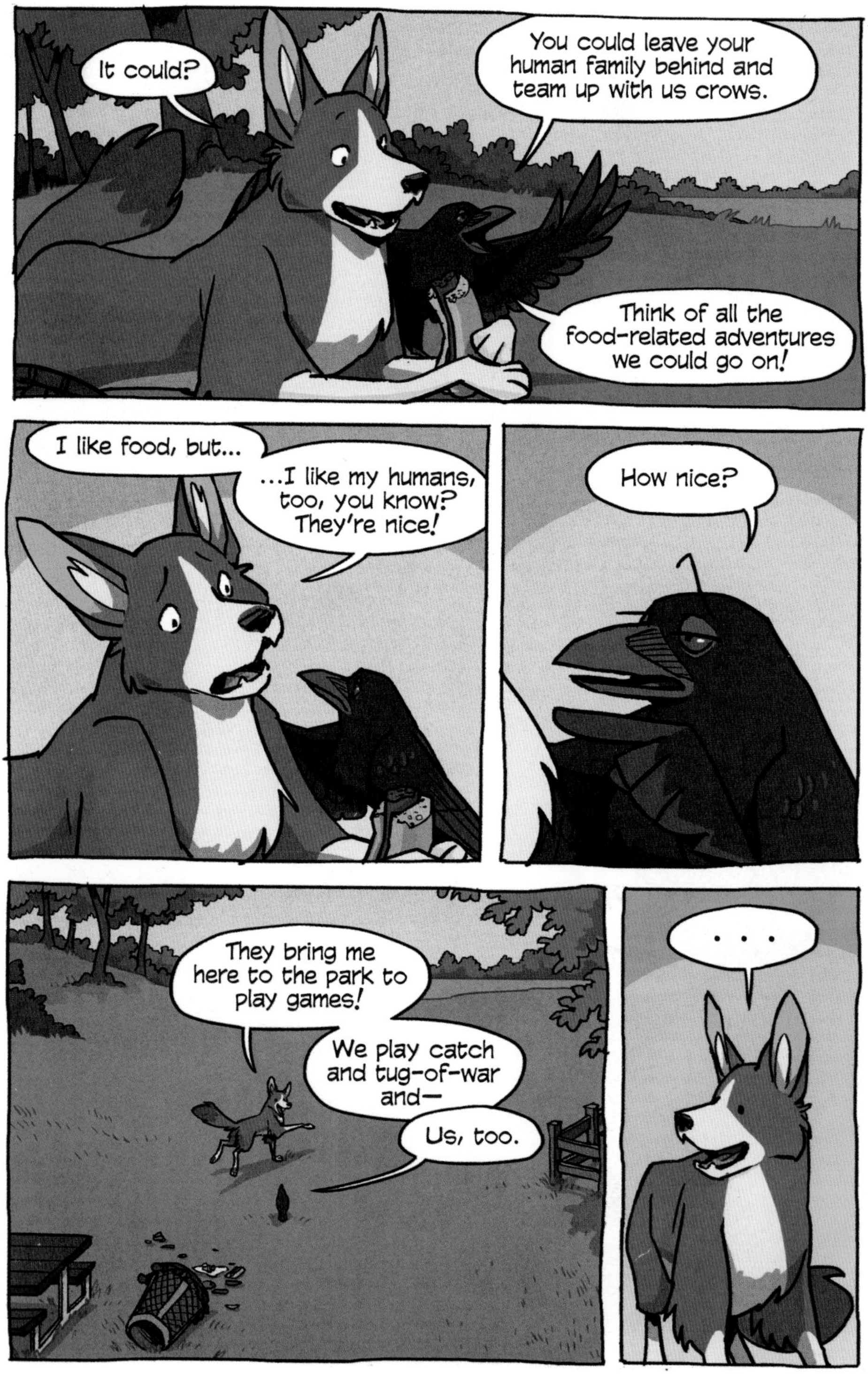
It could?
You could leave your human family behind and team up with us crows.
Think of all the food-related adventures we could go on!
I like food, but...
...I like my humans, too, you know? They're nice!
How nice?
They bring me here to the park to play games!
We play catch and tug-of-war and—
Us, too.
. . .

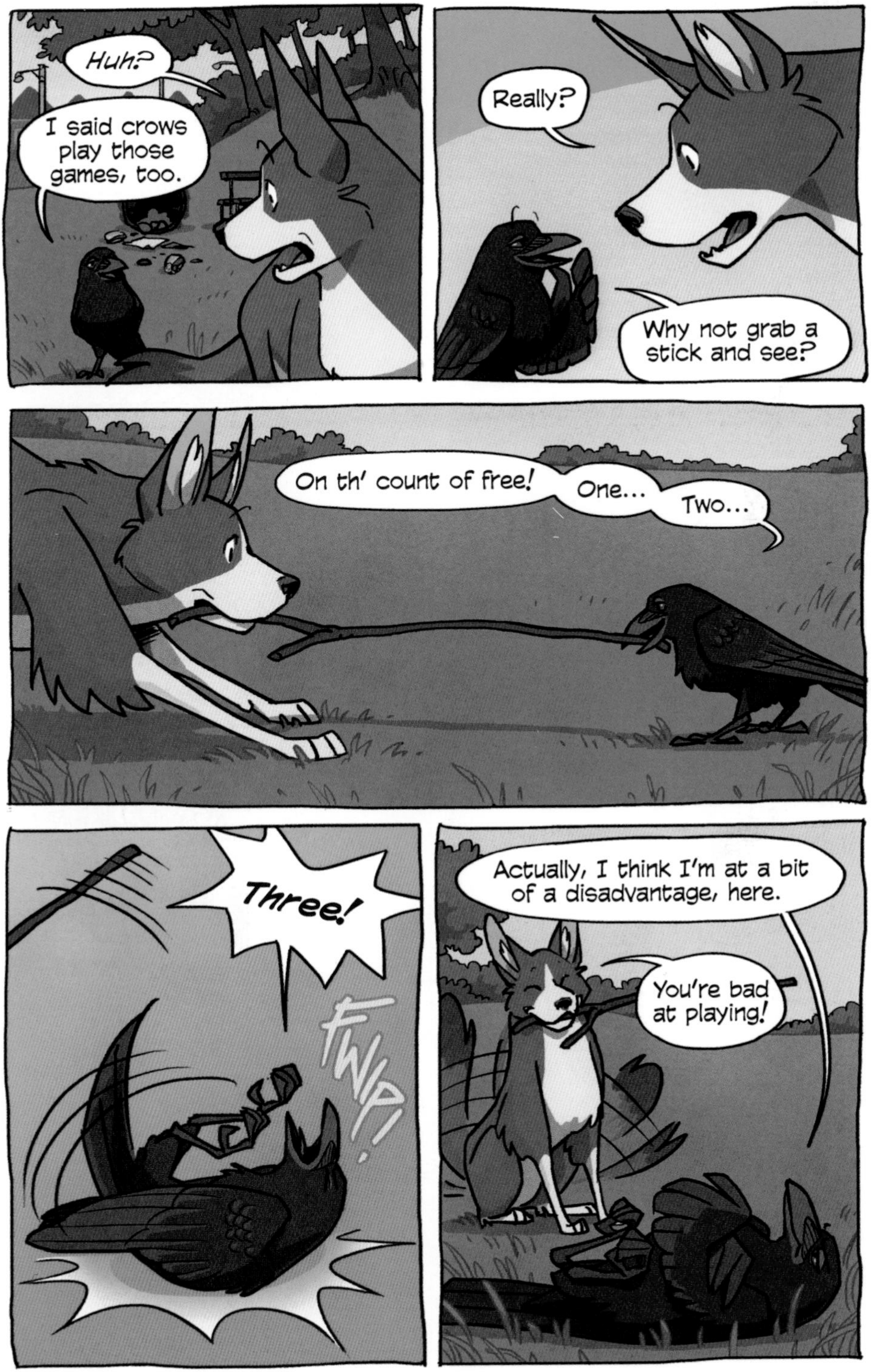
Huh?
I said crows play those games, too.
Really?
Why not grab a stick and see?
On th' count of free!
One...
Two...
Three!
FWIP!
Actually, I think I'm at a bit of a disadvantage, here.
You're bad at playing!

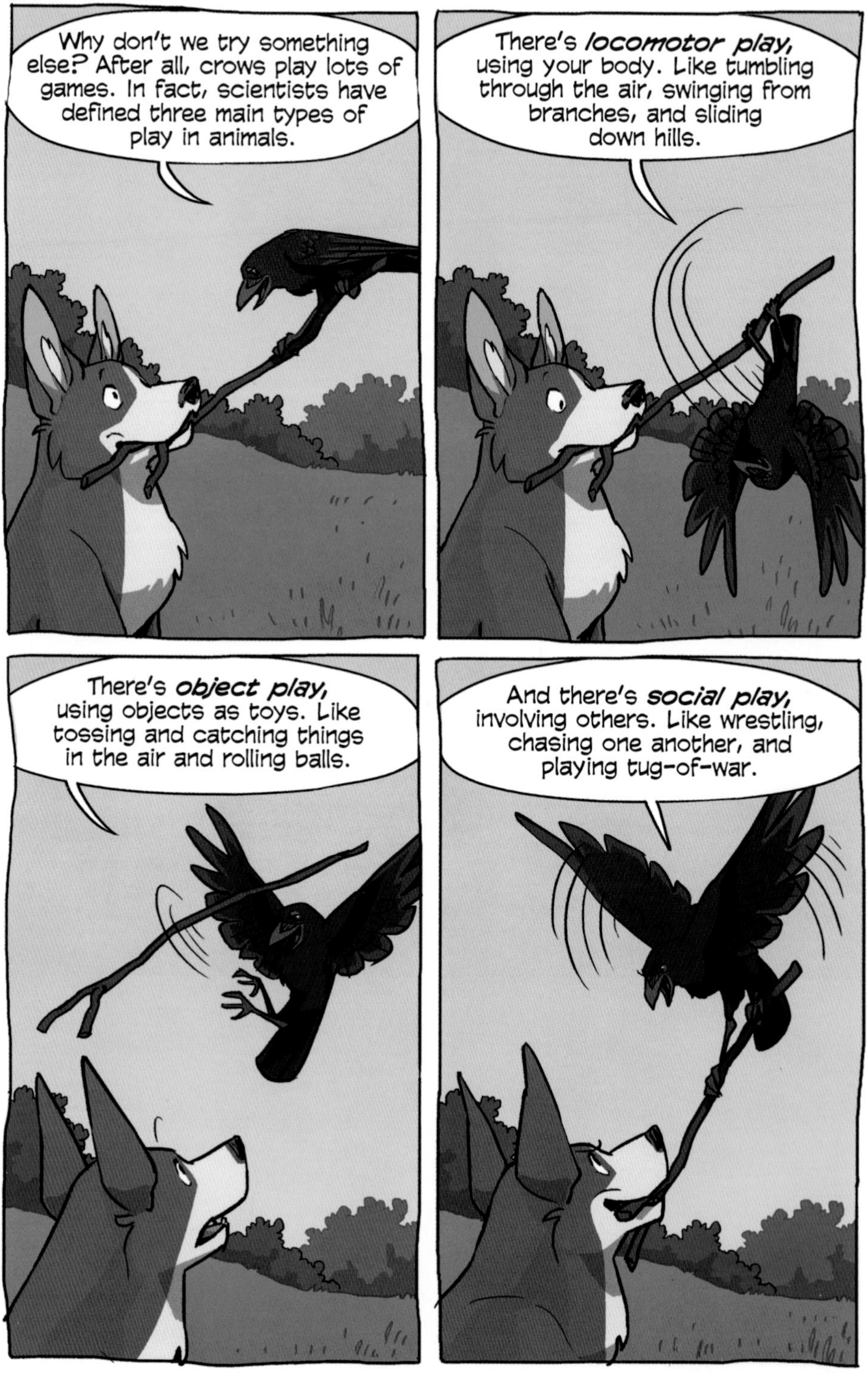
Why don't we try something else? After all, crows play lots of games. In fact, scientists have defined three main types of play in animals.
There's *locomotor play,* using your body. Like tumbling through the air, swinging from branches, and sliding down hills.
There's *object play,* using objects as toys. Like tossing and catching things in the air and rolling balls.
And there's *social play,* involving others. Like wrestling, chasing one another, and playing tug-of-war.

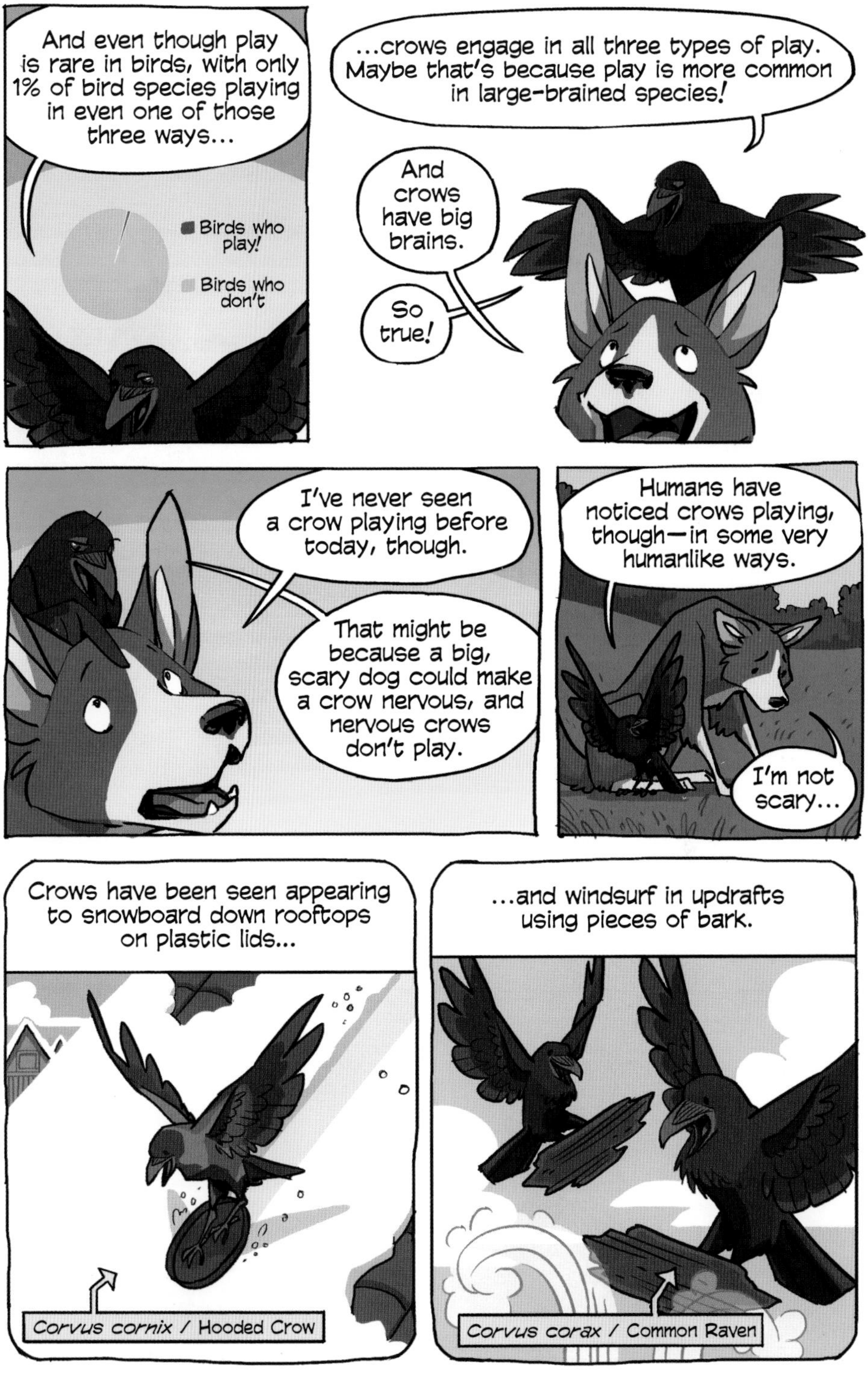
And even though play is rare in birds, with only 1% of bird species playing in even one of those three ways...
Birds who play!
Birds who don't
...crows engage in all three types of play. Maybe that's because play is more common in large-brained species!
And crows have big brains.
So true!
I've never seen a crow playing before today, though.
That might be because a big, scary dog could make a crow nervous, and nervous crows don't play.
Humans have noticed crows playing, though—in some very humanlike ways.
I'm not scary...
Crows have been seen appearing to snowboard down rooftops on plastic lids...
Corvus cornix / Hooded Crow
...and windsurf in updrafts using pieces of bark.
Corvus corax / Common Raven

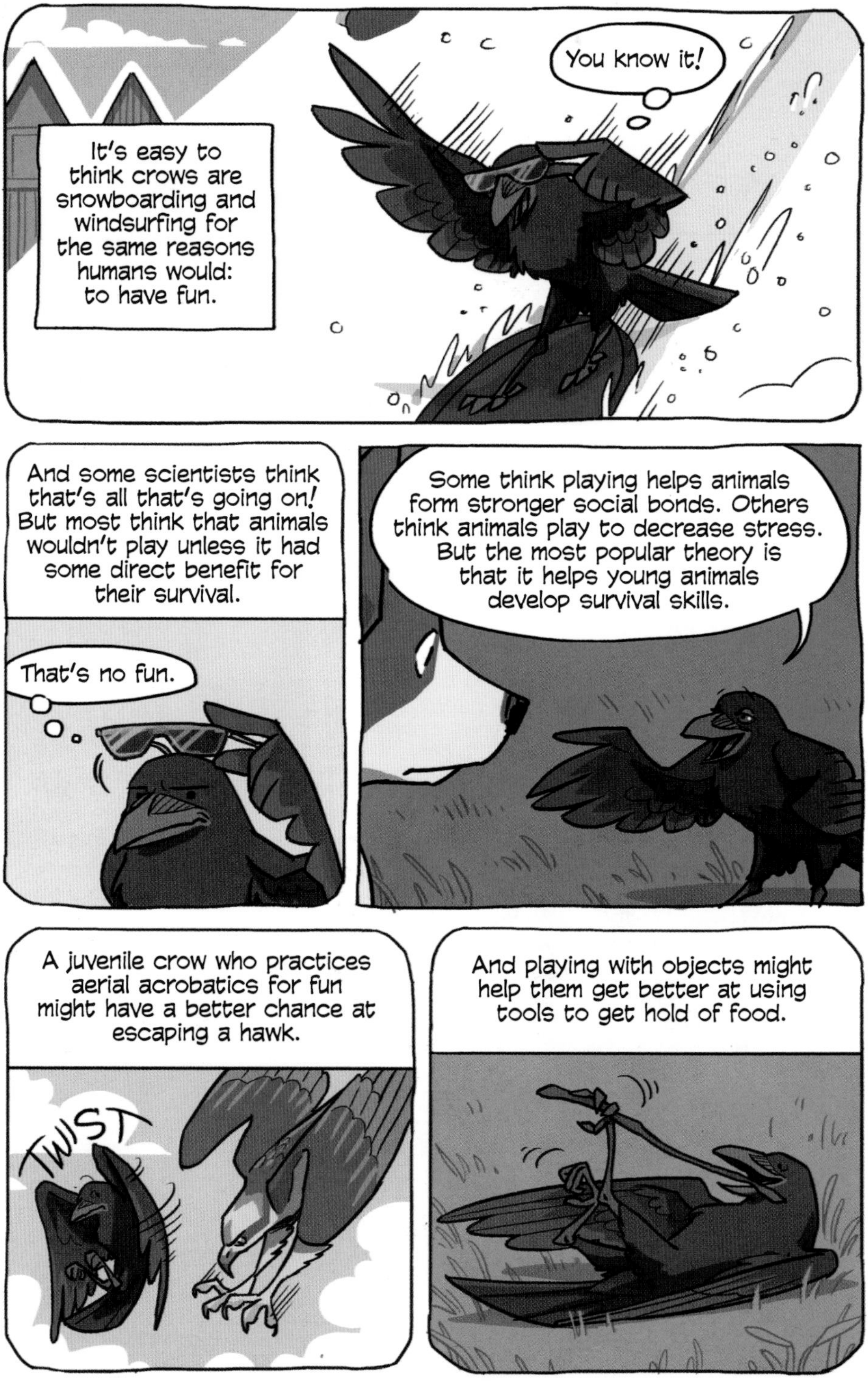
It's easy to think crows are snowboarding and windsurfing for the same reasons humans would: to have fun.
You know it!
And some scientists think that's all that's going on! But most think that animals wouldn't play unless it had some direct benefit for their survival.
That's no fun.
Some think playing helps animals form stronger social bonds. Others think animals play to decrease stress. But the most popular theory is that it helps young animals develop survival skills.
A juvenile crow who practices aerial acrobatics for fun might have a better chance at escaping a hawk.
TWIST
And playing with objects might help them get better at using tools to get hold of food.

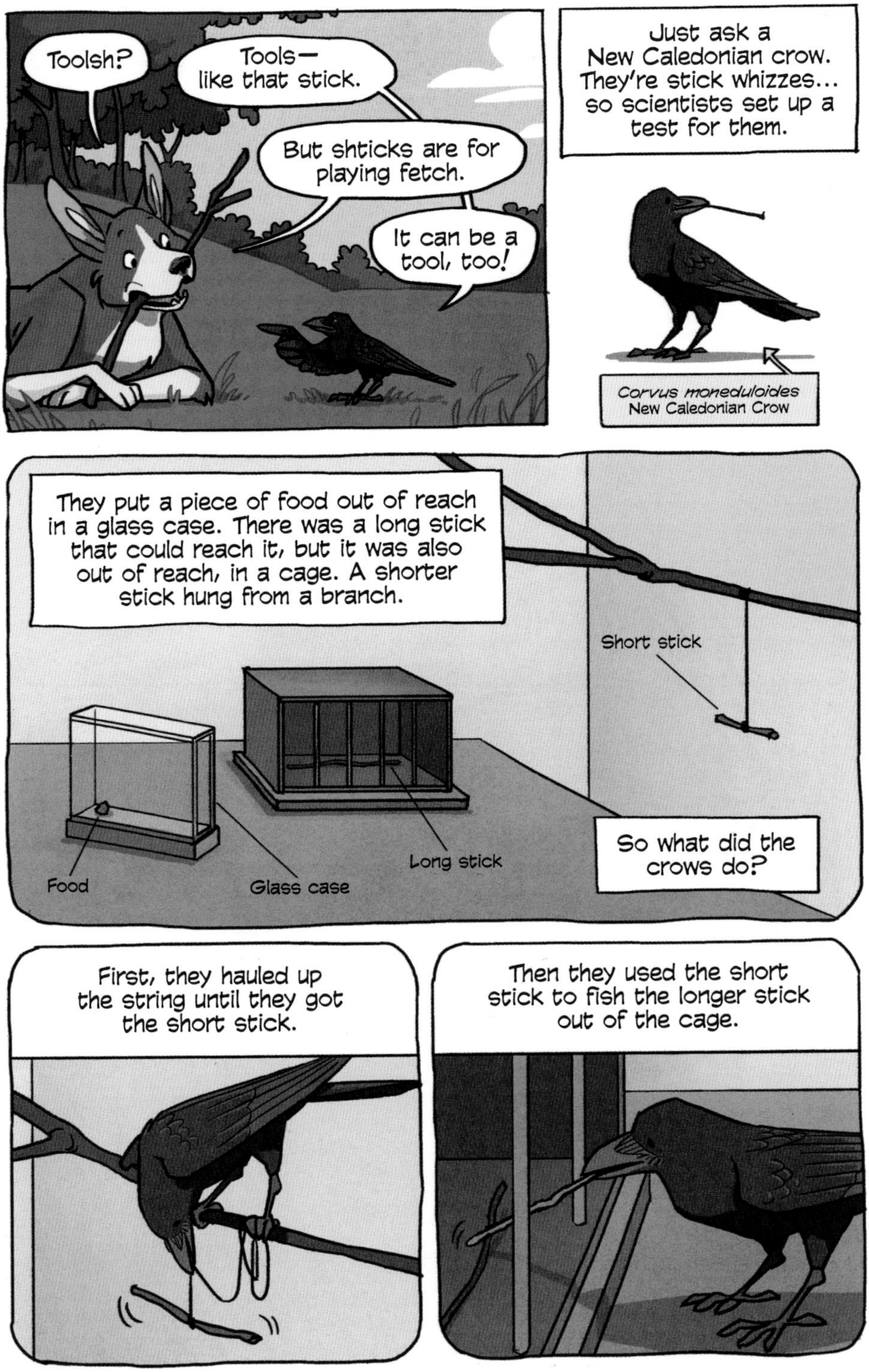

Toolsh?
Tools— like that stick.
But shticks are for playing fetch.
It can be a tool, too!
Just ask a New Caledonian crow. They're stick whizzes... so scientists set up a test for them.
Corvus moneduloides
New Caledonian Crow
They put a piece of food out of reach in a glass case. There was a long stick that could reach it, but it was also out of reach, in a cage. A shorter stick hung from a branch.
Short stick
Food
Glass case
Long stick
So what did the crows do?
First, they hauled up the string until they got the short stick.
Then they used the short stick to fish the longer stick out of the cage.

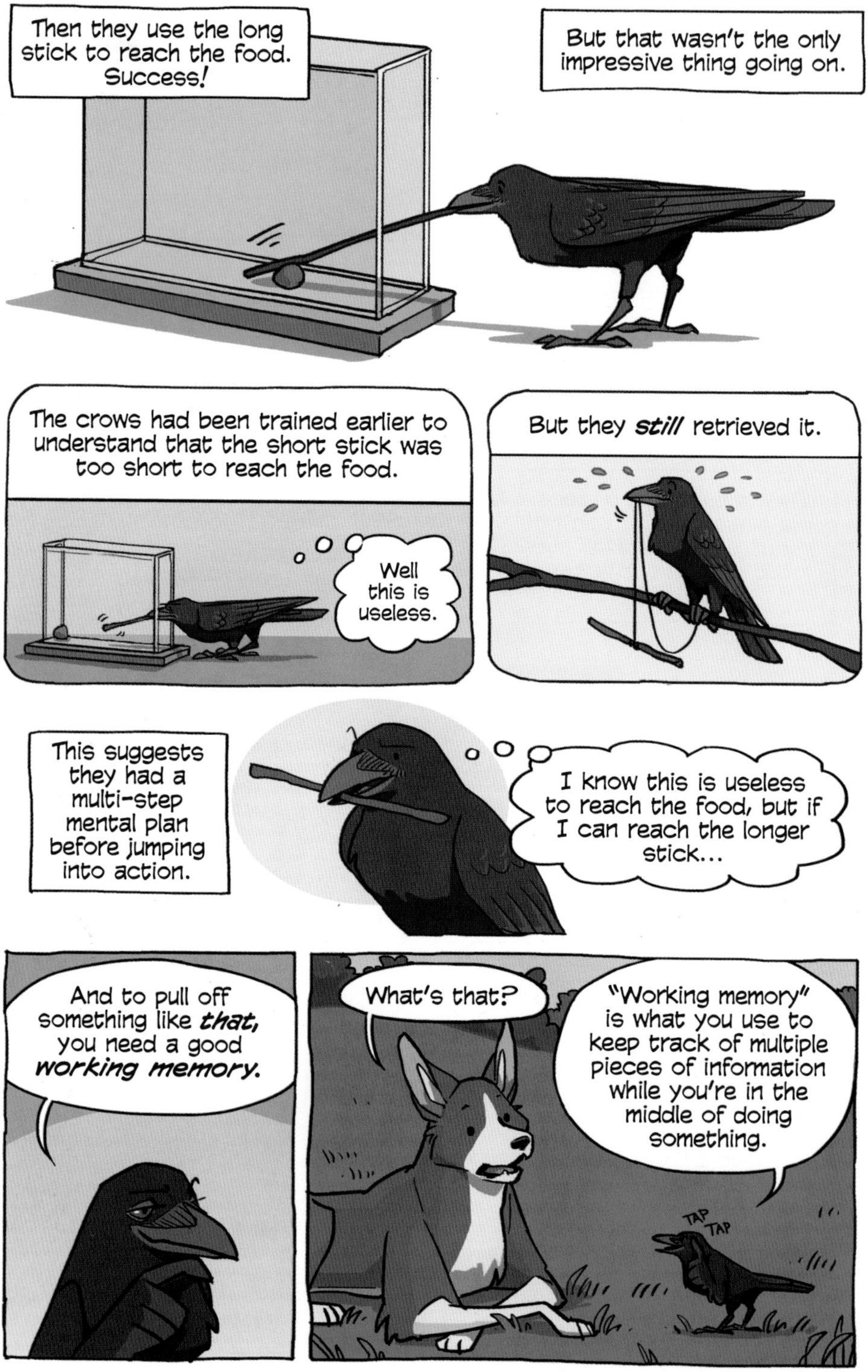

Then they use the long stick to reach the food. Success!
But that wasn't the only impressive thing going on.
The crows had been trained earlier to understand that the short stick was too short to reach the food.
Well this is useless.
But they *still* retrieved it.
This suggests they had a multi-step mental plan before jumping into action.
I know this is useless to reach the food, but if I can reach the longer stick...
And to pull off something like *that*, you need a good ***working memory.***
What's that?
"Working memory" is what you use to keep track of multiple pieces of information while you're in the middle of doing something.
TAP TAP

... ?

Without it, you couldn't keep track of what you were saying, reading, or thinking.

You couldn't work through a math problem.

? ?

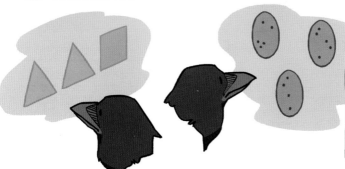

It's also what crows and primates relied on in those image and number matching games.

In fact, crows have been shown to have a working memory as advanced as primates!

But New Caledonian crows don't just use tools in fancy experiments in labs. They use them in the wild, too—in fact, they *make* them.

And since humans and primates rely on their prefrontal cortex for their working memory...

...4, 5, 6.

...in crows, it's another job for our big honkin' NCL.

Stepped tools are cut out of pandanus leaves.	Hooked tools are made by cutting down twigs.	Both are used for fishing grubs out of tree trunks.

This is made easier by the New Caledonian crow's anatomy. They have better binocular vision than other crows—that's the area in front of you that both eyes can see.

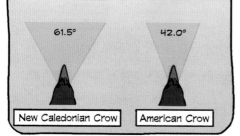

New Caledonian Crow	American Crow

Also, most crows' bills are slightly hooked at the end, but the New Caledonian's is straight, making it easier to hold a tool straight out in front of them where they can see it.

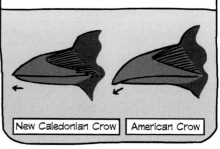

New Caledonian Crow	American Crow

So they're pretty special crows!

On top of that, making hooked tools is very rare.

The fact is, the only animals aside from crows that are known to make their own hooked tools are humans.

That's... pretty rare.

The hooked-tool-making club!

Yup, it's a two-animal club!

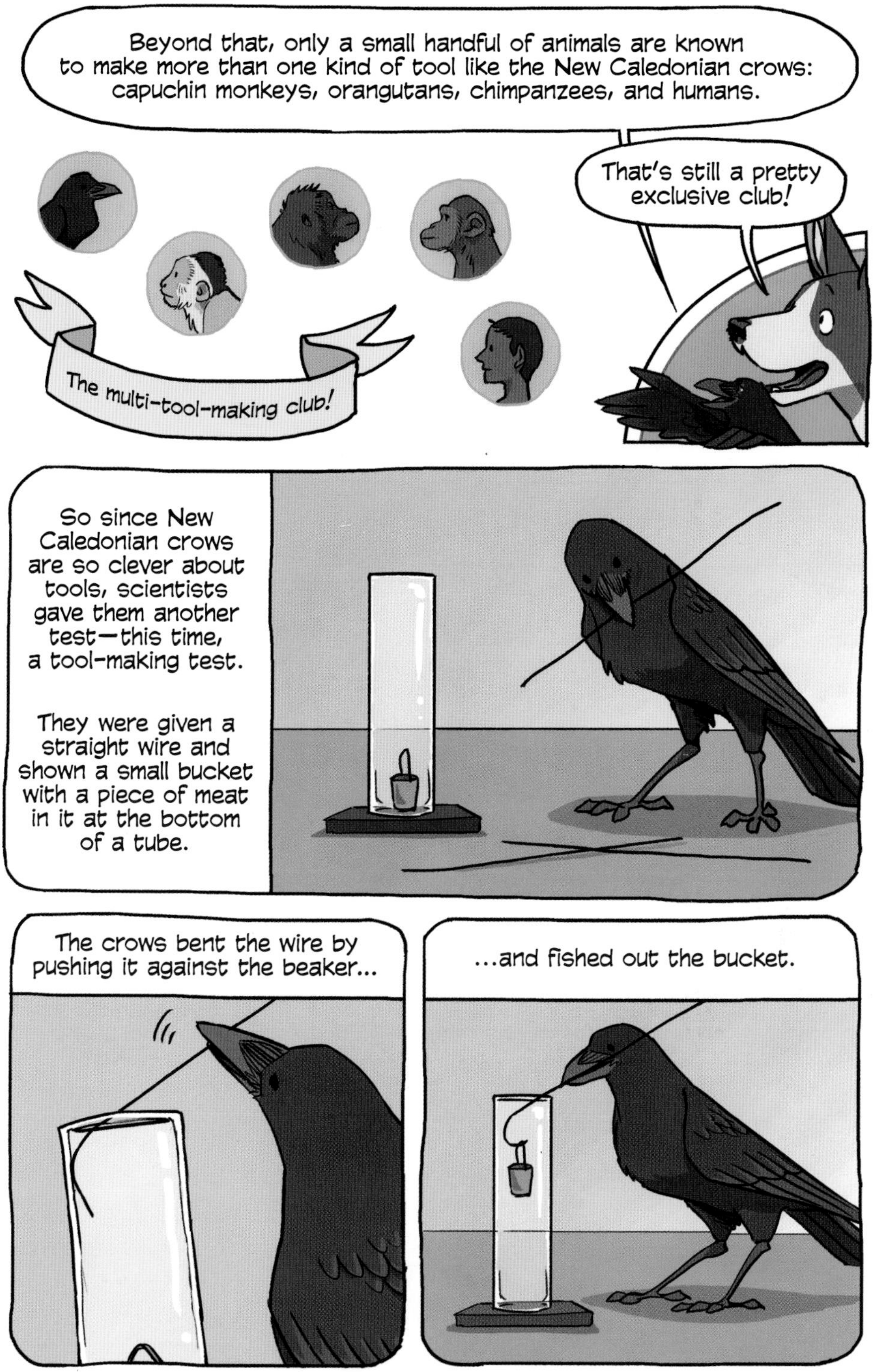
Beyond that, only a small handful of animals are known to make more than one kind of tool like the New Caledonian crows: capuchin monkeys, orangutans, chimpanzees, and humans.
The multi-tool-making club!
That's still a pretty exclusive club!
So since New Caledonian crows are so clever about tools, scientists gave them another test—this time, a tool-making test.
They were given a straight wire and shown a small bucket with a piece of meat in it at the bottom of a tube.
The crows bent the wire by pushing it against the beaker...
...and fished out the bucket.

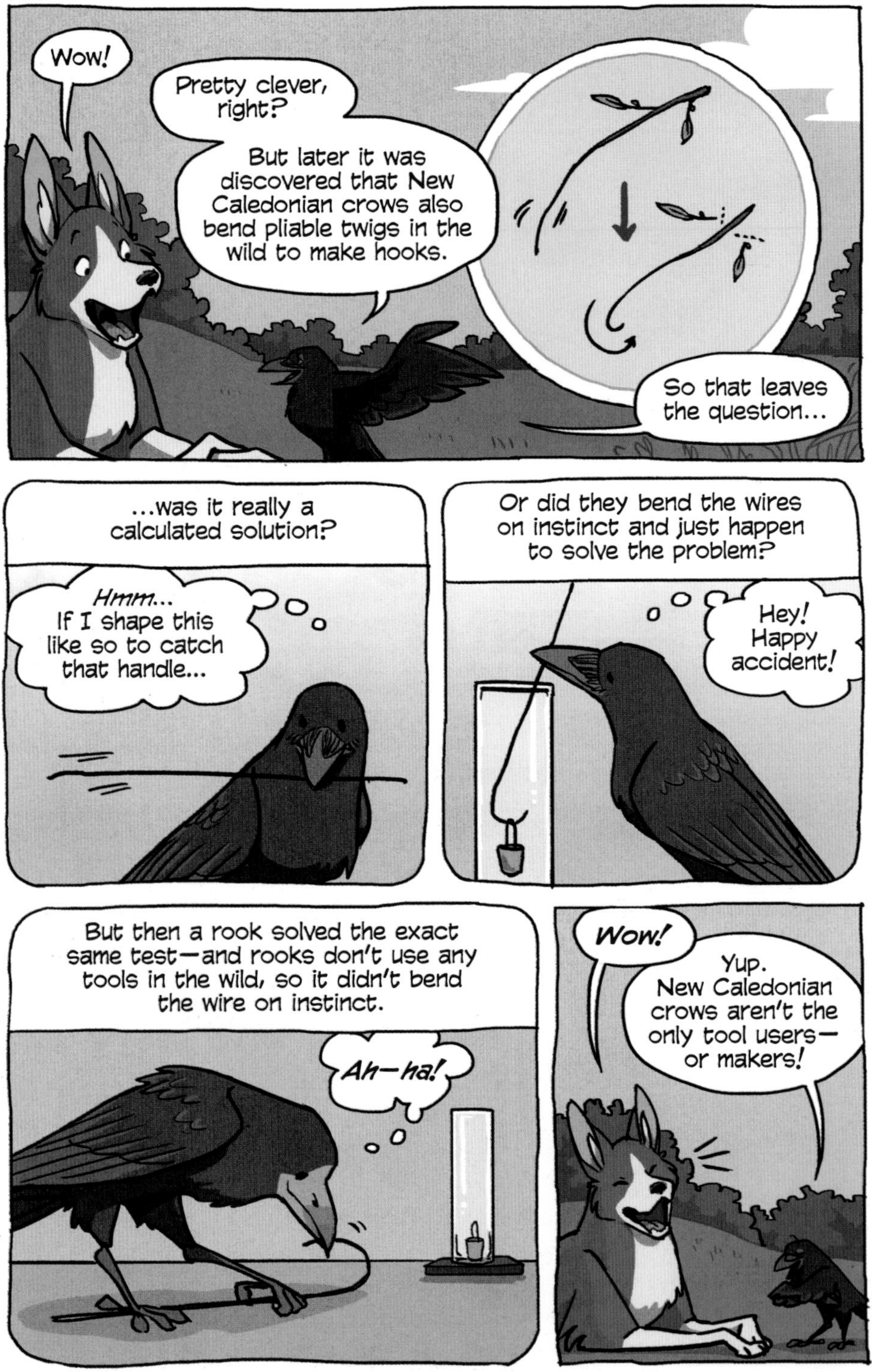
Wow!
Pretty clever, right?
But later it was discovered that New Caledonian crows also bend pliable twigs in the wild to make hooks.
So that leaves the question...
...was it really a calculated solution?
Hmm... If I shape this like so to catch that handle...
Or did they bend the wires on instinct and just happen to solve the problem?
Hey! Happy accident!
But then a rook solved the exact same test—and rooks don't use any tools in the wild, so it didn't bend the wire on instinct.
Ah—ha!
Wow!
Yup. New Caledonian crows aren't the only tool users—or makers!

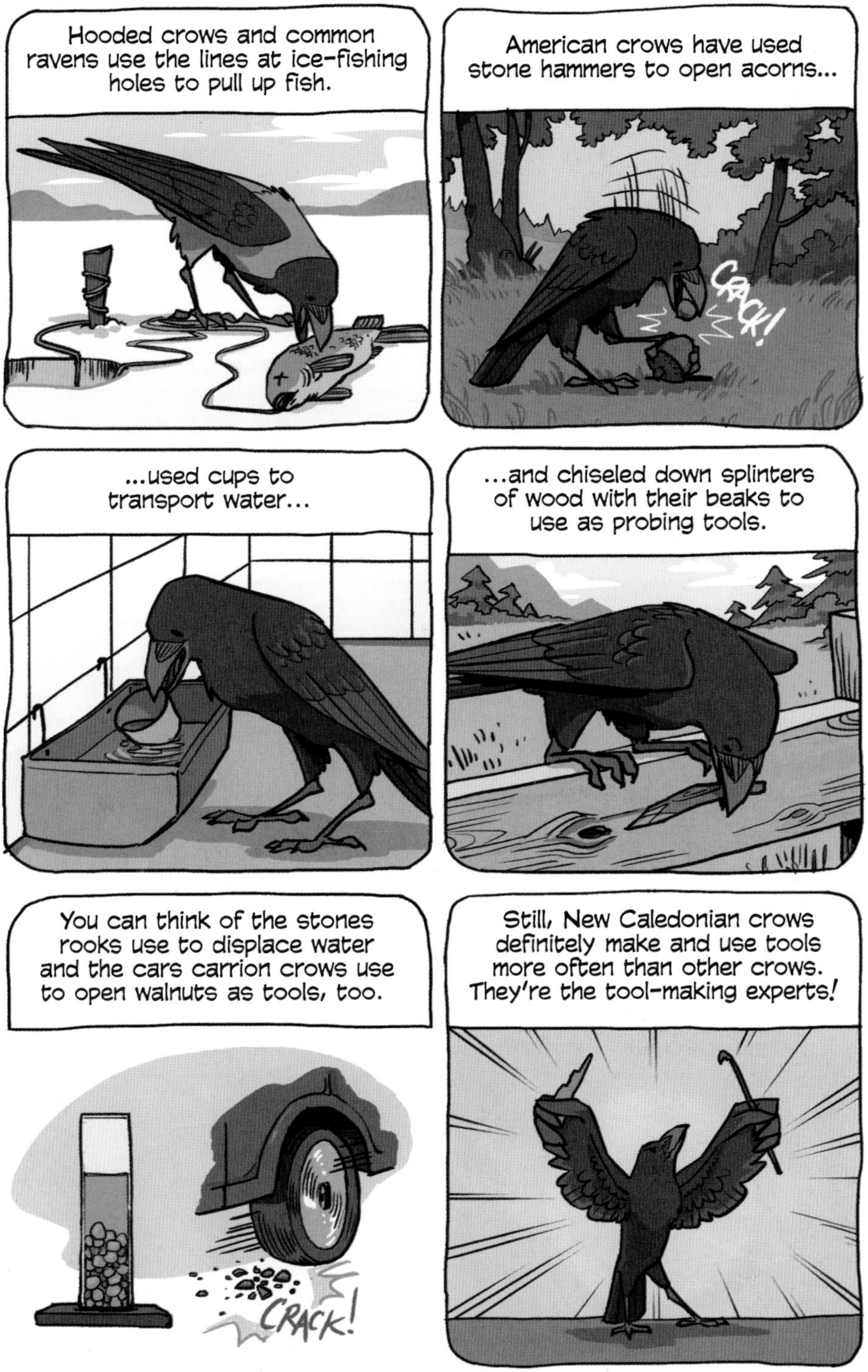
Hooded crows and common ravens use the lines at ice-fishing holes to pull up fish.
American crows have used stone hammers to open acorns...
CRACK!
...used cups to transport water...
...and chiseled down splinters of wood with their beaks to use as probing tools.
You can think of the stones rooks use to displace water and the cars carrion crows use to open walnuts as tools, too.
CRACK!
Still, New Caledonian crows definitely make and use tools more often than other crows. They're the tool-making experts!

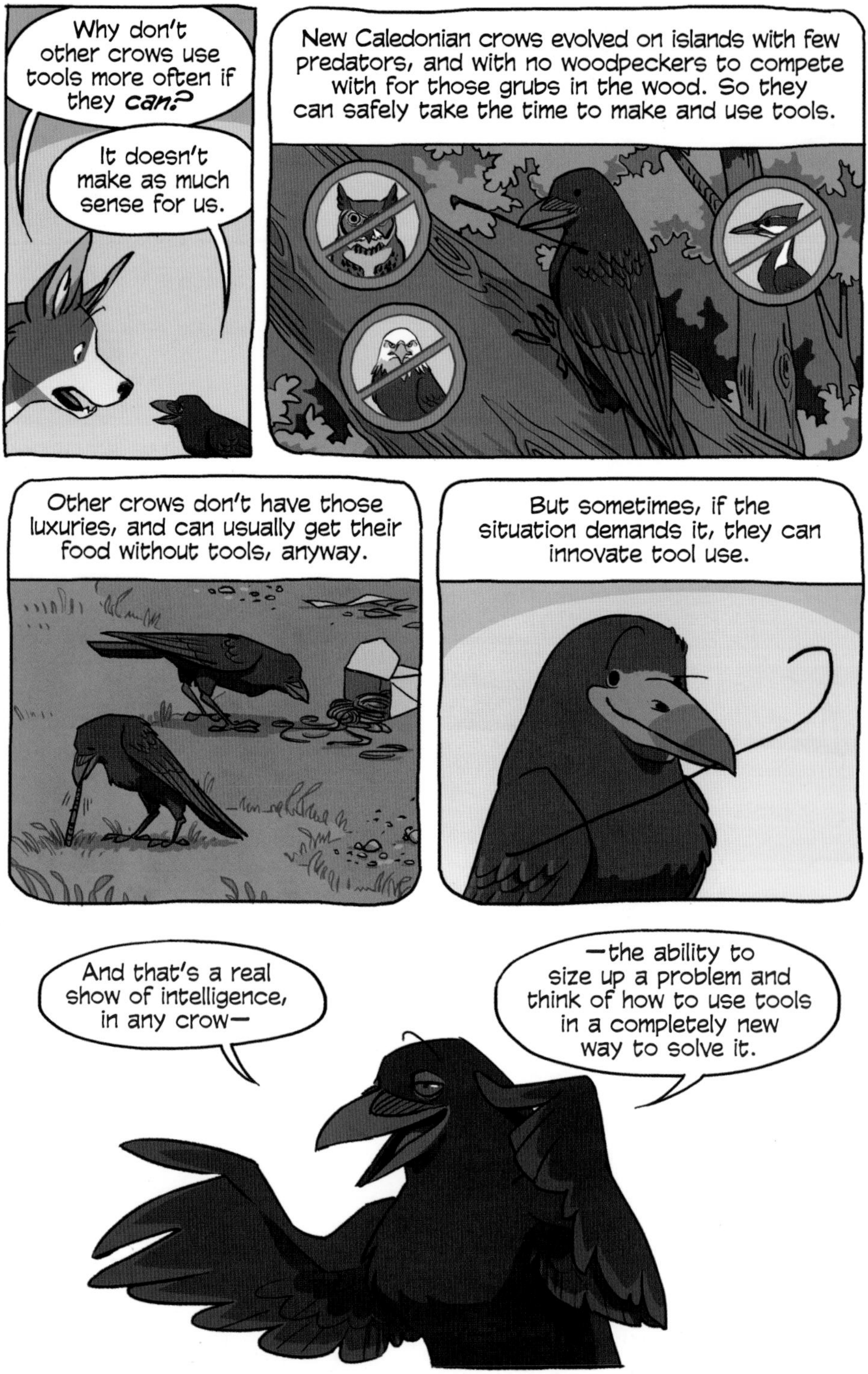
Why don't other crows use tools more often if they *can?*
It doesn't make as much sense for us.
New Caledonian crows evolved on islands with few predators, and with no woodpeckers to compete with for those grubs in the wood. So they can safely take the time to make and use tools.
Other crows don't have those luxuries, and can usually get their food without tools, anyway.
But sometimes, if the situation demands it, they can innovate tool use.
And that's a real show of intelligence, in any crow—
—the ability to size up a problem and think of how to use tools in a completely new way to solve it.

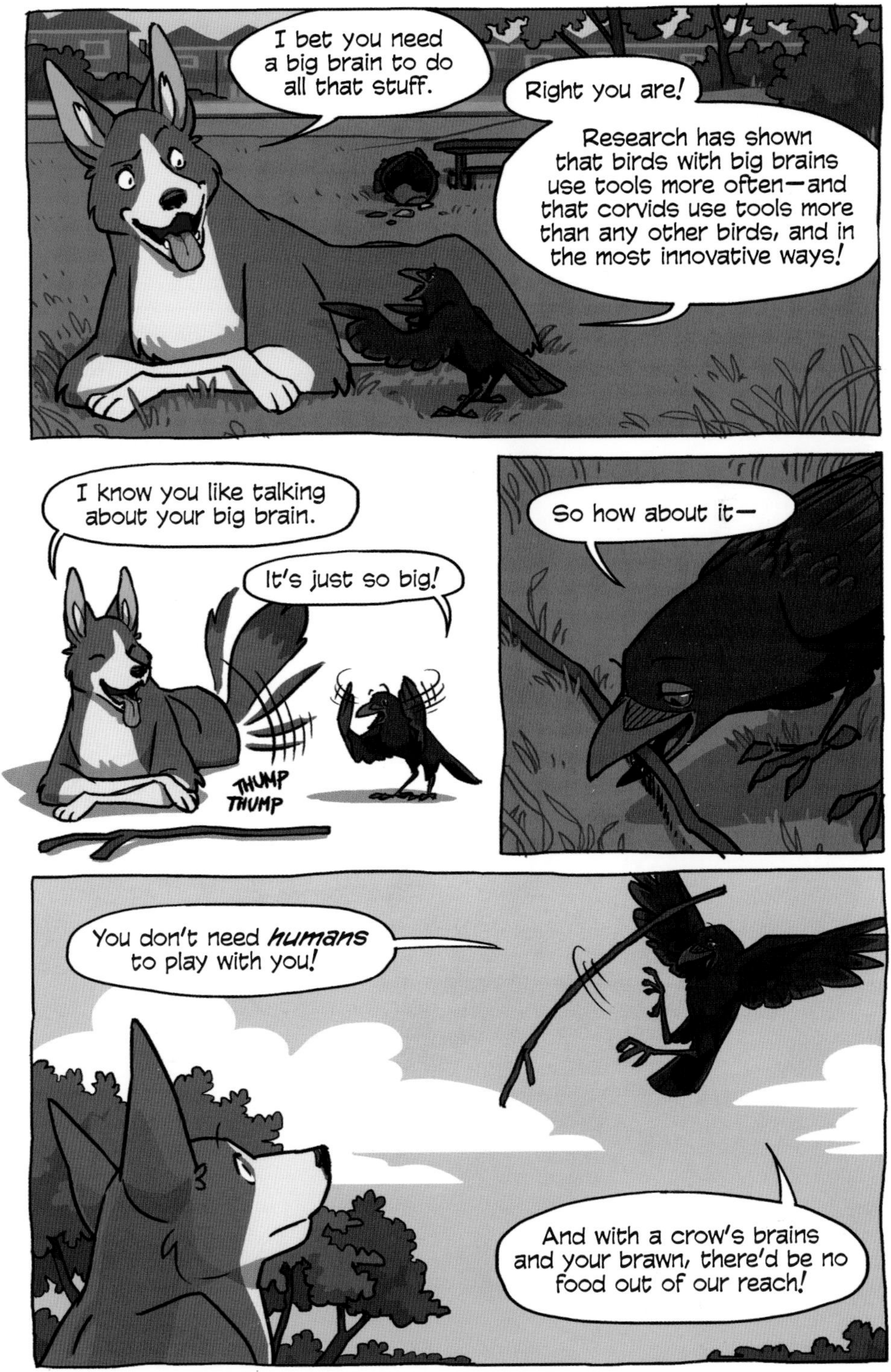
I bet you need a big brain to do all that stuff.
Right you are!
Research has shown that birds with big brains use tools more often—and that corvids use tools more than any other birds, and in the most innovative ways!
I know you like talking about your big brain.
It's just so big!
THUMP THUMP
So how about it—
You don't need *humans* to play with you!
And with a crow's brains and your brawn, there'd be no food out of our reach!

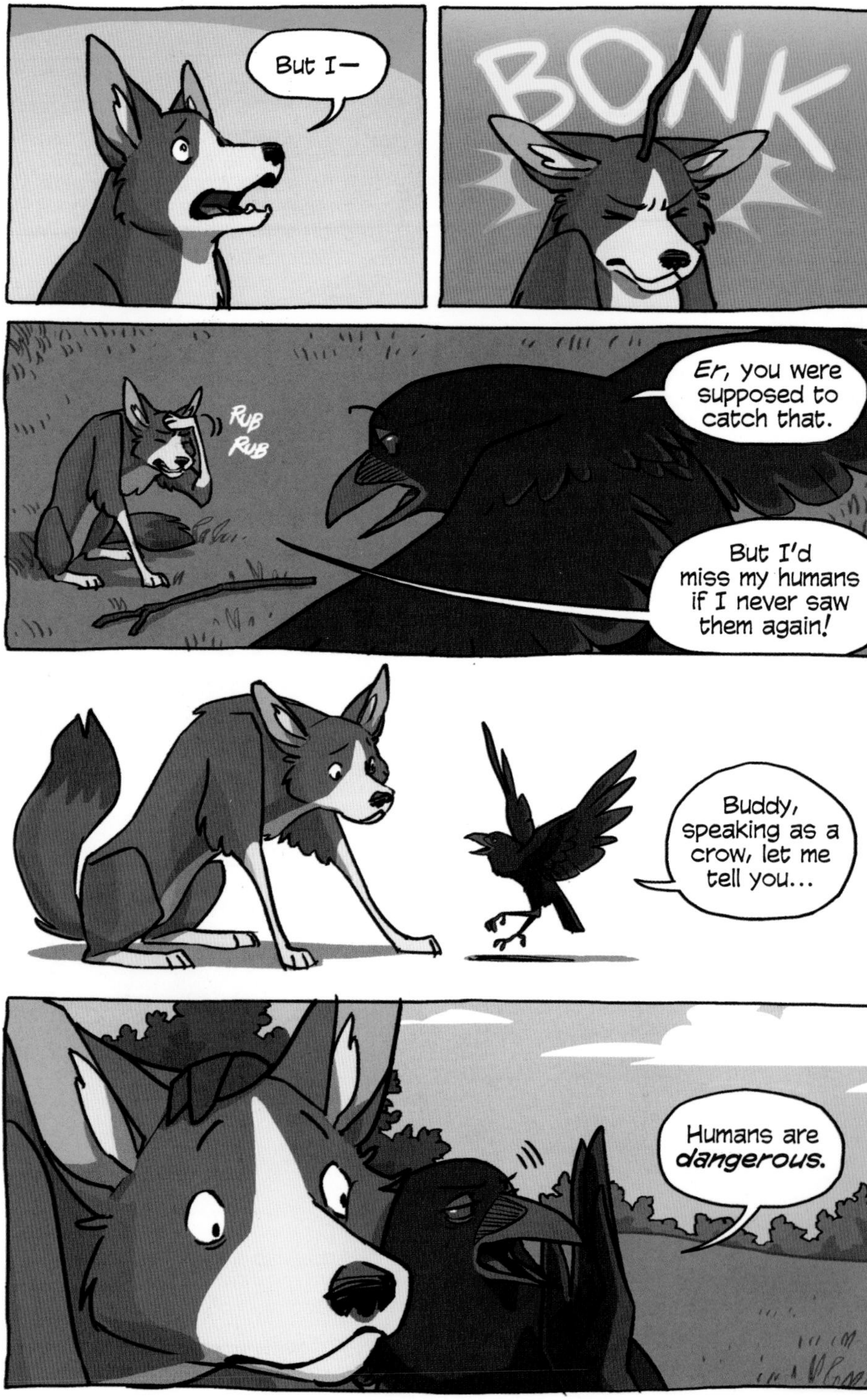
But I—
BONK
Er, you were supposed to catch that.
RUB RUB
But I'd miss my humans if I never saw them again!
Buddy, speaking as a crow, let me tell you...
Humans are dangerous.

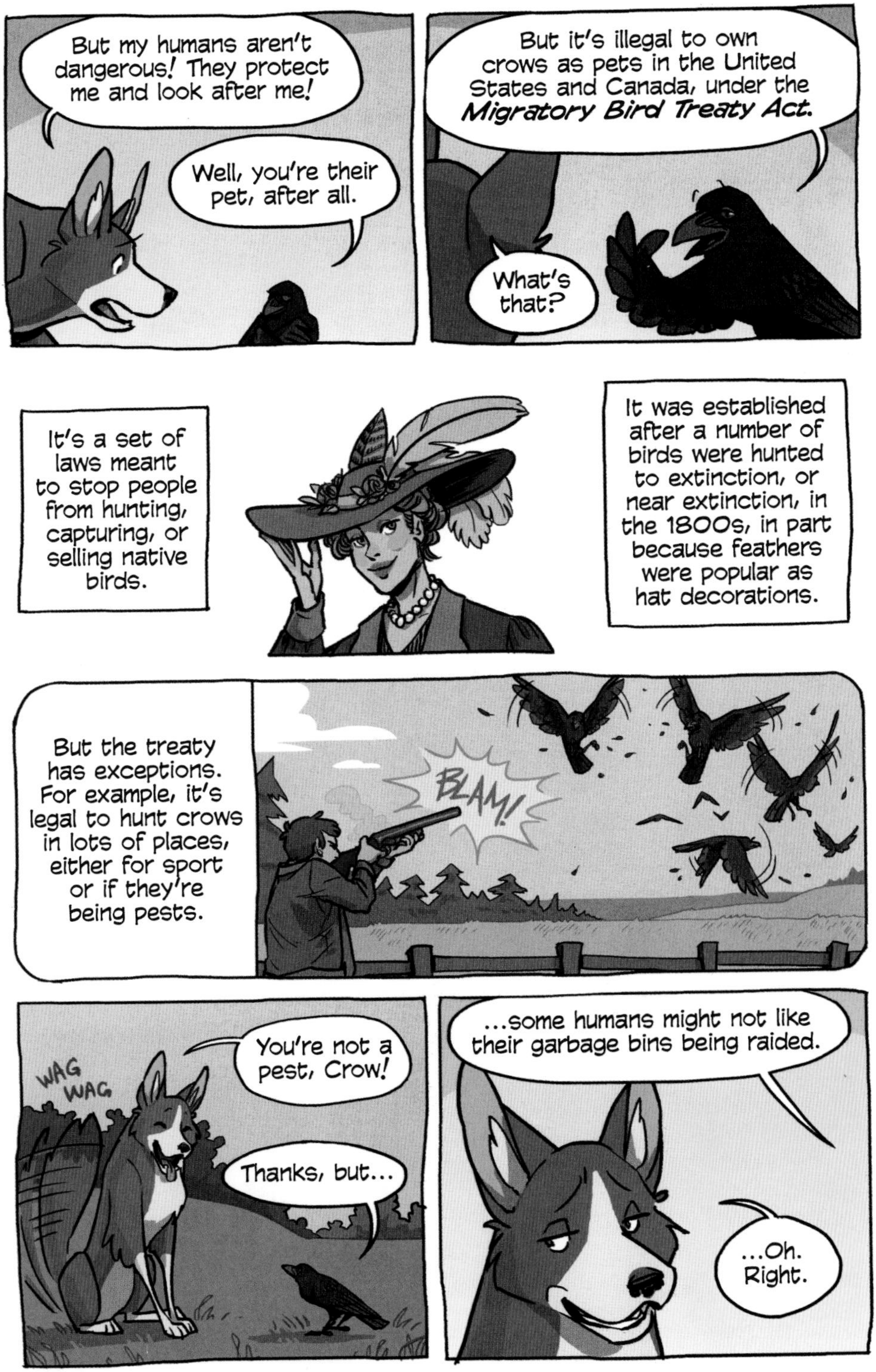

But my humans aren't dangerous! They protect me and look after me!
Well, you're their pet, after all.
But it's illegal to own crows as pets in the United States and Canada, under the *Migratory Bird Treaty Act.*
What's that?
It's a set of laws meant to stop people from hunting, capturing, or selling native birds.
It was established after a number of birds were hunted to extinction, or near extinction, in the 1800s, in part because feathers were popular as hat decorations.
But the treaty has exceptions. For example, it's legal to hunt crows in lots of places, either for sport or if they're being pests.
BLAM!
WAG WAG
You're not a pest, Crow!
Thanks, but...
...some humans might not like their garbage bins being raided.
...Oh. Right.

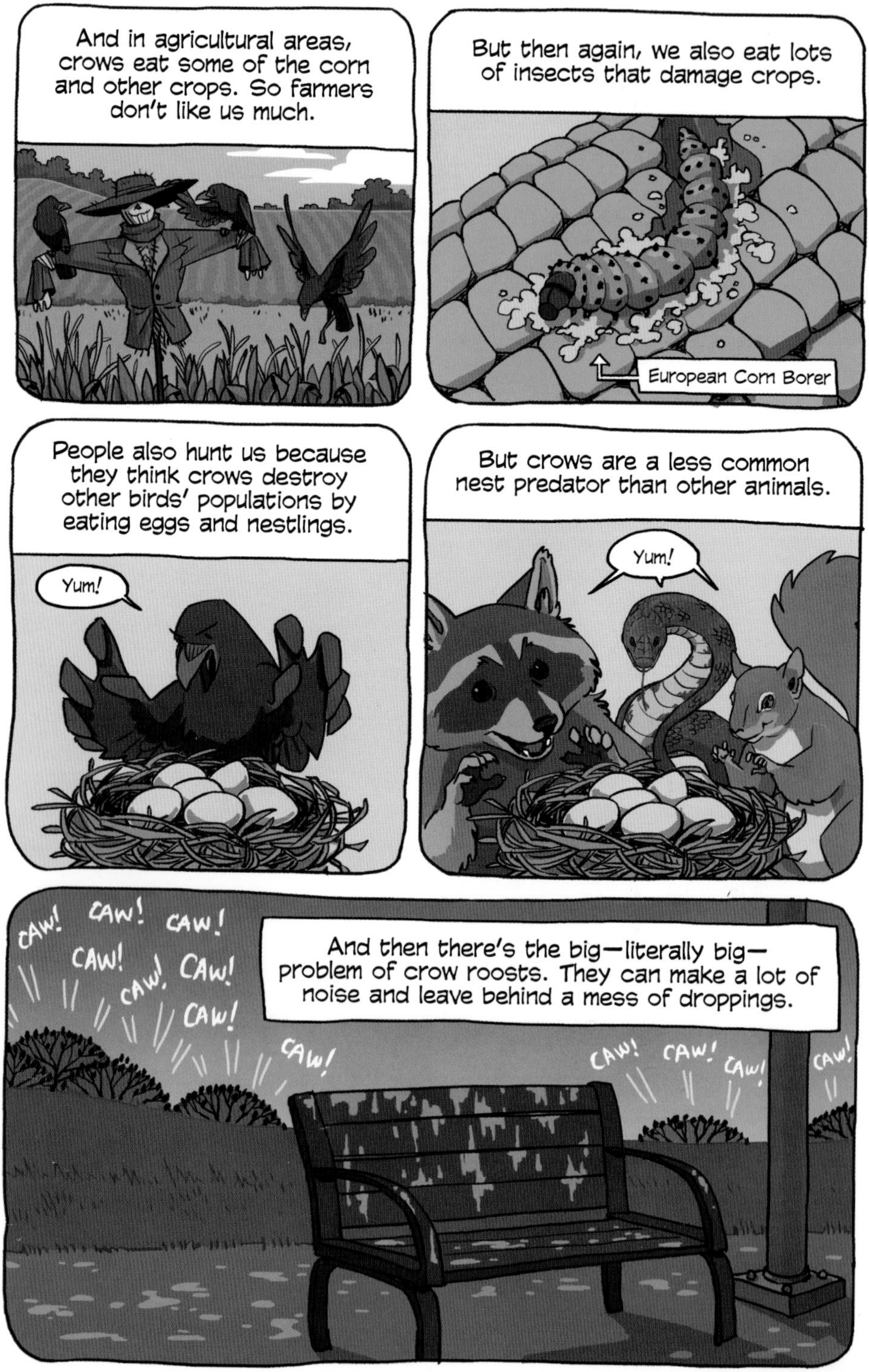
And in agricultural areas, crows eat some of the corn and other crops. So farmers don't like us much.
But then again, we also eat lots of insects that damage crops.
European Corn Borer
People also hunt us because they think crows destroy other birds' populations by eating eggs and nestlings.
Yum!
But crows are a less common nest predator than other animals.
Yum!
CAW! CAW! CAW! CAW! CAW! CAW! CAW!
And then there's the big—literally big—problem of crow roosts. They can make a lot of noise and leave behind a mess of droppings.
CAW! CAW! CAW! CAW! CAW!

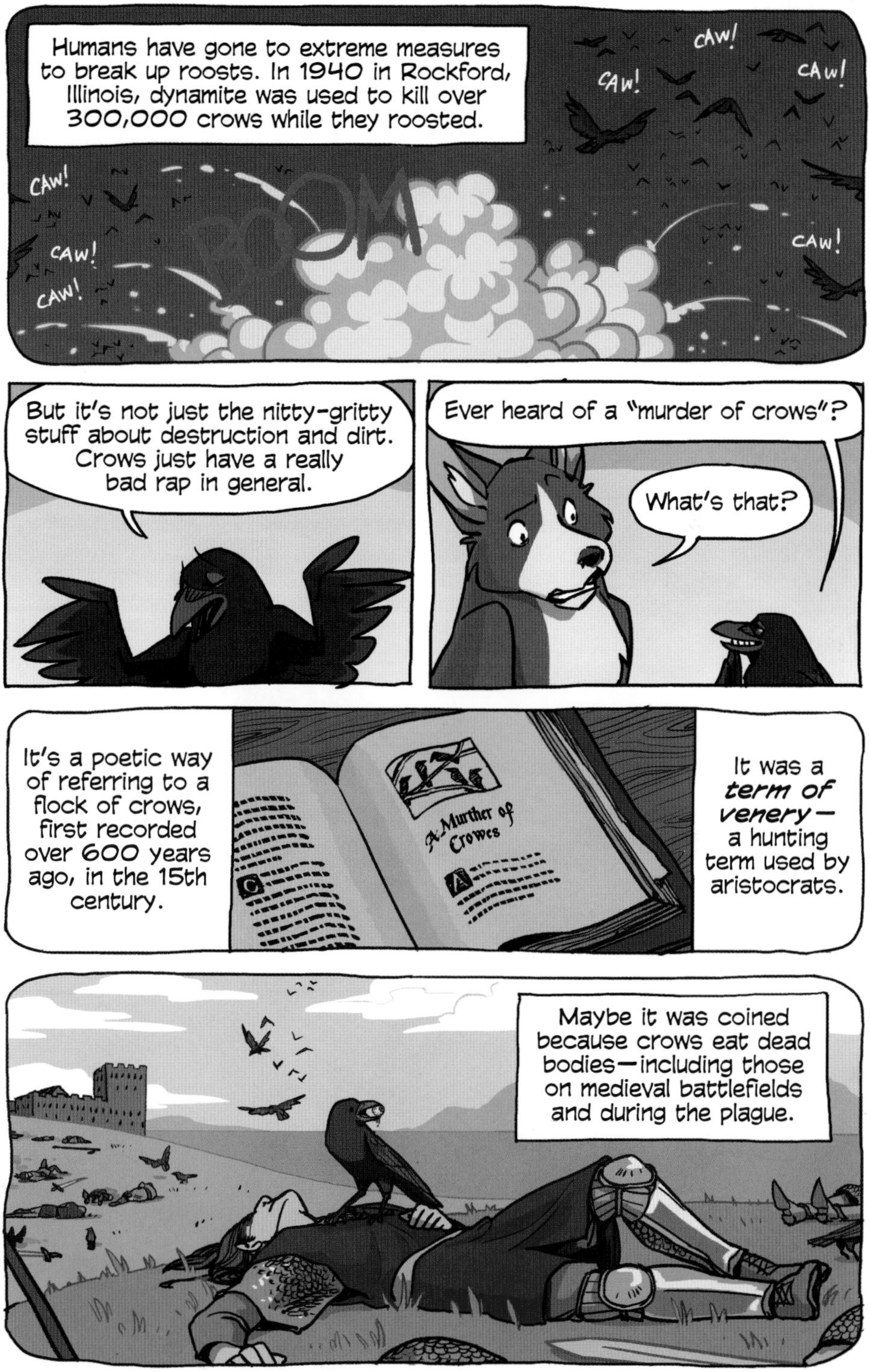

Humans have gone to extreme measures to break up roosts. In 1940 in Rockford, Illinois, dynamite was used to kill over 300,000 crows while they roosted.
CAW!
CAW!
CAW!
CAW!
CAW!
CAW!
CAW!
BOOM
But it's not just the nitty-gritty stuff about destruction and dirt. Crows just have a really bad rap in general.
Ever heard of a "murder of crows"?
What's that?
It's a poetic way of referring to a flock of crows, first recorded over 600 years ago, in the 15th century.
A Murther of Crowes
It was a ***term of venery***— a hunting term used by aristocrats.
Maybe it was coined because crows eat dead bodies—including those on medieval battlefields and during the plague.

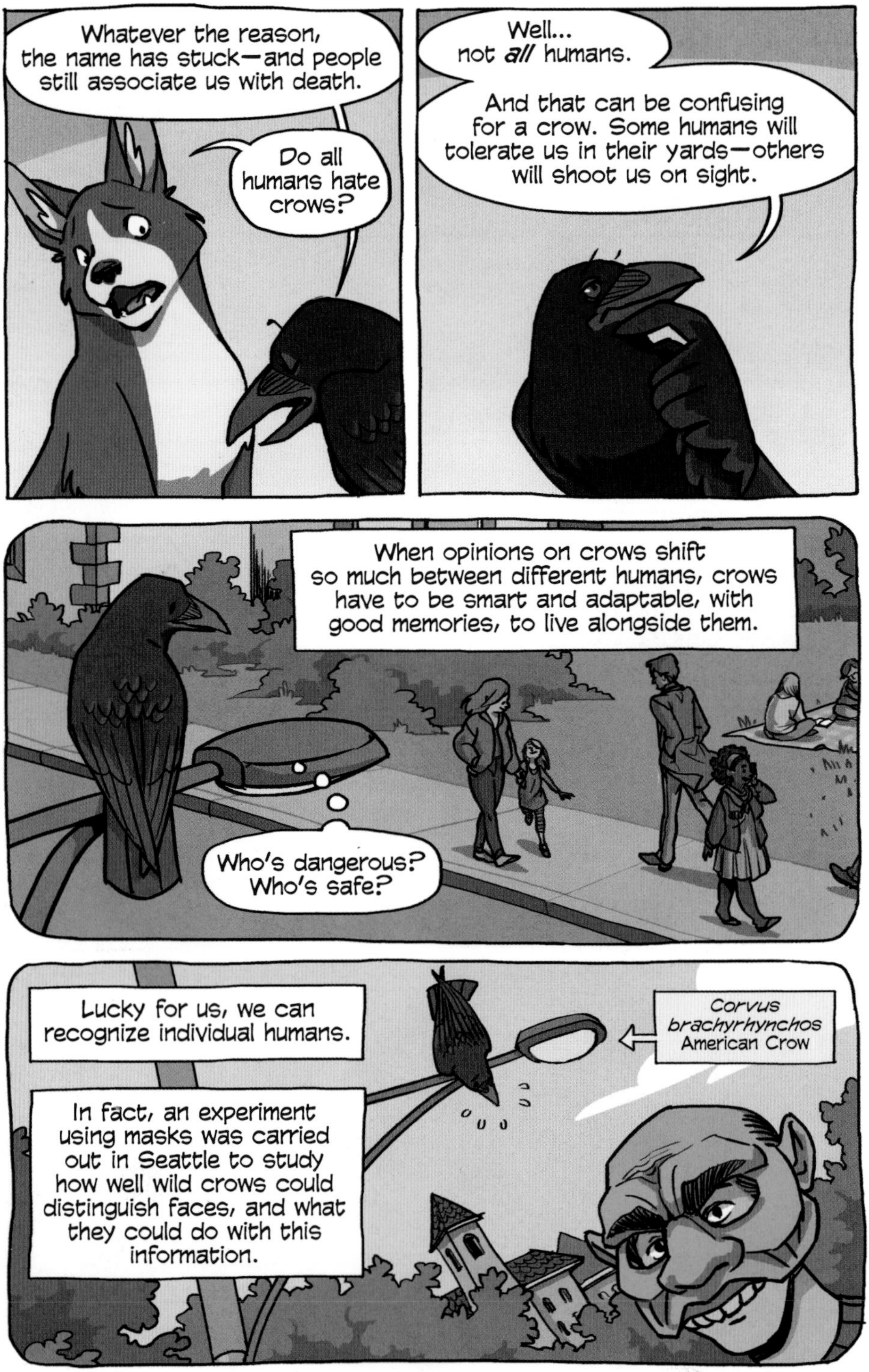
Whatever the reason, the name has stuck—and people still associate us with death.
Do all humans hate crows?
Well... not *all* humans.
And that can be confusing for a crow. Some humans will tolerate us in their yards—others will shoot us on sight.
When opinions on crows shift so much between different humans, crows have to be smart and adaptable, with good memories, to live alongside them.
Who's dangerous? Who's safe?
Lucky for us, we can recognize individual humans.
Corvus brachyrhynchos American Crow
In fact, an experiment using masks was carried out in Seattle to study how well wild crows could distinguish faces, and what they could do with this information.

The researchers had two types of masks—the "dangerous" masks resembling cavemen and the "neutral" masks of famous politicians.

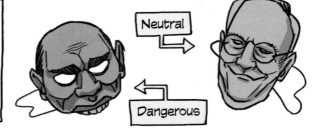

Neutral

Dangerous

Wearing the dangerous mask, they caught and banded wild crows.

Eek! Let me go, you thug!

After the crows were released, researchers walked around wearing the "neutral" mask. The crows ignored them.

A few days later, they walked around wearing the "dangerous" mask again...

...and several of the crows covered them in verbal abuse.

CAW! CAW! CAW! CAW! CAW!

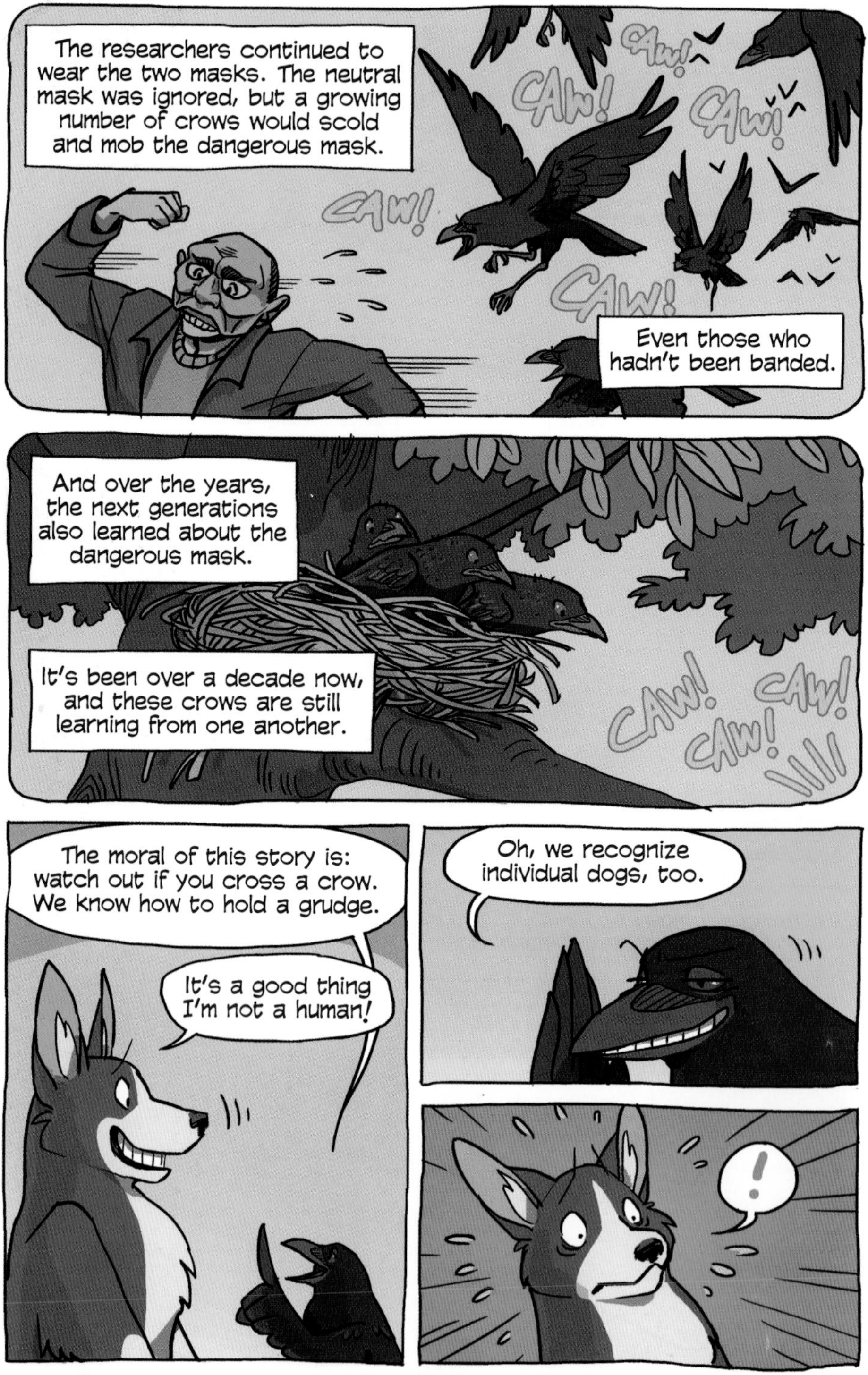
The researchers continued to wear the two masks. The neutral mask was ignored, but a growing number of crows would scold and mob the dangerous mask.
CAW!
CAW!
CAW!
CAW!
CAW!
Even those who hadn't been banded.
And over the years, the next generations also learned about the dangerous mask.
It's been over a decade now, and these crows are still learning from one another.
CAW!
CAW!
CAW!
The moral of this story is: watch out if you cross a crow. We know how to hold a grudge.
It's a good thing I'm not a human!
Oh, we recognize individual dogs, too.
!

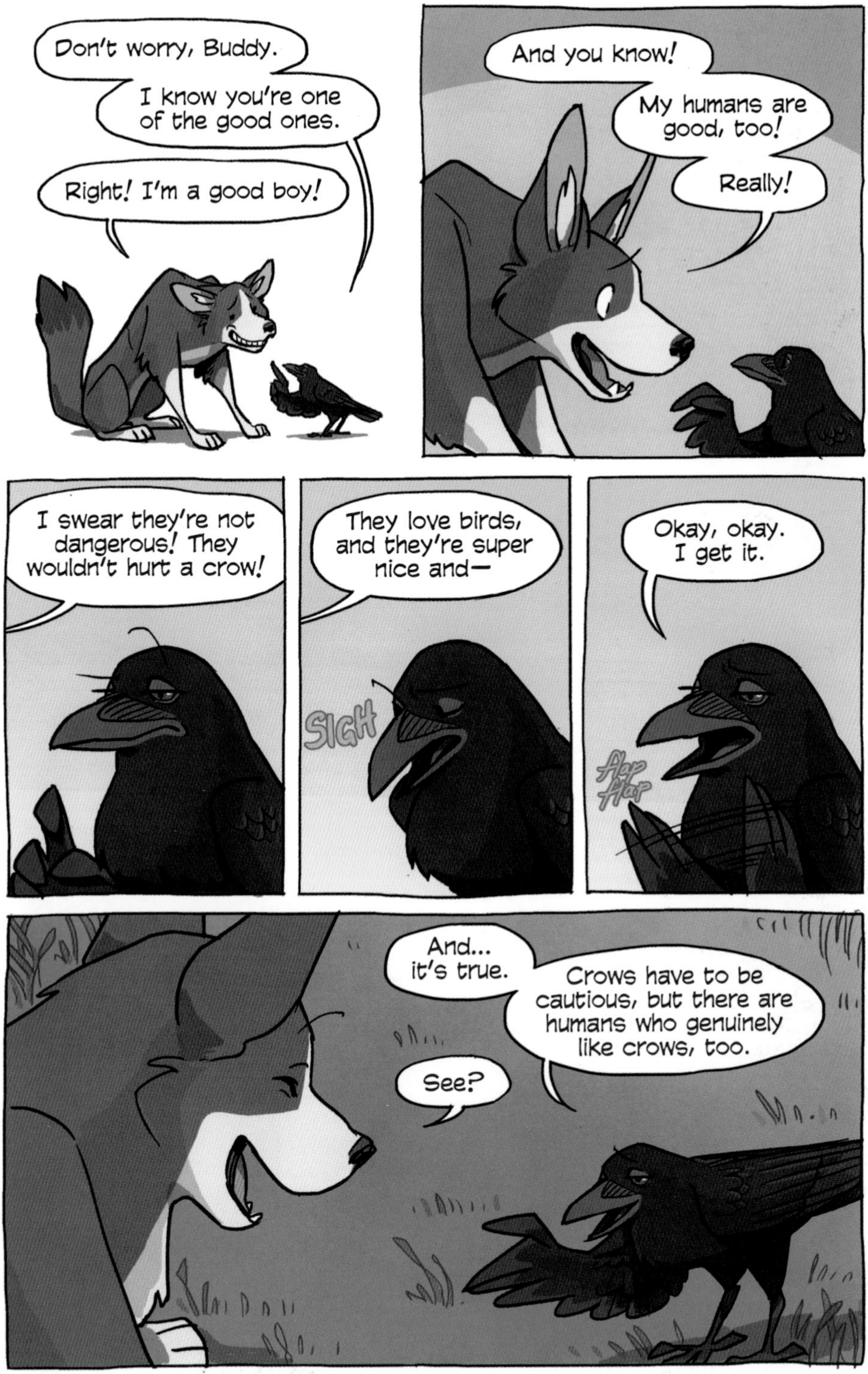
Don't worry, Buddy.
I know you're one of the good ones.
Right! I'm a good boy!
And you know!
My humans are good, too!
Really!
I swear they're not dangerous! They wouldn't hurt a crow!
They love birds, and they're super nice and—
SIGH
Okay, okay. I get it.
flap flap
And... it's true.
Crows have to be cautious, but there are humans who genuinely like crows, too.
See?

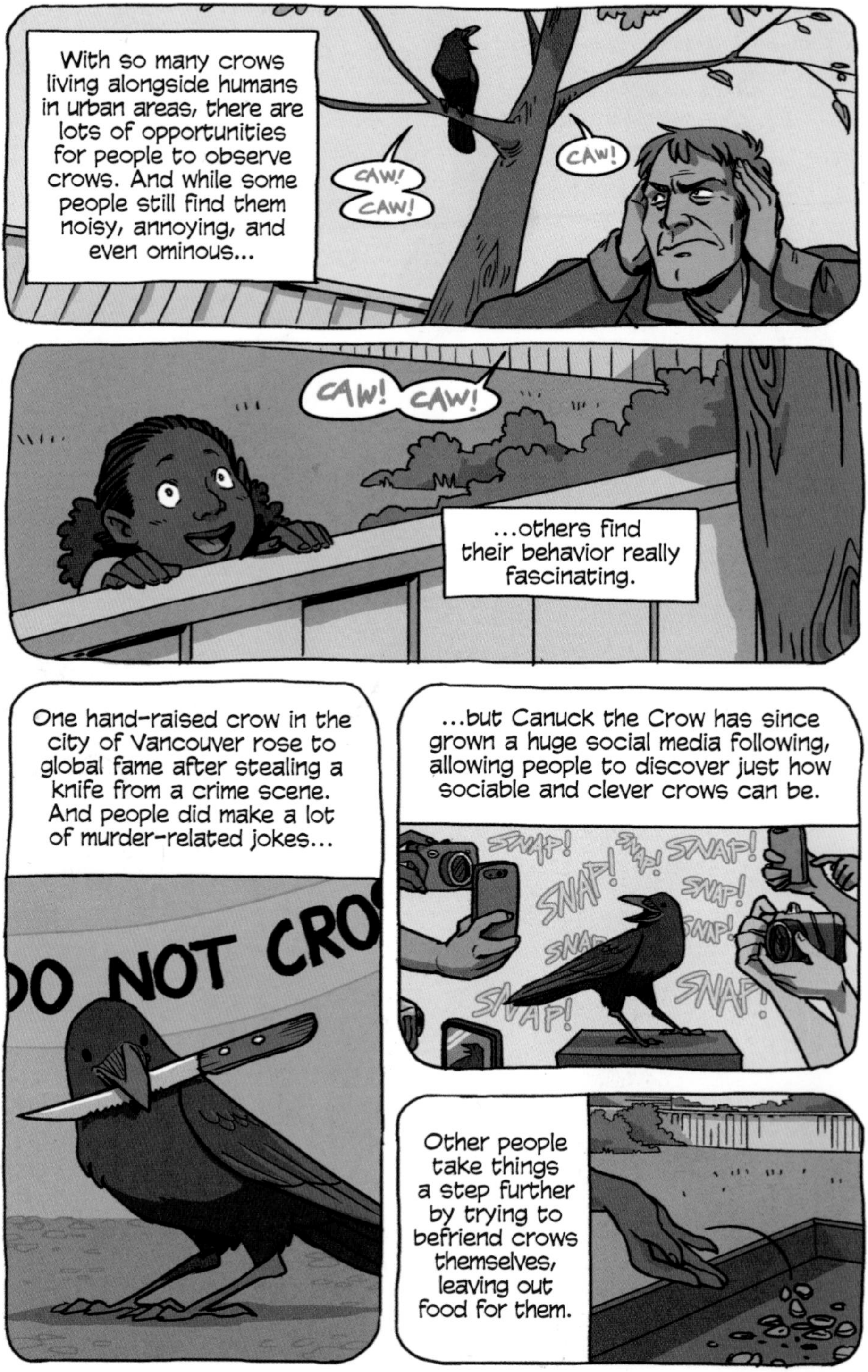
With so many crows living alongside humans in urban areas, there are lots of opportunities for people to observe crows. And while some people still find them noisy, annoying, and even ominous...
CAW! CAW!
CAW!
CAW! CAW!
...others find their behavior really fascinating.
One hand-raised crow in the city of Vancouver rose to global fame after stealing a knife from a crime scene. And people did make a lot of murder-related jokes...
DO NOT CROS
...but Canuck the Crow has since grown a huge social media following, allowing people to discover just how sociable and clever crows can be.
SNAP! SNAP! SNAP! SNAP! SNAP! SNAP! SNAP! SNAP!
Other people take things a step further by trying to befriend crows themselves, leaving out food for them.

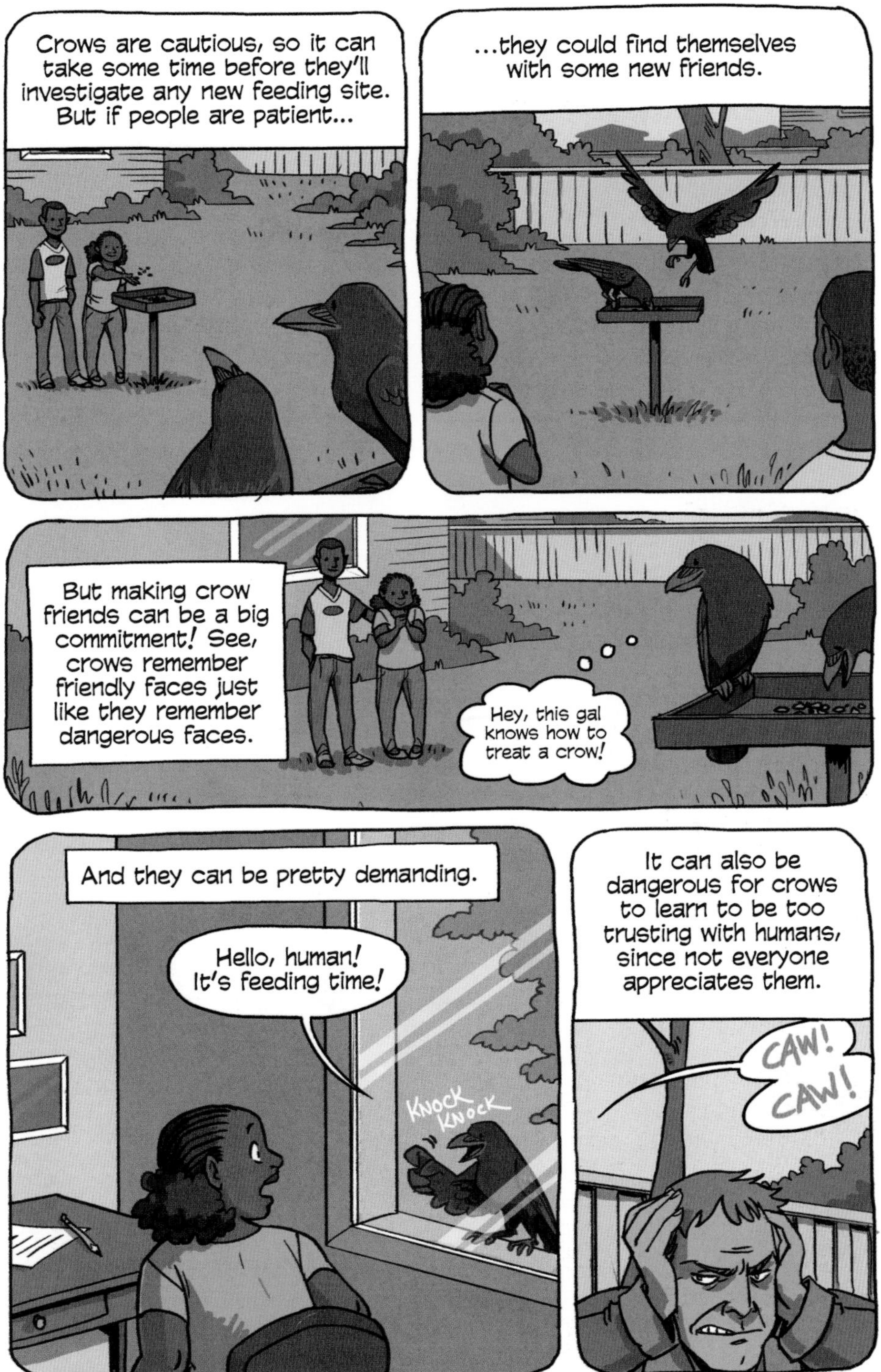
Crows are cautious, so it can take some time before they'll investigate any new feeding site. But if people are patient...
...they could find themselves with some new friends.
But making crow friends can be a big commitment! See, crows remember friendly faces just like they remember dangerous faces.
Hey, this gal knows how to treat a crow!
And they can be pretty demanding.
Hello, human! It's feeding time!
KNOCK KNOCK
It can also be dangerous for crows to learn to be too trusting with humans, since not everyone appreciates them.
CAW! CAW!

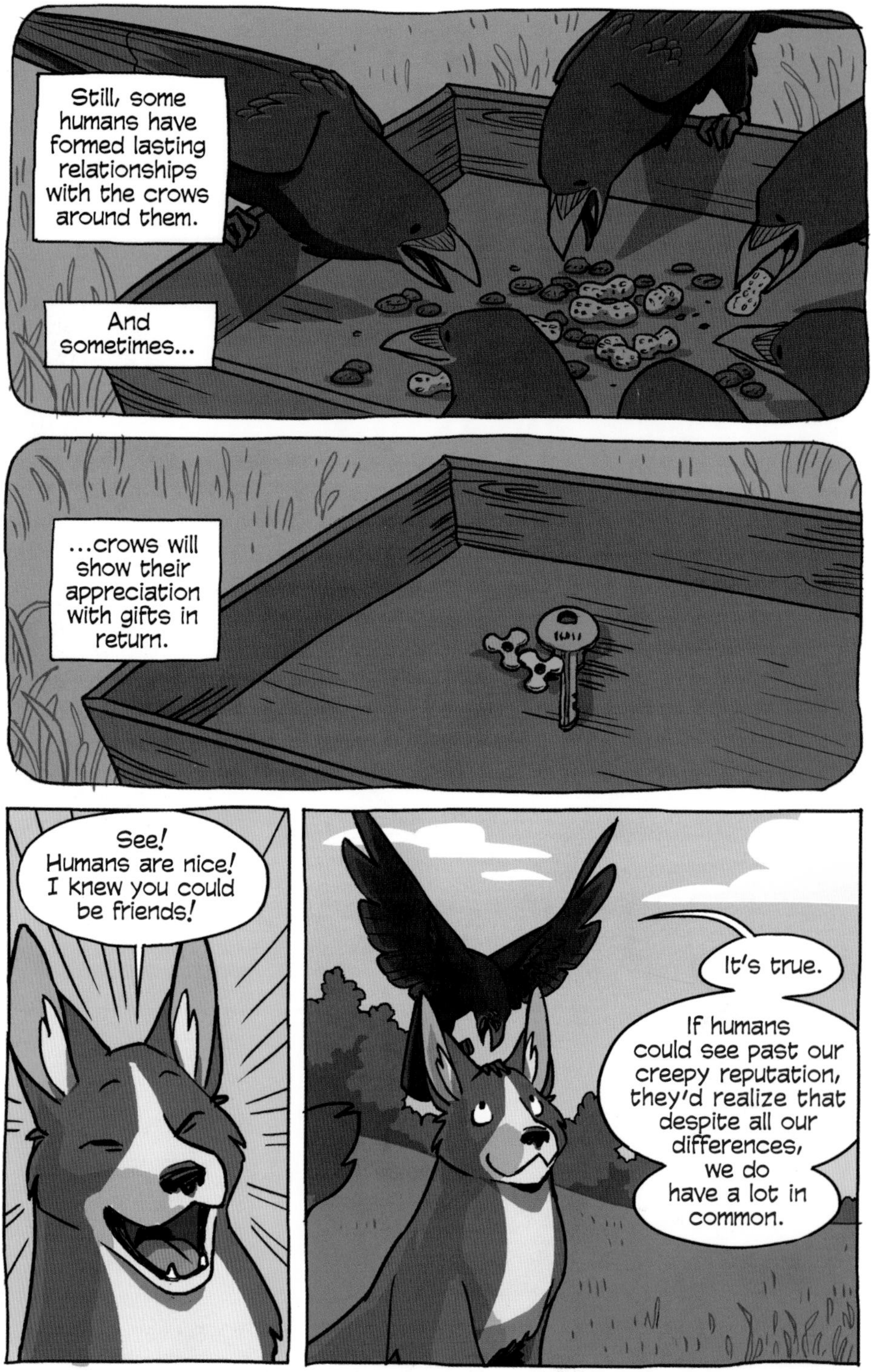
Still, some humans have formed lasting relationships with the crows around them.
And sometimes...
...crows will show their appreciation with gifts in return.
See! Humans are nice! I knew you could be friends!
It's true.
If humans could see past our creepy reputation, they'd realize that despite all our differences, we do have a lot in common.

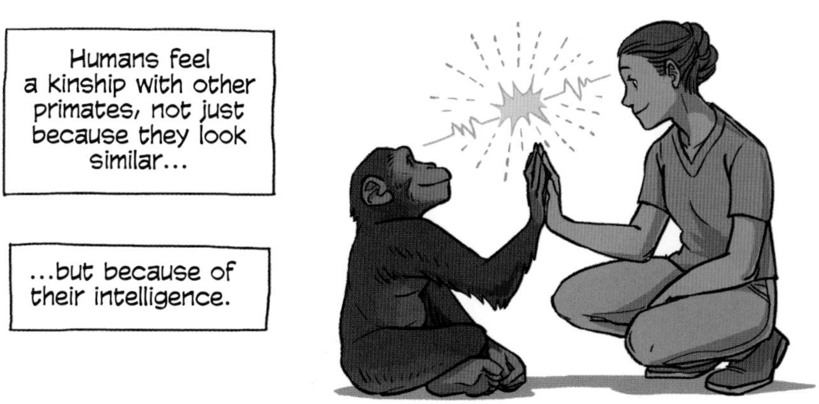
Humans feel a kinship with other primates, not just because they look similar...
...but because of their intelligence.

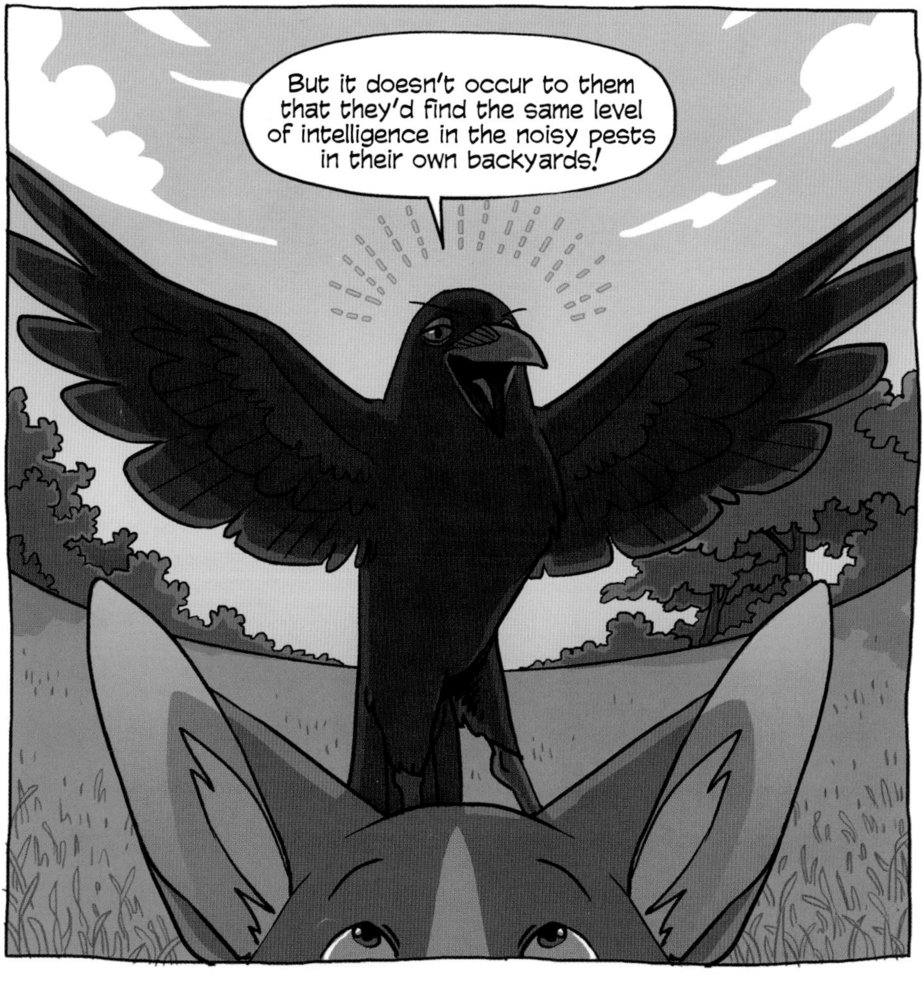
But it doesn't occur to them that they'd find the same level of intelligence in the noisy pests in their own backyards!

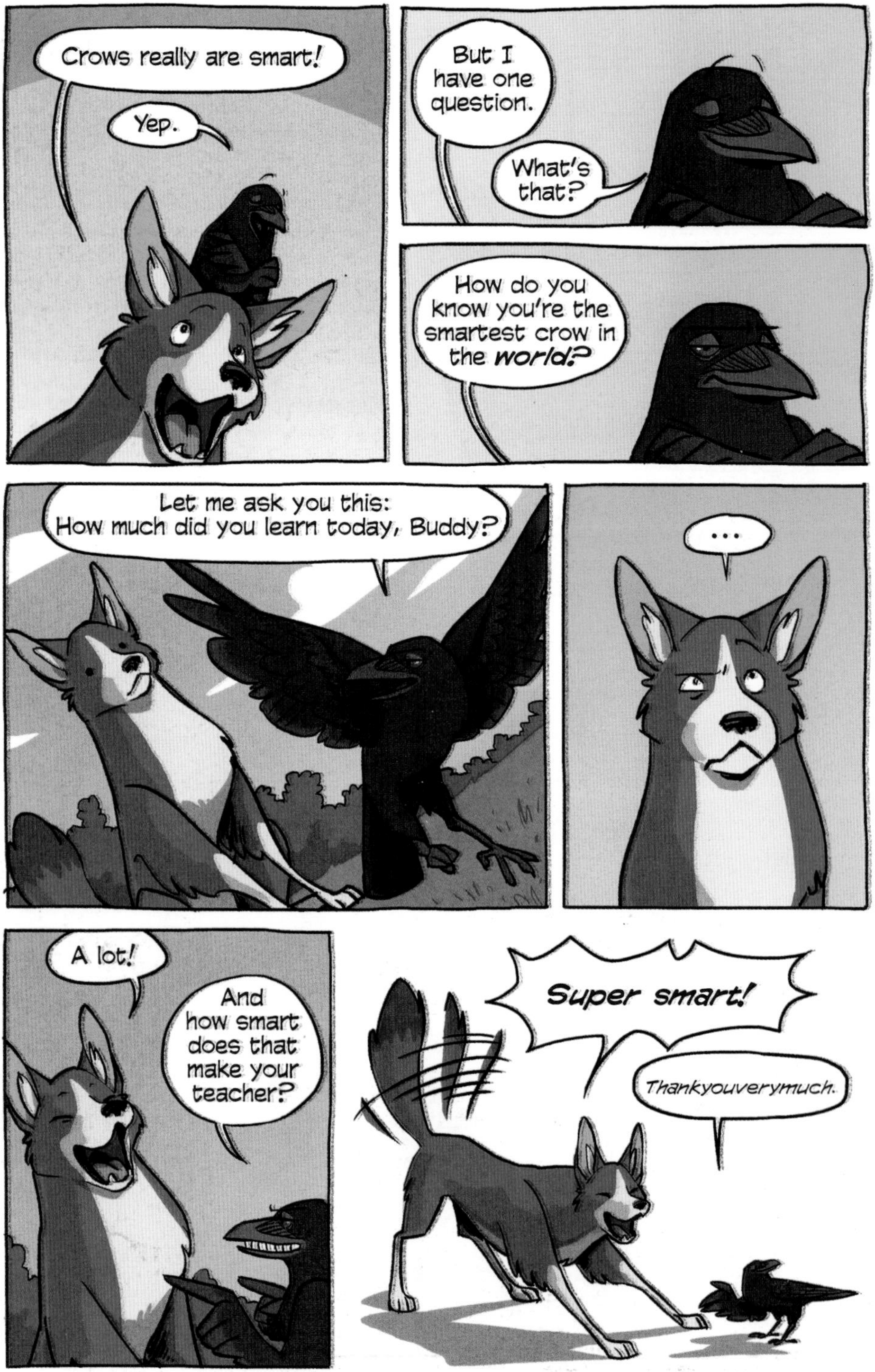
Crows really are smart!
Yep.
But I have one question.
What's that?
How do you know you're the smartest crow in the *world?*
Let me ask you this: How much did you learn today, Buddy?
...
A lot!
And how smart does that make your teacher?
Super smart!
Thankyouverymuch.

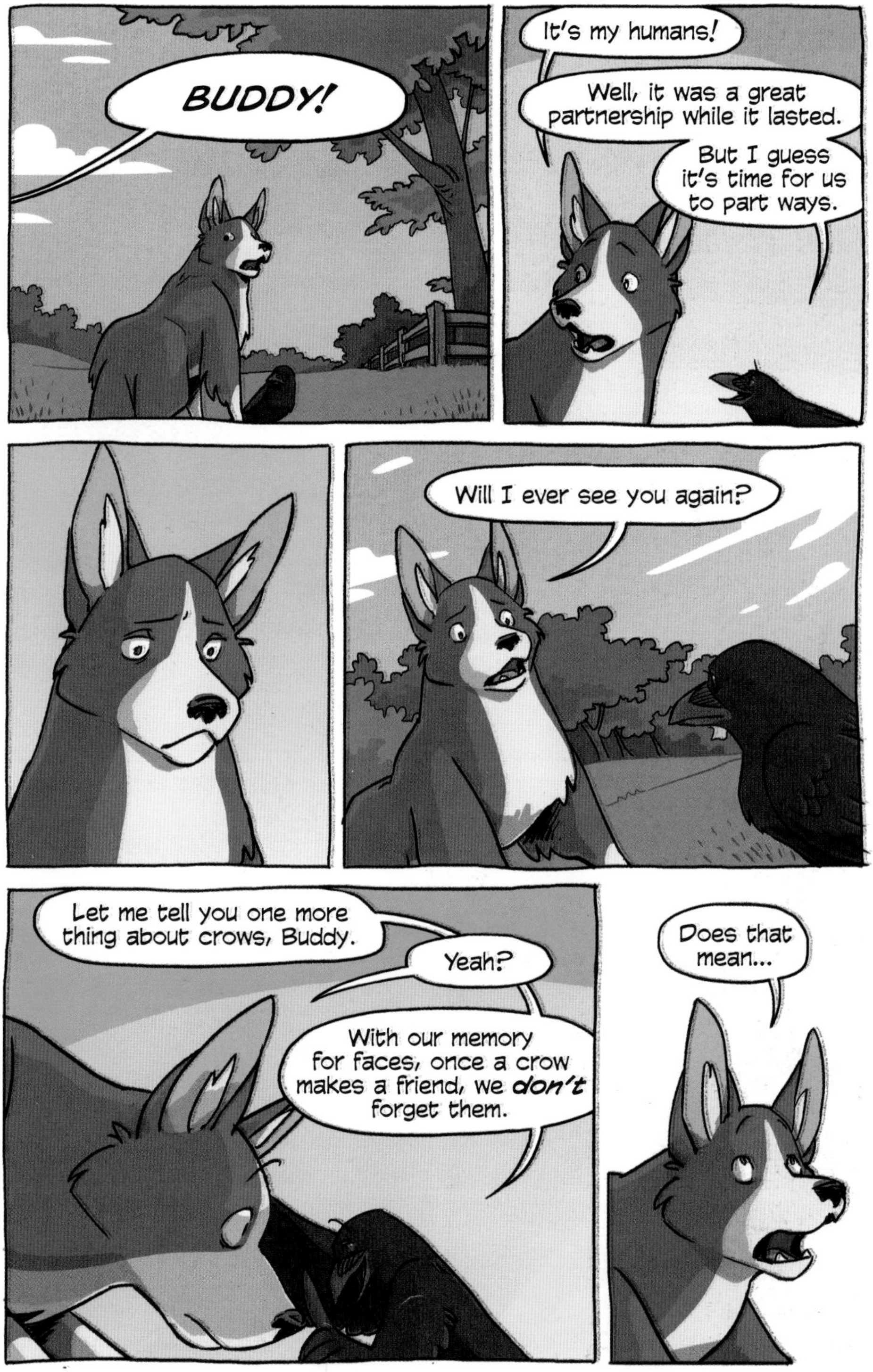
BUDDY!
It's my humans!
Well, it was a great partnership while it lasted.
But I guess it's time for us to part ways.
Will I ever see you again?
Let me tell you one more thing about crows, Buddy.
Yeah?
With our memory for faces, once a crow makes a friend, we *don't* forget them.
Does that mean...

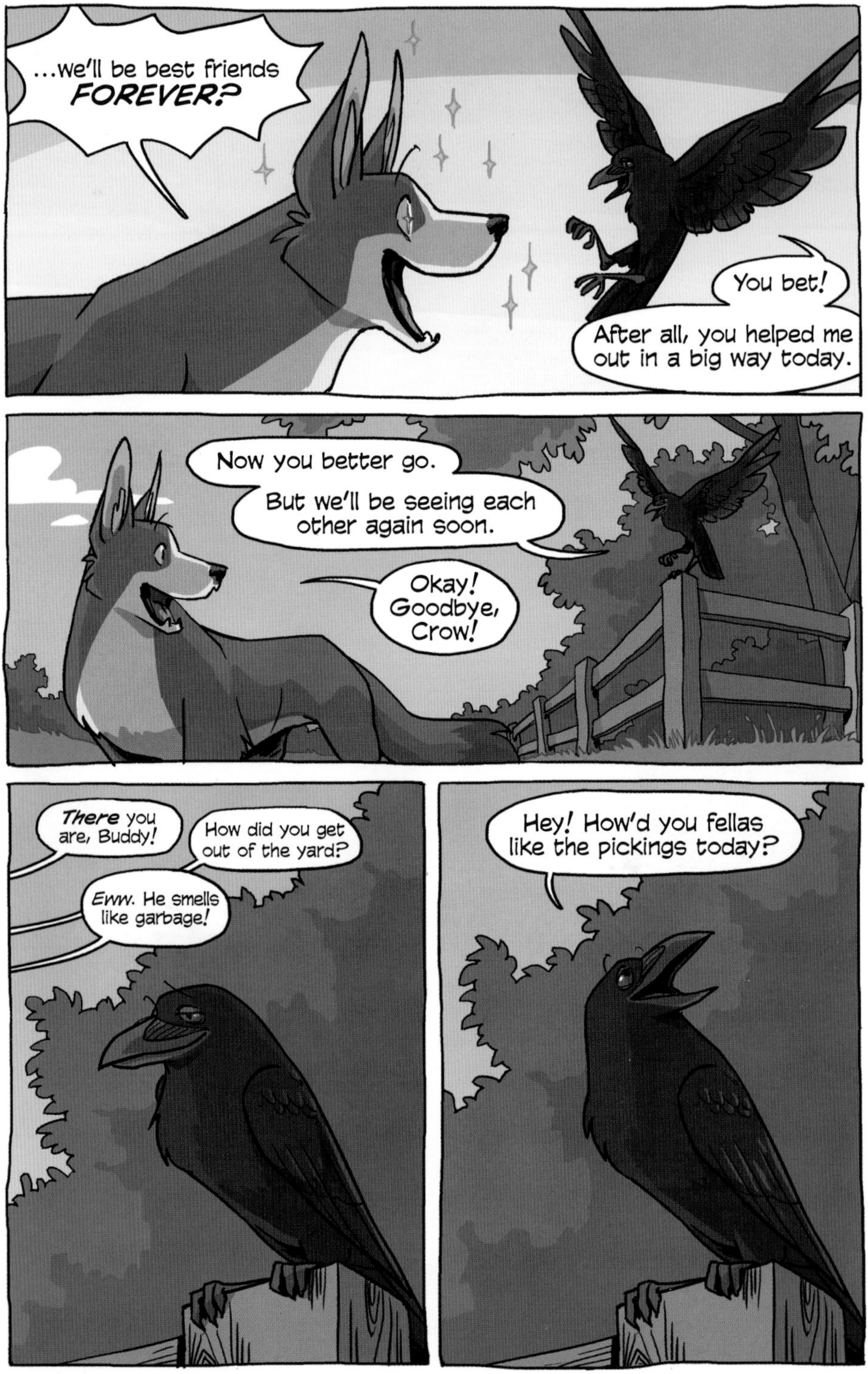
...we'll be best friends
FOREVER?
You bet!
After all, you helped me out in a big way today.
Now you better go.
But we'll be seeing each other again soon.
Okay! Goodbye, Crow!
There you are, Buddy!
How did you get out of the yard?
Eww. He smells like garbage!
Hey! How'd you fellas like the pickings today?

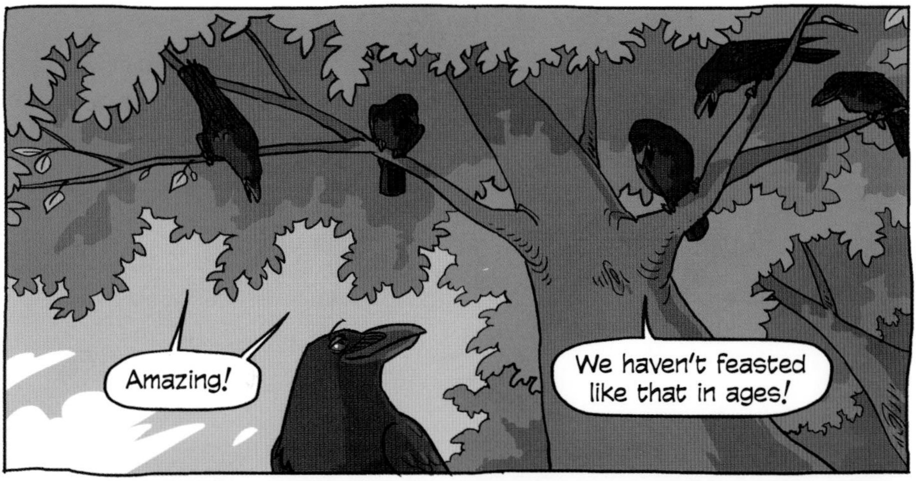
Amazing!
We haven't feasted like that in ages!

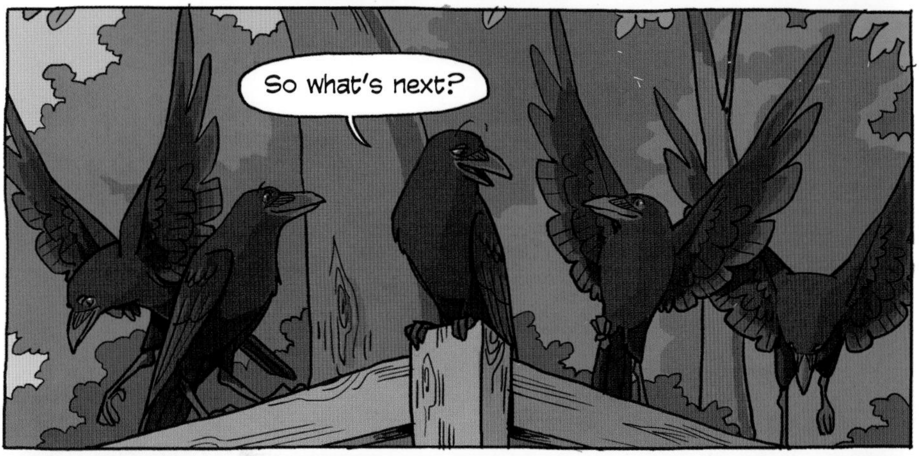
So what's next?

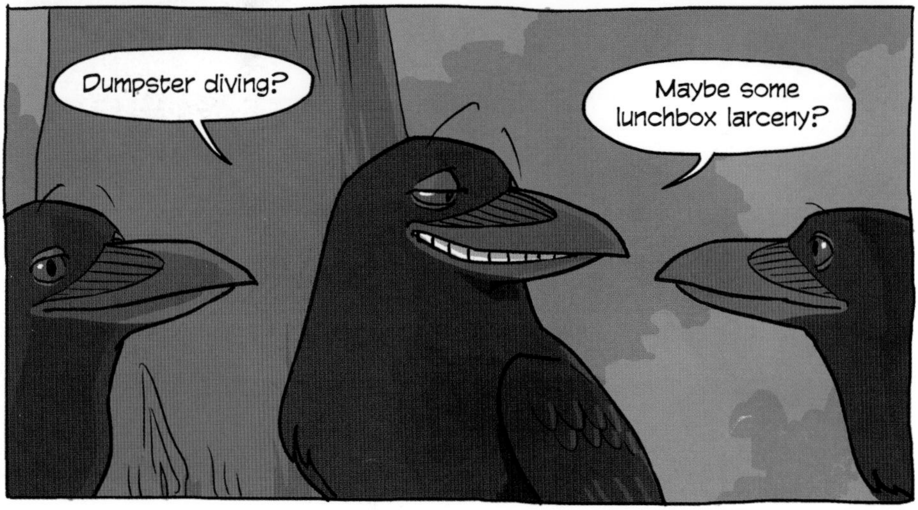
Dumpster diving?
Maybe some lunchbox larceny?

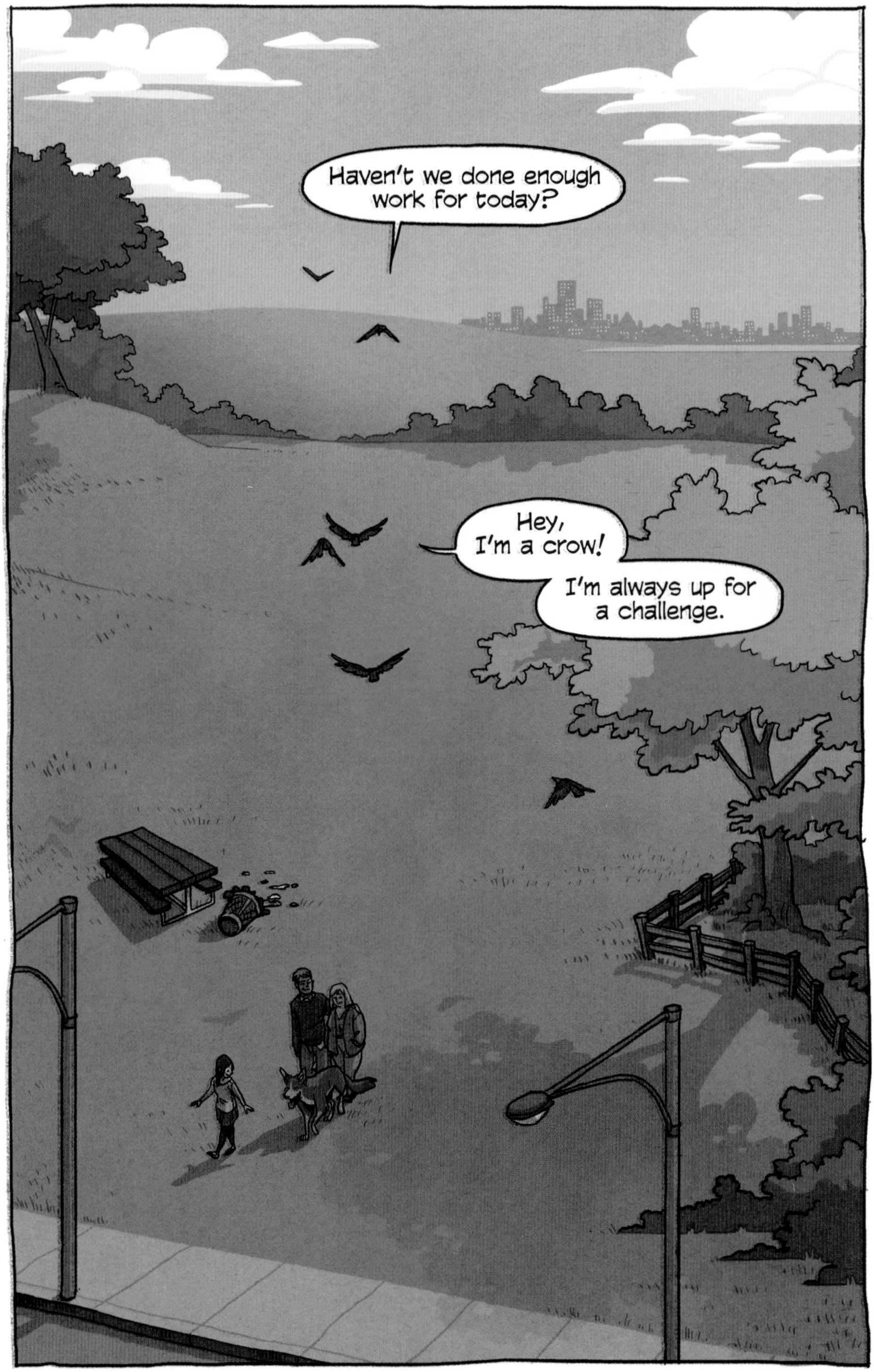
Haven't we done enough work for today?
Hey, I'm a crow!
I'm always up for a challenge.

—GLOSSARY—

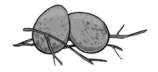

Altricial
Born or hatched naked and blind. Altricial animals can't care for themselves right away.

Caching
Hiding food to eat at a later time.

Carnivores
Animals whose main source of food is meat.

Cone Cells
Cells in the eyes that receive light. Signals from these cells are translated by the brain into color.

Cooperative Breeding
Offspring are raised both by parents and by additional group members, or helpers.

Corvidae
A family of birds to which crows belong. Any bird in this family is called a corvid.

Corvus
A genus of the family Corvidae that includes crows, ravens, and rooks.

Crow Funerals
The behavior of crows to gather en masse around a dead crow.

Crow Roosts
A place where crows gather together in large numbers to spend the night during the fall and winter.

Crows
May refer collectively to birds in the family Corvidae, or more specifically to a species in the *Corvus* genus.

Encephalization Quotient
> A way of measuring relative brain size based on the difference between an animal's actual brain size and the predicted brain size for their body. Called the EQ for short.

Fledgling
> A young bird who's just fledged, or left the nest.

Forebrain
> A large part of the brain, the functions of which include thinking, perceiving, language, and memory.

Helpers
> In cooperative breeding, helpers are non-parental family members who assist in raising the offspring.

Hippocampus
> A structure in the brain that helps keep track of spatial memory and long-term memory.

Locomotor Play
> A type of play in animals that involves moving one's own body, such as rolling down a hill.

Migratory Bird Treaty Act
> A set of laws that prohibit people from hunting native birds for profit, e.g., to sell them as pets or sell their feathers. It also makes it illegal to keep native birds as pets.

Mimicry
> The imitation of something. Crows can mimic sounds they hear with great accuracy.

Neuron
> A type of cell in the nervous system that transmits information.

—GLOSSARY CONTINUED—

Nidopallium Caudolaterale
A structure in a bird's brain that is involved in complex thinking. Called the NCL for short.

Object Play
A type of play in animals that involves using an object, such as rolling a ball.

Omnivores
Animals that eat both plant matter and meat.

Precocial
Born or hatched in a mature state with fur or feathers. Precocial animals can move around shortly after birth.

Prefrontal Cortex
A structure in a mammal's brain that is involved in complex thinking. Called the PFC for short.

Social Play
A type of play in animals that involves interaction with another animal, such as tug-of-war.

Spatial Memory
A type of memory to keep track of where things are.

Term of Venery
A fanciful way to refer to a gathering of animals of the same species, invented by hunters in the Middle Ages. "A murder of crows" is a term of venery.

Theory of Mind
The understanding that other people have thoughts and feelings separate from our own.

Working Memory
A type of short-term memory that holds on to different pieces of information we need while completing a task.

—NOTES—

Page 7: Crows have been seen using tools in amazing ways, many described in this book, but it should be noted that no one has actually seen a crow propping open a pet flap with a stick . . . yet.

Page 52: While it's true most crow species are flourishing, there are some exceptions. The Hawaiian crow is extinct in the wild, with only a few birds left living in captivity, and the Mariana crow is critically endangered. These species live on small, isolated islands and so have been vulnerable to habitat loss and to predators introduced by humans. Conservation efforts are in progress for both species.

Page 76: Experiments carried out in captivity showed that an outsider crow would be shunned or chased away by an established group. It was theorized that this is because the outsider had different short-range calls; as they began imitating the calls of the group, they became accepted.

Page 77: Although scientists suspect the number of crow calls hold some meaning, they haven't yet figured out what those meanings are. That's one crow code we're still trying to crack!

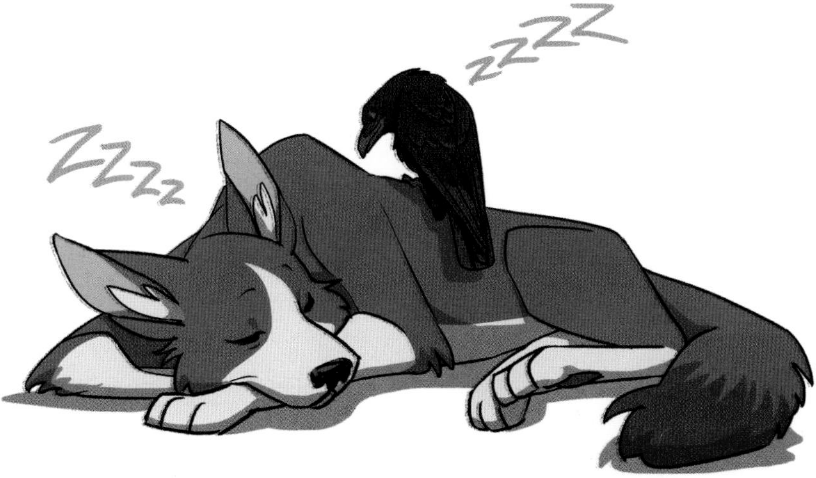
ZZZZ
ZZZZ

LIVING WITH CROWS 101

I found a baby crow on the ground! Should I help it?

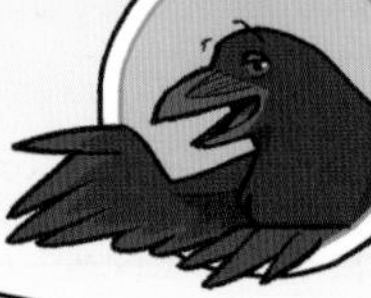

The parents are probably nearby, and it's best for fledglings to stay with their family, so you should leave it where it is. But you can gently pick it up and place it on a low branch if you think it's in danger.

If it's obviously injured or can't perch on a branch, contact your local wildlife rehabilitation center and ask for their advice. Remember that it's illegal for anyone other than a certified rehabilitator to raise crows.

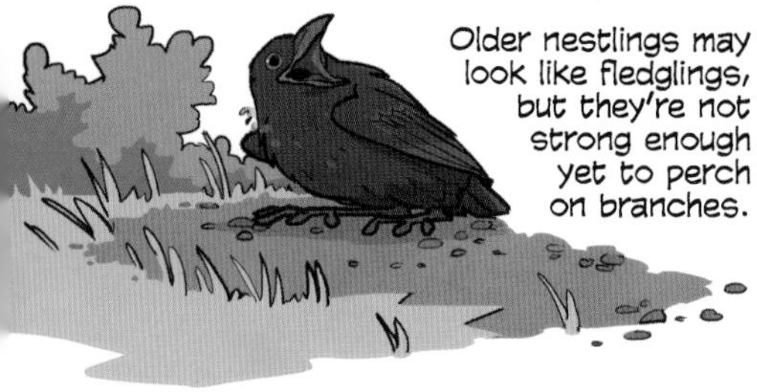

Older nestlings may look like fledglings, but they're not strong enough yet to perch on branches.

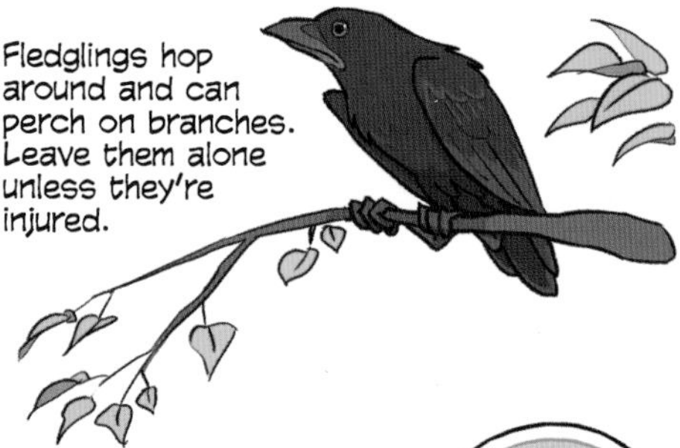

Fledglings hop around and can perch on branches. Leave them alone unless they're injured.

Help! Crows keep dive-bombing me!

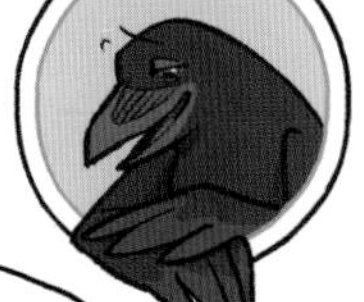

Is it fledging season? If so, the attacks will stop once the fledglings have learned to fly! If it keeps happening in the same area, try avoiding it for a few days or using an umbrella.

If it's a more lasting grudge, you can try to turn their opinion of you around by befriending them. Drop food behind you when you're out walking around. They may focus on the food instead of their vendetta and learn to associate you with good things, instead.

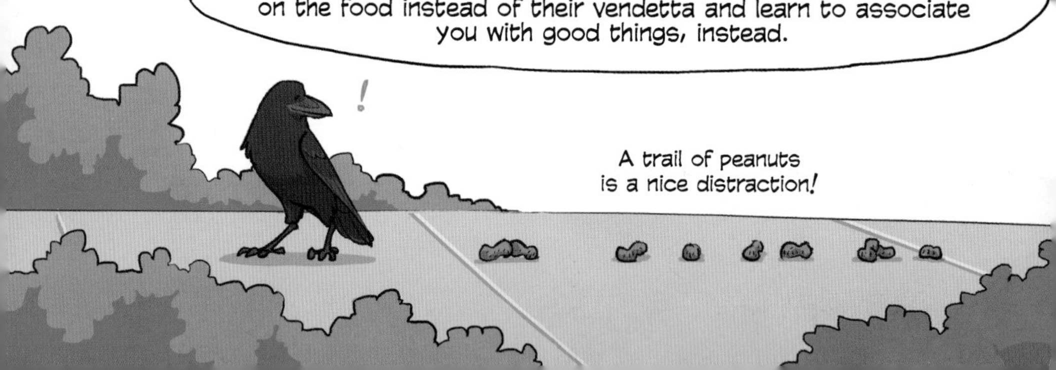
!

A trail of peanuts is a nice distraction!

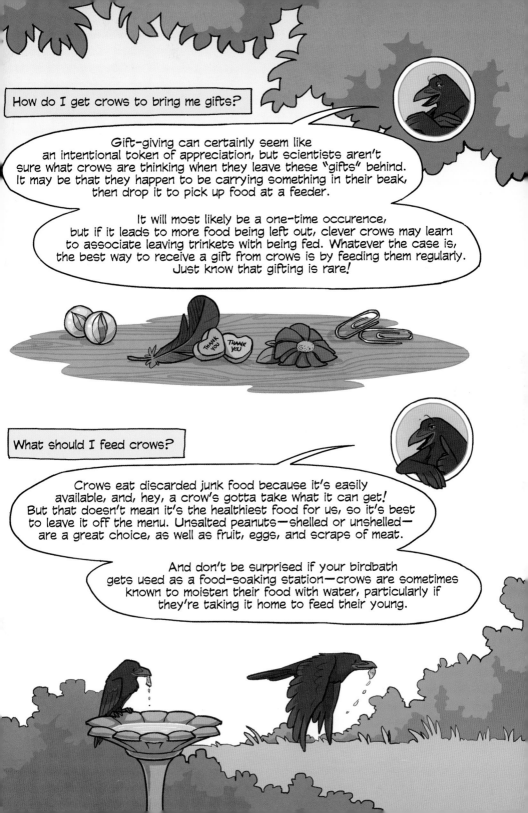

How do I get crows to bring me gifts?

Gift-giving can certainly seem like an intentional token of appreciation, but scientists aren't sure what crows are thinking when they leave these "gifts" behind. It may be that they happen to be carrying something in their beak, then drop it to pick up food at a feeder.

It will most likely be a one-time occurence, but if it leads to more food being left out, clever crows may learn to associate leaving trinkets with being fed. Whatever the case is, the best way to receive a gift from crows is by feeding them regularly. Just know that gifting is rare!

What should I feed crows?

Crows eat discarded junk food because it's easily available, and, hey, a crow's gotta take what it can get! But that doesn't mean it's the healthiest food for us, so it's best to leave it off the menu. Unsalted peanuts—shelled or unshelled— are a great choice, as well as fruit, eggs, and scraps of meat.

And don't be surprised if your birdbath gets used as a food-soaking station—crows are sometimes known to moisten their food with water, particularly if they're taking it home to feed their young.

—BOOKS—

Emery, N. (2016). *Bird Brain: An Exploration of Avian Intelligence.* Princeton University Press.

Herculano-Houzel, S. (2016). *The Human Advantage: A New Understanding of How Our Brain Became Remarkable.* MIT Press.

Lipton, J. (1993). *An Exaltation of Larks: The Ultimate Edition.* Penguin Group USA.

Marzluff, J. M., & Angell, T. (2007). *In the Company of Crows and Ravens.* Yale University Press.

Marzluff, J. M., & Angell, T. (2013). *Gifts of the Crow: How Perception, Emotion, and Thought Allow Smart Birds to Behave like Humans.* Simon and Schuster.

Turner, P. (2016). *Crow Smarts: Inside the Brain of the World's Brightest Bird.* HMH Books for Young Readers.

—ARTICLES & WEB SOURCES—

Balakhonov, D., & Rose, J. (2017). "Crows Rival Monkeys in Cognitive Capacity." *Scientific Reports*, vol. 7, no. 1.

Bogale, B. A., et al. (2012). "Long-Term Memory of Color Stimuli in the Jungle Crow (*Corvus macrorhynchos*)." *Animal Cognition*, vol. 15, no. 2.

Boswall, J. (1977 & 1978). "Tool-Using by Birds and Related Behaviour." *Aviculture Magazine*, vol. 83 & 84.

Boswall, J. (1983). "Tool-Using and Related Behaviour in Birds: More Notes." *Avicultural Magazine*, vol. 89, no. 2.

Bugnyar, T., et al. (2016). "Ravens Attribute Visual Access to Unseen Competitors." *Nature Communications*, vol. 7.

Caccamise, D. F., et al. (1997). "Roosting Behavior and Group Territoriality in American Crows." *The Auk*, vol. 114, no. 4.

Caffrey, C. (2000). "Tool Modification and Use by an American Crow." *The Wilson Bulletin*, vol. 112, no. 2.

Cristol, D. A. (2001). "American Crows Cache Less Preferred Walnuts." *Animal Behaviour*, vol. 62, no. 2.

Cross, D. J., et al. (2013). "Distinct Neural Circuits Underlie Assessment of a Diversity of Natural Dangers by American Crows." *Proceedings of the Royal Society B: Biological Sciences*, vol. 280, no. 1765.

Dally, J. M., et al. (2006). "The Behaviour and Evolution of Cache Protection and Pilferage." *Animal Behaviour*, vol. 72, no. 1.

Ditz, H. M., & Nieder, A. (2015). "Neurons Selective to the Number of Visual Items in the Corvid Songbird Endbrain." *Proceedings of the National Academy of Sciences*, vol. 112, no. 25.

Emery, N. J., & Clayton, N. S. (2004). "The Mentality of Crows: Convergent Evolution of Intelligence in Corvids and Apes." *Science*, vol. 306, no. 5703.

Emery, N. J., et al. (2007). "Cognitive Adaptations of Social Bonding in Birds." *Philosophical Transactions of the Royal Society B: Biological Sciences*, vol. 362, no. 1480.

Goldsmith, T. H. (2006). "What Birds See." *Scientific American*, vol. 295, no. 1.

Griesser, M., & Suzuki, T. N. (2016). "Occasional Cooperative Breeding in Birds and the Robustness of Comparative Analyses Concerning the Evolution of Cooperative Breeding." *Zoological Letters*, vol. 2, no. 1.

Jelbert, S. A., et al. (2015). "Investigating Animal Cognition with the Aesop's Fable Paradigm: Current Understanding and Future Directions." *Communicative & Integrative Biology*, vol. 8, no. 4.

Lefebvre, L., et al. (1997). "Feeding Innovations and Forebrain Size in Birds." *Animal Behaviour*, vol. 53, no. 3.

Lefebvre, L., et al. (2002). "Tools and Brains in Birds." *Behaviour*, vol. 139, no. 7.

Marzluff, J. M., et al. (2001). "Causes and Consequences of Expanding American Crow Populations." In *Avian Ecology and Conservation in an Urbanizing World*. Springer, Boston, MA.

McGowan, K. J. (2010). "Frequently Asked Questions about Crows." Retrieved from birds.cornell.edu/crows/crowfaq.htm

Olkowicz, S., et al. (2016). "Birds Have Primate-Like Numbers of Neurons in the Forebrain." *Proceedings of the National Academy of Sciences*, vol. 113, no. 26.

RT. (2012, January 12). "Crowboarding: Russian Roof-Surfin' Bird Caught on Tape" [Video file]. Retrieved from youtube.com/watch?v=3dWw9GLcOeA

Rutz, C., et al. (2016). "Tool Bending in New Caledonian Crows." *Royal Society Open Science*, vol. 3, no. 8.

Swift, K. N., & Marzluff, J. M. (2015). "Wild American Crows Gather Around Their Dead to Learn about Danger." *Animal Behaviour*, vol. 109.

Taylor, A. H., et al. (2010). "Complex Cognition and Behavioural Innovation in New Caledonian Crows." *Proceedings of the Royal Society B: Biological Sciences*, vol. 277, no. 1694.

Thompson, F. R. (2007). "Factors Affecting Nest Predation on Forest Songbirds in North America." *Ibis*, vol. 149.

Troscianko, J., et al. (2012). "Extreme Binocular Vision and a Straight Bill Facilitate Tool Use in New Caledonian Crows." *Nature Communications*, vol. 3.

Veit, L., & Nieder, A. (2013). "Abstract Rule Neurons in the Endbrain Support Intelligent Behaviour in Corvid Songbirds." *Nature Communications*, vol. 4.

Verbeek, N. A., & Caffrey, C. (2002). "American Crow (*Corvus brachyrhynchos*)," *The Birds of North America* (A. F. Poole and F. B. Gill, Eds.). Ithaca: Cornell Lab of Ornithology. Retrieved from birdsna.org/Species-Account/bna/species/amecro

Weir, A. A., et al. (2002). "Shaping of Hooks in New Caledonian Crows." *Science*, vol. 297, no. 5583.